Fear and the Making of Foreign Policy

D1614957

Fear and the Making of Foreign Policy

Europe and Beyond

Raymond Taras

EDINBURGH
University Press

© Raymond Taras, 2015

Edinburgh University Press Ltd
The Tun – Holyrood Road
12 (2f) Jackson's Entry
Edinburgh EH8 8PJ
www.euppublishing.com

Typeset in 10.5/12.5 Goudy by
Servis Filmsetting Ltd, Stockport, Cheshire,
and printed and bound in Great Britain by
CPI Group (UK) Ltd, Croydon CRO 4YY

A CIP record for this book is available from the British Library

ISBN 978 0 7486 9901 8 (hardback)
ISBN 978 0 7486 9903 2 (paperback)
ISBN 978 0 7486 9902 5 (webready PDF)
ISBN 978 0 7486 9904 9 (epub)

The right of Raymond Taras to be identified as author of this
work has been asserted in accordance with the Copyright,
Designs and Patents Act 1988 and the Copyright and Related
Rights Regulations 2003 (SI No. 2498).

Contents

Acknowledgements

I was told I was born in one of the Gothic towers of the Royal Victoria Hospital overlooking Montreal. A birth in the New World cannot be more Anglo than that. But then I was whisked away, over the mountain, to take up residence in the city of Outremont. It is a wealthy and outré place. Pierre Trudeau, Canada's one colorful prime minister, was raised in a prosperous section of it and attended the Jesuits' Collège Brébeuf nearby.

I lived lower down the slope among normal French Canadians and Hasidic Jews. The 1975 film by Ján Kadár, Lies My Father Told Me, tells the story of life in the streets of the plateau. The upper mountain was only for going tobogganing in winter under the Université de Montréal's ski jump.

One of Outremont's outer boundaries is marked by the businesses opened up along rue Parc by the Greeks of Montreal. Close by lies Mile End, the district through which immigrants have always passed on their path to upward socio-economic mobility. It is here where, a century ago, Little Italy came into existence. The Italian parish of Notre-Dame-de-la-Défense is its most noteworthy landmark. Montreal's stylish bourgeois-bohemian quarter, Plateau-Mont-Royal, abuts the parish.

These were my stomping grounds before I reached my teens. Outremont and its immediate surroundings were dotted with Catholic churches French and English, Anglican churches, Greek Orthodox churches, the synagogues and temples of Orthodox and Reform Jews. Venerable l'église Sainte-Madeleine was the church on our avenue across the street from l'École Lajoie where I went to primary school. The 2011 Quebec film nominated for an Oscar, Monsieur Lazhar, reminds me of school days at Lajoie.

Most grade schools were French and Catholic and administered by the Comité Catholique in Quebec City, until the 1960s Révolution tranquille which indeed germinated a revolutionary idea – setting up a governmental Ministry of Education. Where my parents were born, in Poland, a Ministry *of* Education had been established by King Stanisław August Poniatowski in 1773, the first of its kind in the world.

All we kids in Outremont learned to recognize the different markers of identity well before our Confirmation or Bar Mitzvah. There were so many signs of diversity that the one and only survival strategy was to bond indiscriminately with everyone in the community. That would seem to be the rational and judicious choice. Not unknown was also the inclination to react to difference as Seamus Heaney pithily noted in his poem "Whatever You Say, Say Nothing" concerning 1970s Northern Ireland: "'You know them by their eyes,' and hold your tongue."

Many years later, after I had been living in New Orleans for some time, I was asked by my prospective black landlady, who sang in the local Gospel choir: "Where you from?" To keep things simple, again, I answered: "From Canada." She thought about that for a while, then reassuringly replied: "That be all right, chile, we all God's chillun." Amen.

I express my thanks to these individuals who, over the past five years, have instructed me in fear of different forms: Arda Akçiçek (Ankara), Sergey Akopov (St Petersburg), David Andrews (Claremont, California), Jerzy Bartkowski (Warsaw), Chip Berlet (Boston), Karin Borevi (Uppsala), Estelle Bunout (Lorraine), Sebat Çelik (Diyarbakir), Michael Czerny S.J. (Vatican), Elizabeth Davis (Egham, Surrey), Marie Demker (Gothenburg), Elisabeth Eide (Oslo), Valentina Feklyunina (Newcastle), Rawi Hage (Montreal), Anders Hellström (Malmö), Aleksandra Jasińska (Warsaw), Carsten Jensen (Copenhagen), Riva Kastoryano (Paris), Magdalena Kędzior (Rzeszów), Mikhail Molchanov (Fredericton, New Brunswick), Suzan Mbtwoday (Bergen), Nasar Meer (Strathclyde), Cas Mudde (Athens, Georgia), Peter Olofsson (San Antonio, Texas), Bo Petersson (Malmö), Bashy Quraishy (Copenhagen), Jacek Raciborski (Warsaw), Helena Rytövuori-Apunen (Tampere), Bill Safran (Boulder, Colorado), Yan Sayegh (Lyon), Stanislav Shushkevich (Minsk), Muhammed Siddiq (Berkeley), Mark Silinsky (Washington), Suzuki Michitaka (Okayama), Joanna Szczęsna (Warsaw), Barbara Törnquist-Plewa (Lund), David Wand (Kigali), Marshal Zeringue (New Orleans), and Gwido Zlatkes (Riverside, California).

Students in a Phobias and Foreign Policy course which I have taught at Tulane University beginning in 2008 have put their indelible imprint on this book. I am especially grateful to students who took this course most recently, in 2014, at the University of Warsaw. The majority came from Ukraine and Belarus and they were inspirational in their visions of a peaceful world at a difficult time.

To my favorite people in scholarly publishing at Edinburgh University Press, I extend my gratitude and appreciation to each of you once again.

Years of unfailing support from the two ladies in my life, Marjorie Castle and Gabriela Taras, are what made completion of this book possible. My deep gratitude goes to you. You would think life with a teen would be harder than one with a structural realist.

Raymond Taras

CHAPTER ONE

Fear and suspicion in contemporary politics

MEDITATION ON FEAR

It is rarely a bad idea to turn to classical texts for inspiration and wisdom. The study of fear – "phobology" to use a gauche term – is no exception. Among his diverse achievements, the classical Greek writer Thucydides deserves being called the father of the study of fear. His *History of the Peloponnesian War* has even been described as "a meditation upon fear – its varieties, ubiquity, potency, and even rational necessity."[1]

The beginnings of the study of international relations are usually associated with Thucydides but so should the analysis of fear in politics. This must include how the spread of fear can pose a grave danger to democracy. His book distinguishes many types of fear ranging "from sudden panic to distant suspicion."[2]

Like the many words found in Inuit languages for different kinds of snow, Thucydides employed five different terms (more accurately, word groups) to refer to fear. *Phobos, deos,* and *orrodia* are more general and the more frequently used words he employed.

Classicists suggest that *phobos* signifies a stronger, less rational fear of a present threat. It is the word borrowed from him that is most in usage today. But rather than standing exclusively for fear, phobia is now employed to describe a wide gamut of human passions, not least of which are feelings of animosity, antipathy, antagonism, even hate towards others.

This usage is discernible when we look at the compound word xenophobia. Political scientist Marie Demker succinctly captures its multiple connotations: "xenophobia today is used as shortcut, describing the societal sentiment of distress, agony, antagonism, fear, alarm and suspicion that has come to be a companion of migrant flows to Europe after the end of the cold war."[3]

Deos constitutes a more cerebral fear, an anxiousness about a more distant, ill-defined threat. On occasions, Thucydides uses it interchangeably with

1

phobos so they should not be treated as mutually exclusive. The term *orrodia*, in turn, appears only five times in *History of the Peloponnesian War*, primarily in the quoted speeches of Greek political leaders.

Thucydides made little use of the *ekplexis* and related *kataplexis* word groups. They denote stronger feelings – terror, consternation, even panic. But, when the historian wished to capture a fear evoked by a breakdown in confidence in the state of things, he invoked *hypopsis*. An interrelated word, *hupopsis*, specified anxiety about threats of tyrannical or oligarchic upheavals.[4]

It is Thucydides' idea of *hypopsis* that, I believe, most accurately captures the contemporary politics of fear. It offers a semantic alternative to the generic term phobia which has fallen into misuse. Its literal meaning is "looking underneath the surface" brought on by a suspicion or fear that what may be found underneath will be found to be threatening. Hypopsia therefore represents the condition of being suspicious about the way things or people appear to be. It entails distrust, even deep distrust, which I suggest make up the substance of fear.

The Greek historian's investigation of the causes and effects of fear, and the terminology he developed to approach it, was trailblazing semantically. But it also displayed a prescient awareness of how the emergent system of Athenian democracy collided with human passions and could be destroyed by them.

Today we observe a turnaround in the linkage between fear and democracy as sketched by Thucydides. Contemporary democracies are increasingly surveillance states suspicious and fearful of groups perceived to be threatening to the democratic order. In contrast to Thucydides' logic, today suspicion, surveillance, and democracy mutually reinforce one another.

Thucydides paid particular attention to the part played by fear in international relations – the principal focus of this book. As one example, he cited the emergence of fear as essential to raising the fleet needed to attack Troy. What Brian Calabrese called "a 'panic benefit,' the advantage that a state receives following a sudden, unexpected fear," plays a significant role. It creates "the unity and resolve that develop after the panic and that enable the city to overcome the conditions that caused the panic, usually the threat of invasion."[5] Fear, then, whether arising from within a society or outside it, as in the case of the Greek fear of Persian invasions, has been functional for political leaders.

The presence in society of xenophobia, literally a fear of foreigners but used colloquially an animosity towards them, characterized Greek city-states, none more than Sparta but Athens too. Today, the meanings of xenophobia makes it an often ambiguous and opaque term. Its evolution has parallels with the way in which the concept of anti-Semitism has developed. From a fear of Jews it was expanded to include a dislike of them, then of systematic discrimination against them, and finally the extermination of them. Such semantic fluidity has led to the criminalization of anti-Semitic speech, in particular Holocaust denial, in some European countries.

Unlike anti-Semitism, much xenophobic hate speech targeting specific ethnic and religious groups has not occasioned legislative countermeasures which would criminalize it. Two major subcategories of xenophobia examined in this book are Islamophobia and russophobia but there are other region-specific "phobias con ajetivos" which can be added, for example, anti-yanquismo or Sinophobia.

Like anti-Semitism, xenophobia, and racism, these subcategories are charged phenomena. Associating individuals and groups with these prejudices is likely to shame them. But the terms also can be put to different uses. For example, criticizing specific cultural practices associated with Muslims, such as women wearing full-face veils that can be interpreted as symbols of their subjugation, may be construed as Islamophobia. By this standard the 2014 ruling by the European Court of Human Rights (ECHR) endorsing France's ban on the public wearing of burkas is Islamophobic. If progressive adherents of Euro-Islam agree with this ban they can be attacked as Islamophobes too. In this way, censoring any criticism of Islam may constrain non-Muslims and Muslims alike.[6]

In turn, accusing people of russophobia can lead to unintended consequences. For instance, the Kremlin has skillfully catalogued and disseminated what it regards as russophobic speech in the West to dramatize how Russia is encircled by hostile forces. Many of Russia's most vocal critics are not aware how they unintentionally play into the Kremlin's hands by making negative statements about Russia's politics even if they are fully justified. In this way they contribute to a supposed master narrative of russophobia.[7] These speech acts may hardly be considered russophobic in the West but they may be by sections of Russian society exposed to the Kremlin's information wars.

This brings us to the bane of much social science research: the measurement problem. If we are to use fear as an explanatory variable in politics, a simple Boolean binary may offer the best results: we can categorize a given society in the simple terms of a presence or absence of fear. In a country with many immigrants of Muslim background, the presence of Islamo-hypopsis – distrust of Muslims – and even Islamophobia – hatred of them – is far more likely than one in which there are few such immigrants. Similarly, in a country which neighbors on Russia the presence of russo-hypopsia is all but guaranteed.

Though seemingly banal, these are nevertheless important observations. It is precisely countries most vulnerable to, and most often accused of, Islamophobic or russophobic attitudes that may be fiercest in their denials of their presence. Accusing a country of being incorrigibly phobic evokes the same stubborn defensive mechanism as when calling it racist. Phobia is a polarizing word.

Terms with double-edged uses like Islamophobia and russophobia are problematic, therefore. It is one more reason to dispense with the indiscriminate use of phobia, xenophobia, and its offshoots given the range of meanings and normative biases they evoke. Moreover, they are less likely to be employed in criticism of the West: we rarely hear of "Europhobia" but encounter the gentler term "Euroskepticism" instead.[8] "Skepticism" added as a suffix has its uses, above all because it rules out a hate of Europe.

The presence or absence of skepticism may allow us more precisely to interpret survey results measuring, for example, social distance between ethnic groups in European states. Any perceived distance may reflect skepticism about individuals of immigrant background rather than a hate of them. But skepticism is too overarching, vague, and incongruent to use as a cognate for fear. Hypopsia – digging beneath the surface of things, displaying suspicion and distrust of others – is more apposite. Thus, a precise and measured way of describing citizens' reactions to Russia's intervention in Ukraine in 2014 is russo-hypopsic – a reasoned and profound suspicion of Russia's foreign policy objectives.

To be sure, hypopsia has rarely been employed by English-language writers. One of the few exceptions is philosopher Jacques Rancière's book *On the Shores of Politics* (translated from French). It applied hypopsia to draw contrasts between modern and classical democracy:

> The democratic political subject has a shared domain in the very separateness of a way of life characterized by two great features: the absence of constraints and the absence of suspicion. Suspicion, in Thucydides' Greek, is called *hypopsia:* looking underneath. What characterizes democracy for Thucydides is the rejection of this looking underneath.[9]

As noted earlier, Thucydides did not regard democracy and surveillance as compatible even though he believed in the resilience of democratic systems to manage fear. For Rancière the twenty-first century is marked by the return of old fears, suspicions, even criminality and chaos. They weaken democracy.

Hypopsic attitudes in democracies merit closer analysis, then. The awkward but accurate idea of xeno-hypopsia brands societies riveted by fear, angst, suspicion, and distrust. Instead of a focus on the centrality of trust in modern societies as a number of prominent authors have done,[10] I consider it more valuable to examine distrust and the way it shapes society. We can then reserve xenophobia for descriptions of indisputable intergroup animosity, hostility, and hate. Given that xeno-hypopsia is an unfamiliar and unwieldy term, for stylistic reasons I use it selectively here and employ distrust and suspicion in its place.

4

FEAR ACROSS HISTORY

Up until the sixteenth century fear defined the human condition. It was the product of widespread superstitions, traditions, religious teachings, and unawareness of the laws of natural science.[11] Its influence and pervasiveness was checked in the Age of Reason, beginning in the seventeenth century. Captivation with scientific reasoning as a way of understanding the world steadily grew and formed the core of the eighteenth century's Age of Enlightenment, an intellectual and artistic movement challenging less rational world views.

Fear of the unknown was reduced as more became known about the physical world. Philosopher René Descartes contended that removing fear required appealing to reason. This way people could be persuaded that the threats they perceived were not real, that there was more certainty in confronting fears than in fleeing from them.[12]

It was not in the interests of Church and state, however, to eliminate public fears. Indeed, in 1532 Niccolò Machiavelli elevated fear to a fundamental principle of politics. In his treatise, *The Prince*, he advised that a political leader should learn how to inspire fear in his subjects. Fear allows political authorities to consolidate their power. It is preferable for the Prince to be feared than loved. Machiavelli added that fear is the most constant of the sentiments that citizens have for their ruler. But he warned that fear of rulers should never lead to a hatred of them because this would push the public to a revolt.[13]

Increasing skepticism about the role of fear in the body politic was discernable in the writings of the Social Contract theorists. A century after Machiavelli, Thomas Hobbes still recognized fear as a cornerstone of an inherently artificial political order. Such order helped transform individual fears into collective ones. Presented with a choice between fear and subjugation, Hobbes was sure people would prefer the second.[14]

John Locke, too, accepted that people's fear of one another constituted a characteristic of the state of nature. Fear represented an uneasiness of the spirit, one which could be harnessed constructively to energize politics and help invigorate human collectivities.[15] It was Jean-Jacques Rousseau who broke from this view of the positive role played by fear in politics by holding that fear was not a necessary condition of human interaction. In fact, fear keeps us from recognizing the other as a human being. The hope expressed in *The Social Contract* was that political institutions and laws would help eliminate the fear that humans naturally have of others.

We observe, then, that fear has a lengthy history as an instrument of politics. In early political systems fear and terror were inseparable. Warlords terrified political subjects through means both physical (torture) and psychological (threat of torture).[16] In ancient Athens a punitive political instrument, such as ostracism of dissenters voted upon in the agora by the citizenry, inspired fear and offered deterrence.

"Terror is the curse of man," wrote Fyodor Dostoyevsky, an unusually insightful novelist on the human psyche, in *The Possessed*. Use of terror today seems to be less barbaric and more circumscribed than in earlier historical epochs: the Assyrian empire and its ruthless conquests of foreign lands in the tenth century BC; the Mongol empire founded by Genghis Khan in the thirteenth century and carried on by his successors; the Spanish Inquisition, established in the late fifteenth century and cruelly applied across the expanding Spanish empire; and Robespierre's two-year Reign of Terror four years after the French Revolution.

More sublime and sophisticated ways of inspiring fear have been developed that bypass the need for conjuring up imminent personal physical torture. That was the promise of the celebrated panopticon method of enforcing compliance, developed just four decades after Robespierre's terror by an English philosopher (discussed below). Except for moments of profound crisis and a desperate need for political survival, few political leaders resort to naked terror to evoke fear and compliance among citizens. Today's despots less often turn to terrorizing their publics than claiming they are protecting them from terrorists.

Contemporary political systems led by authoritarian leaders are typically held together by playing on people's existential fears or by evoking new ones. These rulers pose as a Modern Prince and use ploys adapted from Machiavelli's political playbook. By contrast, which dictator today uses fear as a weapon in the way Genghis Khan did? – "Bow to me or die in an ocean of blood."

COSMIC AND EXISTENTIAL FEARS

Bruce Springsteen's "Devils and Dust" sets out the darkness in American society during the George W. Bush years:

> Fear's a powerful thing
> It can turn your heart black you can trust
> It'll take your God filled soul
> Fill it with devils and dust

Sociologist Zygmunt Bauman was no less evocative in writing about this human emotion: "What we fear, is evil; what is evil, we fear."[17]

Whether it emerges from above within elites or from below among citizens, fear has become a legitimate force to be used so as to bring order to modern societies. Both the politics of fear from above and from below typically conflate real and imagined fears in order to produce maximum effects. The fine line separating imagined from real fear is difficult to delineate and depends on the eye of the beholder: one person's imagined fear, let's say of political reprisals, can be another person's real fear.

Fear can become foundational in a society. A century ago literary theorist Mikhail Bakhtin introduced the notion of official fear, an offshoot of the cosmic fear felt by humanity. Lars von Trier's film *Melancholia*, depicting average people going about their everyday business as the inevitability of a planetary collision becomes starker, renders a contemporary view of such cosmic fear.[18] In religious terms, such fear occurs because there is no hiding place from the Father of Creation.

Like its cosmic variant, official fear forms part of the human condition regardless of whether it has been manipulated by authorities or not. For Bakhtin fear was an existential state which could be countered: "Fear is the extreme expression of narrow-minded and stupid seriousness, which is defeated by laughter ... Complete liberty is possible only in the completely fearless world."[19]

Other writers have looked for more precise understandings of fear. Sociologist Michela Marzano contended that "Fear is above all a fear of losing something: someone, oneself, one's way."[20] It originates in a primal attachment to rootedness which if disturbed leads to human anxiety. Writer Simone Weil described this connection:

> To be rooted is perhaps the most important and least recognized need of the human soul. It is one of the hardest to define. A human being has roots by virtue of his real, active and natural participation in the life of a community which preserves in living shape certain particular treasures of the past and certain particular expectations for the future.[21]

When an individual's need to belong to a community is denied, we enter the realm of a politics of exclusion. The organization of a community into in-group and out-group becomes real.

Bauman agreed that fear reflects an existential state. He also believed that attachment to human company was a catalyst of fear rather than a palliative for it:

> ... the perception of human company as a source of existential insecurity and as a territory strewn with traps and ambushes tends to become endemic. In a vicious circle of sorts, it exacerbates in its turn the chronic frailty of human bonds and adds further to the fears that frailty is prone to gestate.[22]

Fear as an existential state is linked to a gamut of human emotions such as a need for attachment and company. A vivid illustration of fear's interconnectedness with other passions is provided in Sara Ahmed's *The Cultural*

> ## Box 1.1 Depoliticizing fear in the interests of unity
>
> Understanding the objects of our fear as not political renews us as a collective. Afraid, we are like the audience in a crowded theater confronting a man falsely shouting fire: united, not because we share similar beliefs or aspirations, but because we are equally threatened. Were we to understand the objects of our fear as truly political, we might argue about them, as we do about other political things. We might find ourselves less united than we thought. Some of us might sympathize with the grievances of our foes; others might not see them as so implacable or dangerous. By removing these objects from the controversies of politics, however, we achieve political unity – and renewal.
>
> Source: Corey Robin, *Fear: The History of a Political Idea* (New York: Oxford University Press, 2006), p. 6.

Politics of Emotion. The book traces the interweaving of bodies, pain, hate, fear, disgust, and shame. Stories of pain circulate throughout the public domain and feelings of bodily injury are transformed into hate for those others suspected of being the sources of pain. "Figures of hate" – immigrants, foreigners, terrorists – are bundled together into a common threat. Fear of these figures is heightened by the thought that they may one day pass near us. The terrorist can be anyone or everywhere, Ahmed argues, elevating fearfulness to a perpetual state. As with fear, disgust, too, brackets objects together. In turn, expressions of shame bond a community together through speech acts that apologize to others for shameful acts committed in the past.[23]

Suffering a traumatic episode has long been identified as an important factor in the making of fear. Political psychologist Vamik Volkan spoke of chosen traumas in describing events that shock the social system. He explained how psychic recollections, whether real or imagined, of past grievances or glories can transmit intense feelings and fanaticized expectations across generations about, as well as psychological defense mechanisms against, unacceptable ideas (Box 1.1). These processes maintain structures of ancient hatreds and traumatic pasts reinforced by newer hegemonic narratives about power.[24]

Such psychological transformations are often helped along by a category that Jacques Lacan called the master signifier. It consists of the following process: the master puts the slave to work by using signifiers to which the latter's identity is intricately bound: for example, his or her nation, culture, religion, gender.[25] The master signifier conjures up anxiety and fear in the subject.

8

Cultural theorist Slavoj Žižek popularized the master-signifier idea by examining the figure of the shark in the 1975 American film *Jaws*. Like illegal immigrants, the shark arrives on our shores from the sea. It arouses fears and enables expressions of ordinarily repressed impulses within a society. Žižek's insight was to claim that the shark as master signifier does not precede the various attempts to speak of it but is the after-effect of the failure to do so.[26] In this way, unspoken, repressed fears provide deep meaning for society and structure its shape.

Chosen traumas are important to citizens' perceptions of their societies. An analysis of the terrorist attacks in London in 2005 and Norway in 2011 suggested how these traumatic events were "so shocking that they disrupt our previous understandings of how the world is constituted – they fully disturb our sense of ontological security, our security of being, thus heightening levels of existential anxiety."[27] Both events resulted in expressions of disbelief, astonishment, doubt, and incredulity.

Treatment of such traumas may require recourse to past shared experiences entailing a reconstruction of previous traumatic or glorious events. They may serve as powerful identity signifiers to counter a sudden sense of insecurity and vulnerability. Authorities can exploit the public's need for security by normalizing the exclusionary positioning of perceived out-groups.[28] Thus, a candid discussion of the dangers of the shark, or of outsiders, becomes the after-effect of having stuck to an earlier taboo on speaking about it.

The prevalence of fear in contemporary Western societies started a process called securitization. Once set in motion, it may even arouse stronger threat perceptions. Securitization theory is associated with the Copenhagen School of international relations. The first step in the process involves a speech act: by talking security about an issue, a political actor moves a topic out of the realm of ordinary politics into an arena of exceptional security concerns. In the process, an actor legitimizes the use of extraordinary measures to counter a socially constructed threat. The threat can then be dealt with swiftly and without the normal democratic rules and regulations of policy-making becoming impediments. The object no longer has a given meaning but becomes anything that the securitizing actor says it is.[29]

Solely by voicing a security threat and having another actor agree with such abracadabra, something gets done about a problem: "It is by labelling something a security issue that it becomes one."[30] An illustration of this process is the securitization of immigration which reclassifies the intake of immigrants from the realm of economics (labor markets), human rights (family unification), and humanitarian concerns (refugee policies) into the specter of threats to a receiving society and the countermeasures needed to contain them. Most of the fear and hypopsia examined in this book involve citizens' reactions to those they construct as foreigners.

9

FEAR IN PHILOSOPHY

Many philosophers have taken an interest in the role played by fear in the ordering of society. Jeremy Bentham, the founder of modern utilitarianism, who died in 1832, may be the most influential as a result of his idea of building a device he called the panopticon. In Greek mythology Panoptes was a hundred-eyed giant and, it follows, a vigilant watchman. Bentham applied the term panopticon to a design for a prison in which inmates would be confined to solitary cells built in a circle around a central tower. They would not be able to see each other or the tower guards but would develop a sense that they were continuously under observation.

Bentham was convinced that, once released, the prisoner, having an ingrained feeling of being under constant scrutiny, would avoid any behavior that could be regarded as criminal because he would immediately be apprehended.[31] This vision of a society pacified by fear and citizens paralyzed with fright was subsequently developed in George Orwell's dystopian novel *1984*.

Philosopher Michel Foucault's thought was influenced by the panopticon idea. In *Discipline and Punish: The Birth of the Prison*, Foucault adopted it as a metaphor for modern punitive societies engaged in far-reaching surveillance of citizens. Writing forty years before Edward Snowden's revelations about the United States's National Security Agency, Foucault took note of the evolution of a disciplinary society extending from "a sort of social 'quarantine,' to an indefinitely generalizable mechanism of 'panopticism.'"[32]

Foucault linked the fear that is an outgrowth of being constantly observed by authorities to a theory of power he called governmentality. This structure of power was commonplace in today's Western liberal democracies, he claimed. Instead of viewing power as a hierarchical, top-down practice of the state, he expanded the forms of social control to include disciplinary institutions such as prisons, schools, and hospitals.

For Foucault forms of knowledge were also part of governmentality in that citizens internalized selective discourses which guided their behavior. The knowledge acquired by active citizens allowed them to become auto-correcting selves much in the way that panopticon prisoners behaved. Under liberal governmentality fear could be decentralized and individualized, thereby making for more efficient social control.[33]

An important lesson to draw from Foucault is how surveillance techniques need not inspire fear of authorities but instead can becoming reassuring. This is especially true when individuals feel they are assisting in the carrying out of surveillance. This is why Žižek's essay, "Fear Thy Neighbor as Thyself!" is significant: it broadens the spectrum of groups and individuals we need to fear. For Žižek fear drives us further apart and its final result is often isolation.

Much like Foucault, Žižek is interested in how politics and power conceal themselves in modern society. Affairs of state have become increasingly depoliticized and desensitized. In this context fear performs a positive func-tion: "with the depoliticized, socially objective, expert administration and coordination of interests as the zero level of politics, the only way to intro-duce passion into this field, to actively mobilize people, is through fear, a basic constituent of today's subjectivity."[34]

Žižek contends that today's politics renounces the basic constitutive principle of past politics which was based on universal moral axioms. Contemporary politics resorts to fear as the definitive mobilizing principle:

... fear of immigrants, fear of crime, fear of godless sexual depravity, fear of the excessive state itself, with its burden of high taxation, fear of ecological catas-trophe, fear of harassment. Political correctness is the exemplary liberal form of the politics of fear. Such a (post-) politics always relies on the manipulation of a paranoid *ochlos* or multitude: it is the frightening rallying of frightened people.[35]

Even tolerance is for Žižek a product of fear rather than open-mindedness. Our understanding of tolerance is determined in great part by "an obsessive fear of harassment." It leads to a concern with avoiding being stigmatized which will occur if we violate the code of political correctness.[36]

Žižek also shows how the Western world inspires fear not just within its own publics but also in other ones. Describing Muslim reactions to Denmark's 2005 cartoon controversy (where the Prophet Muhammad was depicted as a bomb carrier), he contends that the term Occidentalism – the counterpart to Edward Said's Orientalism – accurately conveys how the worst features of the West come to define it and inspire contempt in the East (Box 1.2).

Box 1.2 Occidentalism

Those who propose the term "Occidentalism" as the counterpart to Edward Said's "Orientalism" are right up to a point: what we get in Muslim countries is a certain ideological vision of the West which distorts Western reality no less, though in a different way, than the Orientalist vision distorts the Orient. What exploded in violence was a web of symbols, images and attitudes, including Western imperialism, godless materialism, hedonism, and the suffering of Palestinians, and which becomes attached to the Danish cartoons. This is why the hatred expanded from the caricatures to Denmark as a country, to Scandinavia, to Europe, and to the West as a whole.

Source: Slavoj Žižek, *Violence: Six Sideways Reflections* (London: Picador, 2008), pp. 51–2.

Globalization has many sides – economic, cultural, political, normative. Žižek tells us that it also subsumes fear and hate. Accordingly he writes how "dark xenophobia" stretches "today from the Balkans to Scandinavia, from the U.S. to Israel, from Central Africa to India: ethnic and religious passions are exploding, and Enlightenment values receding. These passions have always been there, lurking; what's new is the outright shamelessness of their display." In a society "in which racism and sexism have been rendered unacceptable and ridiculous . . ., imagine that, step by step, although the society continues to pay lip service to these norms, they are de facto deprived of their substance."[37]

The logic which undergirds the rise and spread of "dark fear" in countries' domestic and international politics is the main subject of this book.

ETHICS AND FEARS

In Europe fear of the foreign can have many targets: a minority group, an immigrant community, a neighboring nation, even a different civilization. As already noted, Bakhtin dismissed it as an extreme expression of narrow-mindedness and stupid seriousness. But it stems from a legitimate human urge to belong and to be rooted.

Fear arises when a dominant national narrative describing "homeliness" – Sigmund Freud's celebrated concept of *Heimlich*[38] – is disrupted by an encounter with the excluded Other.[39] The "unhomeliness" and "uncanniness" – *unheimlich* – of Others are embodied in phenomena both familiar and alien – "something which ought to have remained hidden but has come to light."[40] It comes to light through a hypopsic outlook – suspicion that compels people to dig beneath surface appearances.

The concept of *l'inquiétante étrangeté* – "worrying strangeness" – is an apt descriptor of European fears about faraway locals. They can be defined as first- and second-generation immigrants born in, or current citizens of, European states who educe alien and exotic imagery in the majority national group. They remind majority group members of the contingent nature of hospitality extended towards strangers.[41] Sociologist Frank Furedi has accurately captured these feelings in his idea of "a world of risky strangers." This world has been expanding owing to our growing estrangement from others: "Not only are more people seen as strangers but they are also seen as potentially threatening to our security."[42]

In the presence of greater numbers of strangers the national *Heimlich* narrative begins to exclude those who had already legally become the included. It creates for citizens who are viewed as faraway locals what can be called an "Otherland" – a special place in a homeland set aside for the socially and culturally marginalized, for those regarded as not belonging.[43]

12

In the 1960s moral philosopher Emmanuel Levinas developed a code of ethics concerned with hospitality towards strangers. He argued that our inability to approach the other may be the source of many episodes of horror and violence found in human history. For Levinas violence was paradoxically the result of a striving for unity because unity can be achieved only by excluding anyone considered disruptive.[44]

Forming a totality is possible, then, only through exclusion of the other. Almost tautologically, Levinas explains that the other is precisely that which cannot be included in a totality; the other is other, incomprehensibly and unreasonably so. It is treated as someone who cannot be reduced to familiar categories or easily assimilated into "my" conceptual framework. "The other upsets the balance: disturbs the order of alike phenomena I impose on the world to understand it." As one Levinas critic put it, "A stranger receives my open-armed welcome only if and when he distances himself from his strangeness and transforms into what I think he should be."[45]

There is nothing "unnatural" about rejection of the other. Psychoanalysis identifies stranger-anxiety in infants as the earliest manifestation of our rejection of others. At about six months a child has become so bonded in a love relationship, typically with a parent, that the appearance of others in its life is cause for fear. "Attachment theory also highlights an infant's need for proximity to an attachment figure, cultivating an affective bond, and establishing a 'secure base.'"[46]

Levinas's ethical reflections on fear were particularly influential on the work of Bauman, a sociologist whose focus was less on what united a society than what divided it. Bauman critiqued a "community which doesn't have to worry," one built not on positive moral values inherent within a community but, rather, on a pragmatic urge to exclude everyone and everything considered undesirable or dangerous. Such a community was like that of Mont-Saint Michel in France: "simultaneously a cloister and an inaccessible, closely guarded fortress."[47]

For Bauman what binds the smug residents of such a community are not shared values but joint fear. A consequence is the loss of the basic human skill of interacting with strangers. Yet even such a Mont-Saint-Michel does not produce an integrated social unit. A defining characteristic of "liquid modernity" is how "Contemporary fears, anxieties and grievances are made to be suffered alone."[48]

Bauman went on to describe the othering that takes place in the immigration policies of affluent European countries. They are today based on economic rather than country-specific criteria. Fortress Europe is a ghetto with acceptance criteria that are no longer country specific because state borders in a liquid Europe are unclear – it is, instead, the economic standing of people which has become decisive. People today viewed as suspect are those looking for relief from economic hardship. They are excluded from our fortress because, while the affluent are welcome, the penniless who will cost us are not.[49]

Migration scholar Mikael Spång focused his attention on the insider-outsider cleavage integral to immigration policy and how it is linked to questions in moral philosophy. He writes: "Some argue that immigration should only be considered from the moral point of view – what is in the equal interest of every person – while others argue that utility and collective goals play a central role in democratic decision-making."[50] Utilitarian considerations are juxtaposed with moral principles, therefore.

Spång brings democratic ideals into the equation on the reception of foreigners. Concern with the effects of immigration policy on others not members of the demos embodies "important democratic virtues, particularly in an immigration policy context where those affected have no voice and where their interests and rights are largely defended by organizations on an advocacy basis." Unlike migration scholars stressing the moral case for liberal immigration policy, he agrees that "democratic legitimacy involves collective goals and that demos has a right to control entrance to and residence in the state on the basis of arguments relating to democratic self-government." For him, "A balance needs to be struck between demos's right to decide about immigration policies and the rights of migrants concerning entrance to and residence in the state."[51]

Ethical issues have generally dominated public debates about strangers. Advocates of immigration and social integration policies which may promote the common good, such as triggering economic development, have been subject to charges of cynical pragmatism. The ethical–utilitarian divide is usually liminal though ethics is the force that will more quickly identify and condemn evidence of exclusion, fear and hate of foreigners.

So far, I have concentrated on the role of fear and hypopsia in politics. The process leading to the transformation of fear and distrust of strangers into hatred of them entails complex psychological stages and requires an analysis beyond the scope of this book. But philosopher Cornelius Castoriadis's examination of the two faces of hatred can serve as an invitation to probe deeper into the subject.

For Castoriadis one face of hatred is the flip side of European self-love or narcissism. Colonialism expanded the European sense of self-worth and moral superiority. Examples can be grandiose self-ascribed national role conceptions in leading European states: in France *la mission civilisatrice*, in Britain the white man's burden, in Germany the notion *am deutschen Wesen soll die Welt genesen* ("the German spirit shall heal the world"). While they played a negligible part in nineteenth-century European colonization, Nordic and Central European states also may be shaped by inflated self-worth and moral superiority: Sweden's self-regarding gold standard of human rights and Poland's historic sense of serving as *antemurale christianitatis* – the eastern fortress of Christian civilization. Castoriadis contended that affirmation of Europe's civilizational mission simultaneously pointed to the purported non-value of non-white Europeans.

The second face of hatred was what Castoriadis called unconscious self-hatred. The presence of the other became a cipher for European self-doubt and ontological insecurity.[52] Hatred of the other, especially observable in racism, had its origins in "psychical self-hatred."[53] Hatred of others can thus be the product of self-loathing and insecurity.

Self-love and self-hatred are deep psychological structures which can drive people to adopt hostile attitudes towards those not like themselves. Acting out this hostility requires additional facilitating mechanisms: organizations, leaders, collectivities, programs, a specific country, a particular time. The Third Reich furnishes the most obvious case. But this book is concerned with understanding why twenty-first century Europe has become a land – like many others – of fears. It does not make the case for calling Europe lands of hate.

EUROCENTRISM

Like other parts of the world, Europe is characterized by a collection of national fears. It is present across Western, Central, and Eastern Europe as well as Nordic and Mediterranean Europe because "national fear arises from fear of a spectral past, from the grief and pain of historical ghosts that will not rest."[54]

National fear never sleeps. European states' fears of their inner demons as well as of encroaching strangers, have had an impact not just on the social cohesion of individual states but on intra-European relations. If, in the year 2000, European elites boasted about the successes of integration among member states, today, attention is drawn to its divisions. Shared fear can contribute to the process of *e pluribus unum*. But insecurity can also produce more hypopsic relations between European states in addition to increased fear about neighboring regions.

In the aftermath of Europe's financial crisis that surfaced in 2007, conflicting explanations of what had triggered it pitted Northern European countries, most significantly Germany, against Mediterranean ones – Portugal, Spain, Italy, and Greece. The Northern narrative pointed to the South's insolence, graft, and extravagance; the Mediterranean one highlighted the lending practices, predatory capitalism, and unlevel playing field favored by the North. The North–South rift in Europe remained a valence issue well after the endangered euro had been secured.

15

In *Why Europe Fears its Neighbors*, political scientist Fabrizio Tassinari explained what he saw as increasing distance between European states. He believed that Europeans were becoming alarmed by their neighbors' values. Here is some evidence. Survey results published before Russia's military involvement in Ukraine in 2014 indicated that two out of three Europeans were concerned by Russia's role as their principal energy provider and by its behavior towards neighboring countries. But russo-hypopsia is commonplace so let me refer to other cases. About 70 percent of respondents in France and Germany believed that Turkey had values so different from the West that it could not be regarded as Western. Two-thirds of the survey sample in Italy, the Netherlands, and Spain considered greater interaction between the Muslim and Western worlds as threatening.

Tassinari concluded, then: "Name one of the countries neighboring Europe, and it is quite likely that the average European citizen will at best associate it with gaping cultural or economic differences and at worst with the barbarians at the gate."[55] Eurocentrism, alongside traditional ethnonationalisms in Europe, have therefore fueled perceptions of division and disunity.

In its efforts to promote enlargement and integration, the European Union has, at times inadvertently, reinforced Eurocentrism by underscoring the supposed uniqueness of European values and identity. Claims that Europeanness stands for freedom, tolerance, inclusion, democracy, rule of law, and human rights – norms allegedly not inherent to other world civilizations – appear quizzical given Europe's nineteenth-century history of colonialism and twentieth-century history of world wars. Official Euro-discourses meticulously avoid identifying fear as a feature of European identity, yet it lurks under the surface.

Cultural studies specialist Mitja Velikonja offered a mordant takedown of the Eurocentric phenomenon: "The infinitely reproduced mantras of the new European meta discourse have caught on and become normalized within all spheres of social life: in politics, in the media, in mass culture, in advertising, in everyday conversations."[56] To illustrate EU-based centrism he titled his chapters EUtopia, EUldorado, EUgoism, and EUreka.

European Union elites' claims of exceptionalism are anchored in a primordial understanding of the purported time-honored existence of a European family of nations. It may be labeled a civilizational chauvinism. Let me document this by citing EU elites' discourse supporting Ukraine's wish to sign an association agreement with the EU in 2013–14. At a late 2013 European Union Summit, European Council President Herman Van Rompuy was hyperbolic in praising Maidan activists in Kiev who waved "the European flag, and its stars of hope, without a hint of cynicism." European Commission President José Manuel Barroso, making a case for appearing the most Eurocentric member of the European Union establishment, added: "When we see European flags in the streets of Ukraine in a very cold temperature we can't resist saying it's part of the European family."[57] The civilizational dichotomy juxtaposing "members of the family of Europeans braving the cold to wave flags" and those others who are not waving European flags was stark and raised fears among those excluded and left behind.

Politicians describing Ukraine as already belonging to an extended European family were implicitly contrasting it to Russia which did not. Swedish foreign minister Carl Bildt, one of the architects of the EU's Eastern Partnership initiative, repeated the "EUmantra" that "Ukraine is a European country, and it belongs within the European family of nations."[58] He implied that it was natural for it to associate with the EU but reject membership in the Russian-led Eurasian Customs Union which, paradoxically, is in geographic, civilizational, and nominal terms a broader, more inclusive "big tent" than the European Union is.

Eurocentrism is an exclusionary perspective, therefore, and it trades on public fears which stress the salience of the divide between civilization – "us" – and barbarism – "them." It produces blowback and pushback in much of the non-European world. This includes not just Euroskepticism within Europe but Euro-hypopsia – distrust of Europe – elsewhere.

Postcolonial theorists are particularly well positioned to question Europe's supposed civilizational exceptionalism. Singling out the exclusionary character of European philosophy Gayatri Spivak observed "how Kant foreclosed the Aboriginal; how Hegel put the other of Europe in a pattern of normative deviations and how the colonial subject sanitized Hegel; how Marx negotiated difference."[59]

Writing about the same time, Dipesh Chakrabarty weighed in on the "first in Europe, then elsewhere" contention. In *Provincializing Europe* he made this bold statement:

> No major Western thinker has publicly shared Francis Fukuyama's "vulgarized Hegelian historicism" that saw in the fall of the Berlin wall a common end for the history of all human beings. The contrast with the past seems sharp when one remembers the cautious but warm note of approval with which Kant once detected in the French Revolution a "moral disposition in the human race" or Hegel saw the imprimatur of the "world spirit" in the momentousness of that event.[60]

While acknowledging the contribution of Western liberal values, he contrasted them with actual European political practices: "The European colonizer of the nineteenth century both preached this Enlightenment humanism at the colonized and at the same time denied it in practice."[61] Chakrabarty went further: "Historicism – and even the modern, European idea of history – one might say, came to non-European peoples in the nineteenth century as somebody's way of saying 'not yet' to somebody else." What did this mean? "Not yet civilized enough to rule themselves," he explained.[62]

Andre Gunder Frank's *ReOrient* represents a different effort to decenter Europe. Its objective is to provide a "holistic universal, global, world history – 'as it really was'" which would turn "Eurocentric historiography and social theory upside down by using a 'globological' perspective."[63] Like postcolonial critics, Gunder Frank rejects the Eurocentrism inherent to the works of European philosophers such as Karl Marx, Max Weber, Arnold Toynbee, Karl Polanyi, and Fernand Braudel. Similar to Spivak, he wished to construct a "different paradigmatic perspective" which would place not Europe but Asia "at the helm of history."[64] Already in 1998 the author was certain that the center of the world economy was ineluctably returning to the Middle Kingdom, China.

Eurocentrism today is discernable in EU claims that it constitutes the civilizational repository of ideas and practices of tolerance, inclusion, human rights – the gamut of values that is more accurately termed *universal values*. As the studies we have reviewed indicate, Eurocentrism inevitably involves processes of othering and placing peoples in a hierarchy. It projects internationally what has been occurring in Europe: fears and distrust of Roma, rootless migrants, Jews, Turks. Fears writ large and fears writ small share a common source – an inflated European valorization of itself.

Fear from above, fear from below

To assert that fear pervades politics is only a partial truth. Contemporary political systems suffer from other pathologies including, paradoxically, a sense of omnipotence. Marzano has written: "Western society appears today to be split between, on the one hand, valorization of omnipotence and will and, on the other, an obsessive fear of everything which eludes or seems to elude control."[65]

Concurrent yet contradictory beliefs in today's societies are that just about everything can be mastered but also that many events emerge over which we have no control. The sense of control and the sense of fear are interlocked in a dialectical relationship. As noted above, in politics the sense of control can be reinforced by the manipulation of fear. If in authoritarian systems this appears self-evident, in democracies the connection between the two is more elusive.

Elites infrequently refer to fear by name. The effectiveness of the politics of fear from above, conducted by elites, lies in creating the atmosphere out of which fear emerges. The most successful cases of the politics of fear may therefore be when the concept never comes up. Fear is a powerful tool when silence surrounds it.

Thomas Jefferson may have spoken about fear. He is reputed to have said that when people fear the government there is tyranny. When the government fears the people there is liberty. Deliberate and systematic top-down manipulation of fear produces, by this logic, a form of political tyranny. Conversely when grassroots movements threaten the political establishment we see the signs of liberty. Even if Jefferson never made this distinction, it is valuable to reflect on how elites' fear of the people may play positive functions.

The politics of fear from below may be emancipatory but carries dangers. A democratic system *eo ipso* is prone to the influence of xenophobes because elections should give the demos a decisive voice in the selection of leaders and policies. Some groups in society may become so empowered as to become the entrepreneurs of fear. The marginalized, uneducated, unskilled, unemployed are identified as dependable political sources for the rise of exclusionary nationalism. These groups are not all that different from the lumpenproletariat and the peasantry identified by Marx as the social strata striking fear into the hearts of progressive classes.

It is tautological to say that, in authoritarian systems, the policy preferences of the political elite become that of the state. These systems are often associated with discriminatory and repressive policies towards minorities at home and antipathies towards neighboring nations. But democratic systems are also susceptible to the xenophobic temptation. By definition they register public opinion more sensitively, including when such opinion subsumes a fear of foreigners. Democracy may be a double-edged sword, therefore.

In international politics, "A democratic franchise may bias a society toward a more pacific foreign policy [. . .] Supposedly it does so by enfranchising those whom war is least likely to benefit or whose ingrained taste for it is far less pronounced."[66] Equally it may do just the reverse: trigger belligerence towards another state.

Let us consider a case that we develop in Chapter 5. If much of the public were to express anti-Russian attitudes, as in much of Central Europe in 2014, it may lead not just to electoral success for a party campaigning on a russo-hypopsic platform. It may also entrust foreign policy-making to nationalist actors who advocate a confrontational approach to the nation's perceived historical foe. Xeno-hypopsia at home and abroad can be particularly influential in a democracy, therefore. "Demagoguery works best where the demos has some influence."[67] The type of demagoguery most likely to have resonance is that targeting an unpopular foreign nation or a disliked minority at home. Projected to foreign policy, such demagoguery can produce irrational security fears, unrealistic national interests, and eventually a confrontational policy towards a distrusted nation.

In the United States the political use of fear is usually associated with economic and political elites.[68] Particularly after the 2001 terrorist attacks, threat perceptions became an integral part of official discourse, media reporting, and the rapidly growing securitization industry. The war on terror launched by President George W. Bush – the war *of* terror as film character *Borat* misspeaks to Oklahoma rodeo fans – involved raising Americans' sense of threat levels, graphically illustrated by the color codes employed by the State Department in the years following the terrorist attacks. Fear has led to the rapid expansion of many industries – gated communities, security companies, and firearms – which exploit Americans' personalized fears planted in them by elites. Yet there are grounds to characterize American society as more consumed by fearlessness than fear, as Chapter 7 suggests.

The United States was not the only country whose perceptions of threat increased early in the twenty-first century. But in Europe threat perceptions were different, associated more with identity than security, and did not give rise to massive securitization-related industries. To be sure, as with the US, a civilizational divide emerged pitting Europe against the Islamic world. But the greatest perceived threat originated not from Islamic jihadism but from large-scale Muslim immigration to Europe. In its extreme variation, it was the specter of a future Eurabia, a Europe controlled by the Arab world. Coupled with a more general European malaise stemming from the rise of East Asia and financial crisis at home, fear began to spread across the European Union.

Europe's politics of fear appear less to entail top-down elite manipulation of citizens. Indeed, EU elites stick to a master narrative of Europe's radiant future. What is unique is bottom-up mobilization of swathes of society against an unresponsive political establishment holding to policies of liberal immigration and far-reaching cultural diversity. Many political leaders of individual EU states acknowledged this backlash and a number dropped the term multiculturalism from their vocabulary; they realized such a formulation of diversity management was a vote loser. By contrast, at the European Union governance level, elites had little to fear from bottom-up pressures stressing fear of loss of identity, breakdown of social cohesion, and an ever-increasing surplus of low-skilled labor. They were insulated from grassroots pressure to be responsive to public preferences because their sinecure and selection did not depend on citizens' views.

In Europe today the entrepreneurs of fear are most frequently the leaders of right-wing, populist, nationalist, and sometimes single-issue anti-immigrant political parties. These entrepreneurs are often the products of xenophobic grassroots political organizations. Some are opportunistic and see advantage in employing xenophobic discourse to expand and diffuse their organizational base. Xenophobia is Žižek's shark in the sea, a master signifier permitting social anxiety to crystallize.

Right-wing parties may instrumentalize xenophobic ideas because they can serve as code for anti-elite politics. If European political elites champion immigrant-based diversity and multiculturalism, anti-immigrant rhetoric amounts to anti-elite rhetoric. Anti-immigrant parties in Europe can be seen then as contesting what Samuel Johnson (1709–84) called the dictatorship of the prevailing orthodoxy, in this instance the dictatorship of cultural diversity.[69]

Skilled entrepreneurs of fear exploit ethnic, linguistic, and religious cleavages to promote their political careers. Sometimes described as ethnic entrepreneurs, they played a prominent role in the Balkans' wars of the 1990s. More recently, the 2014 elections to the European Parliament illustrated how populist xenophobic leaders and their parties have become "mainstreamed" and more widespread, a familiar phenomenon found across all of Europe.[70] Outside the European Union, ethnic entrepreneurs in Kiev, Simferopol, and Donetsk in 2014 played critical parts in worsening Ukraine's political crisis.

CASE STUDIES

Three country studies of the influence of fear on politics are featured in this book: France, Poland, and Sweden. Each considers how public fears affect domestic policies, such as on immigration and social integration. But the case studies also examine how fears may end up shaping foreign policy, too, such as on relations with other countries implicated in fear narratives.

In the three cases, the years 2006 and 2007 are turning points when opposition parties ousted incumbents and in power took different policy courses than their predecessors. In Sweden in 2006 Fredrik Reinfeldt's Moderate Party-led conservative alliance replaced the Social Democratic-led government and pursued less liberal domestic and foreign policies. The alliance remained in power until 2014 but imprinted a changed political landscape.

In France in 2007 Nicolas Sarkozy was elected president, replacing Jacques Chirac. Here, too, important changes followed even though both presidents belonged to the same right-of-center party. Sarkozy was seen as more of a game changer, *l'homme de rupture*, than his Socialist Party successor, François Hollande, who defeated him in the 2012 election.

In 2007 also Poland's nationalist government, led by Jarosław Kaczyński, was ousted by a center-right liberal party headed by Donald Tusk. Jarosław's twin brother Lech was the country's president until he was killed in an air crash in 2010. Changes in policy and style after the Kaczyńskis were stark; Tusk was an authoritative prime minister until he resigned in 2014 to become president of the European Council.

The shift to conservatism in Sweden, away from conservatism in Poland, and to a different kind of conservatism in France share a common feature. Congruence between domestic and foreign policies that followed the three turnovers may have been strengthened in these countries after 2006–07. The influence of domestic factors on foreign policy appeared to grow: an increase

21

in French citizens' fears of Muslim immigrants, a decrease in Polish public fear of neighboring Russia, more adventurous Swedish government policies shaking traditional preferences for consensus and security. The devil lies in the details, and evidence from these countries in these time periods is presented in Chapters 4 to 6.

In France the *Front National* (FN), headed by Marine Le Pen, is one of Europe's most radical fear-inciting parties. In Poland the opposition Law and Justice party (PiS) represents a traditional nationalist Roman Catholic right-wing movement that raises fears about a secularizing European Union, a resurgent Russia, and a more influential Germany. It is the closest Poland has to a parliamentary-based populist movement. In Sweden the rise of the Sweden Democrats (SD), a party which draws attention to the country's problems in integrating immigrants, its declining social cohesion, and its muddled national identity, is another example.

This study asks whether citizens' distrust of groups they construct as foreigners living within their societies or in neighboring states has an impact on their states' foreign policies. Specifically can public hypopsia shape unfriendly foreign policy towards the targets of distrust?

A threefold typology of "strangers" structures this book. First are members of immigration-based communities. The case of France focuses on attitudes towards migrants and their descendants who originate from the Maghreb and Sahel regions of Africa. Another case is the effect on foreign policy of Swedish images of war refugees coming from Iraq and Syria. Do suspicions of these refugees put pressure on Sweden to mediate conflicts in Iraq, Syria, and elsewhere or do they have no discernable impact?

The second set of imagined strangers is made up of people living in neighboring countries. For Poland, Russians and Russia have historically evoked hypopsic attitudes. Case studies similar in design not conducted here could have been French citizens' attitudes towards, and historical memories of, Germans and Germany; and Swedish society's views of Danes and Denmark which may assume a normative and cultural rift between the two wider than the Øresund.

The final part of the typology is composed of the historic minorities often framed as "strangers." Examples are Bretons in France, Roma in Poland, and Saami in Sweden. There is no foreign policy resonance to such types of hypopsia so this linkage is not examined in this book. But the persistence of anti-Semitism in European states directed at established Jewish communities is considered.

This typology points to how today in these three countries fear of certain groups has greater potential foreign policy implications than fear of others. Fear of Muslims living in France has the potential to affect its relations with Muslim-majority states; hypopsia of neighboring Russia can have an impact

22

on Poland's relations with Russia; and Sweden's relations with the countries of origin of Middle Eastern asylum-seekers may be affected by domestic opinion.

CONCLUSIONS

Napoleon Bonaparte claimed that only two forces unite men: fear and self-interest. In certain conditions fear and self-interest may develop simultaneously. Thucydides recognized that fear is a factor shaping interstate relations but added that it was not the sole or chief one. The hope of gain was a stronger force than the fear of loss. Maximizing profits and rents is a defining feature of the early twenty-first-century economic order. The politics of fear, suspicion, and surveillance are largely harnessed in the service of the 1 percent at the pinnacle of the socio-economically unequal global system.

A characteristic of this world system is increasing hypopsia shown by the less well off towards the least well off. This structured suspicion is seen in global migration. We inhabit a world of unparalleled migration of peoples – south to north and east to west but also now north to south and west to east. Fear and distrust of strangers may represent the most atavistic way today that Napoleon's fear and self-interest collude.

What is distinct in recent years is how the politics of fear from below in Europe contest politically correct strictures on how to regard the stranger. This politics follows the codicil of the Duke of Albany which concludes Shakespeare's King Lear:

> The weight of this sad time we must obey;
> Speak what we feel, not what we ought to say.

To speak what we feel – it is a combination of cosmic, official, and existential fears that people wish to speak of – has for some time been discouraged. But this taboo is being broken and the implications for domestic and international politics are significant.

It is how public fear and national interests within a country interact to shape its foreign policy behavior that is the concern of this book. In an interdependent kaleidoscopic world, where the sanctity of state borders is repeatedly challenged, the divide between what is internal and what is external to a state is being eroded. As writer Fatima Mernissi put it at the end of the cold war, "Our fin-de-siècle era resembles the apocalypse. Boundaries and standards seem to be disappearing. Interior space is scarcely distinguishable from exterior."[71]

The next chapter describes how the field of international relations has itself become concerned with trying to connect domestic factors including cultural ones with foreign policy.

Notes

1. William Desmond, "Lessons of Fear: A Reading of Thucydides," *Classical Philology*, 101 (2006) p. 359, http://eprints.nuim.ie/827/1/William_Desmond.pdf
2. Brian E. Calabrese, *Fear in Democracy: A Study of Thucydides' Political Thought* (Ann Arbor, MI: ProQuest, UMI Dissertations Publishing, 2008), p. 17.
3. Marie Demker, "Attitudes toward immigrants and refugees: Swedish trends with some comparisons." Paper presented at the International Studies Association 48th Annual Convention, 28 February 2007, Chicago, p. 2.
4. This typology is from Calabrese, *Fear in Democracy*, pp. 19–21. A caveat is in order: other studies of Thucydides' vocabulary of fear do not include *hypopsis* in their list of words associated with fear. See Desmond, "Lessons of Fear;" Pierre Huart, *Le vocabulaire de l'analyse psychologique dans l'oeuvre de Thucydide* (Paris: Klincksiek, 1968); and Jacqueline de Romilly, "La crainte dans l'oeuvre de Thucydide," *Classica et Mediaevalia*, 17 (1956), pp. 119–27.
5. Calabrese, *Fear in Democracy*, p. 39.
6. For more see Raymond Taras, *Xenophobia and Islamophobia in Europe* (Edinburgh: Edinburgh University Press, 2012).
7. Valentina Feklyunina, "Constructing Russophobia," in Ray Taras (ed.), *Russia's Identity in International Relations: Images, Perceptions, Misperceptions* (London: Routledge, 2012), pp. 98–100.
8. But see Polish historian Andrzej Wierzbicki, *Europa w polskiej myśli historycznej i politycznej XIX i XX wieku* (Warsaw: Wydawnictwo TRIO, 2009), Chapter 3.
9. Jacques Rancière, *On the Shores of Politics* (London: Verso, 2007).
10. A sweeping sycophantic study is Francis Fukuyama, *Trust: The Social Virtues and the Creation of Prosperity* (New York: Free Press, 1996). See also Bo Rothstein, *The Quality of Government: Corruption, Social Trust, and Inequality in International Perspective* (Chicago, IL: University of Chicago Press, 2011).
11. Lucien Febvre, *Le problème de l'incroyance au XVIeme siècle* (Paris: Albin Michel, 1947).
12. René Descartes, *Passions of the Soul* (Indianapolis, IN: Hackett, 1989), art. 45.
13. Niccolò Machiavelli, *The Prince* (Harmondsworth: Penguin, 2003), Chapter XVII.
14. Thomas Hobbes, *Leviathan* (Harmondsworth: Penguin, 1982), Book II, Chapters 17–19.
15. John Locke, *Second Treatise of Government* (Mineola, NY: Dover, 2002). It was published in 1689.
16. See Gérard Chaliand and Arnaud Blin (eds), *The History of Terrorism: From Antiquity to Al Qaeda* (Berkeley, CA: University of California Press, 2007); Randall Law, *Terrorism: A History* (Cambridge: Polity Press, 2009). See also Jean Delumeau, *La peur en Occident* (Paris: Livre de poche, 1978).
17. Zygmunt Bauman, *Liquid Fear* (Cambridge: Polity Press, 2006), p. 54.
18. Mikhael Bakhtin discussed by Zygmunt Bauman, *Wasted Lives: Modernity and its Outcasts* (New York: John Wiley, 2004), pp. 46–53.
19. Mikhail Bakhtin, *Rabelais and His World* (Bloomington, IN: Indiana University Press, 1984), p. 41.

20. Michela Marzano, *Visages de la peur* (Paris: Presses Universitaires de France, 2009), p. 44.
21. Simone Weil, *The Need for Roots: Prelude to a Declaration of Duties Towards Mankind* (London: Routledge Classics, 2001), p. 43. For an analysis of the psychological bases of fear, especially factors occurring in childhood, see my *Xenophobia and Islamophobia in Europe* (Edinburgh: Edinburgh University Press, 2012), pp. 8–16.
22. Bauman, *Liquid Fear*, p. 132.
23. Sara Ahmed, *The Cultural Politics of Emotion* (New York: Routledge, 2004), p. 15.
24. Vamik Volkan, *Bloodlines: From Ethnic Pride to Ethnic Terrorism* (Boulder, CO: Westview, 1997).
25. Jacques Lacan, *The Four Fundamental Concepts of Psycho-analysis* (New York: W. W. Norton, 1981), note 8.
26. Slavoj Žižek, *Living in the End Times* (London: Verso, 2011), p. 68.
27. Catarina Kinnvall, "European Trauma: Governance and the Psychological Moment," *Alternatives: Global, Local, Political*, 37 (2012), p. 269.
28. Catarina Kinnvall, "Trauma and the politics of fear: Europe at the crossroads," in Nicolas Demertzis (ed.), *Emotions in Politics: The Affect Dimension in Political Tension* (London: Palgrave, 2013), pp. 143–66. In the same volume see also Jack Barbalet and Demertzis, "Collective fear and societal change," pp. 167–85.
29. Rita Taureck, "Securitization theory and securitization studies", *Journal of International Relations and Development*, 9 (2006), pp. 53–61.
30. Ole Wæver, "Aberystwyth, Paris, Copenhagen: New 'Schools' in Security Theory and their Origins between Core and Periphery." Paper presented at the annual meeting of the International Studies Association, Montreal, 17–20 March 2004, p. 13.
31. Miran Božovič, (ed.), *The Panopticon Writings* (London: Verso, 1995).
32. Michel Foucault, *Discipline and Punish: The Birth of the Prison* (New York: Vintage, 1995), p. 216.
33. Michel Foucault, *Naissance de la biopolitique: Cours au Collège de France (1978–1979)* (Paris: Gallimard & Seuil, 2004). See also Foucault, "Governmentality," in Graham Burchell, Colin Gordon, and Peter Miller (eds), *The Foucault Effect: Studies in Governmentality* (Chicago, IL: University of Chicago Press, 1991), pp. 87–104.
34. Slavoj Žižek *Violence: Six Sideways Reflections* (London: Picador, 2008), p. 40.
35. Ibid., p. 41.
36. Ibid.
37. Slavoj Žižek, "Barbarism with a Human Face," *London Review of Books* (8 May 2014), p. 36.
38. Sigmund Freud, "The 'Uncanny,'" in *The Standard Edition of the Complete Psychological Works of Sigmund Freud* (New York: Vintage, 1999), vol. XVII (1917–19): *An Infantile Neurosis and Other Works*, pp. 217–56.
39. Deborah Lea Madsen, "'The Exception that Proves the Rule'?: National Fear, Racial Loathing, Chinese Writing in UnAustralia," *Antipodes*, 23:1 (2009), p. 17.
40. Freud, "The Uncanny," p. 241.
41. See Ray Taras, *Europe Old and New: Transnationalism, Belonging, Xenophobia* (Boulder, CO: Rowman and Littlefield, 2010), Chapter 4.
42. Frank Furedi, *Culture of Fear Revisited* (London: Bloomsbury Academic, 2006), p. 115.

43. A Chinese-language literary journal published in Australia is titled *Otherland*.
44. Emmanuel Levinas, *Totalité et infini: essai sur l'extériorité* (The Hague: Martinus Nijhoff, 1961), IX–XII.
45. Anonymous author, "Hospitality and its Ambivalences: on Zygmunt Bauman," *Hospitality & Society*, forthcoming 2015.
46. See Inge Bretherton, "The Origins of Attachment Theory: John Bowlby and Mary Ainsworth," *Developmental Psychology*, 28, no. 5 (1992), pp. 759–75.
47. Zygmunt Bauman, *Liquid Modernity* (Cambridge: Polity Press, 2000), p. 91.
48. Ibid., p. 148.
49. Bauman, *Liquid Fear*, p. 5.
50. Mikael Spång, "Svensk invandringspolitik i demokratiskt perspektiv", *Current Themes in IMER Research*, 8 (Malmö: Malmö University IMER, 2008), pp. 170–1.
51. Ibid.
52. Cornelius Castoriadis, "Reflections on Racism," *Thesis Eleven* 32, no. 1 (1992), pp. 1–12.
53. Stathis Gourgouris, "On Self-Alteration," *Parrhesia*, 9 (2010), p. 9.
54. Deborah Lea Madsen, "The Exception that Proves the Rule? National Fear, Racial Loathing: Chinese Writing in 'UnAustralia,'" *Antipodes*, 23, no. 1 (2009), p. 21.
55. Fabrizio Tassinari, *Why Europe Fears its Neighbors* (Santa Barbara, CA: ABC–CLIO, 2009), pp. 2–3.
56. Mitja Velikonja, *Eurosis: A Critique of the New Eurocentrism* (Ljubljana: Peace Institute, 2005), p. 8.
57. "EU stands by 'family member' Ukraine," BBC News website, 20 December 2013, http://www.bbc.com/news/world-europe-25467738
58. "Bildt hopes 2014 will be better year for Ukraine," *KyivPost* website, 30 December 2013, https://www.kyivpost.com/content/ukraine/swedish-foreign-minister-i-hope-2014-will-be-better-year-for-ukraine-when-the-country-334439.html
59. Gayatri Chakravorty Spivak, *A Critique of Postcolonial Reason: Toward a History of the Vanishing Present* (Cambridge, MA: Harvard University Press, 1999), p. x.
60. Dipesh Chakrabarty, *Provincializing Europe: Postcolonial Thought and Historical Difference* (Princeton, NJ: Princeton University Press, 2000), p. 3.
61. Ibid., p. 4.
62. Ibid., p. 8. "Not yet" is taken from Martin Heidegger, *Being and Time* (New York: Harper Perennial, 2008), Division II.
63. Andre Gunder Frank, *ReOrient: Global Economy in the Asian Age* (Berkeley, CA: University of California Press, 1998), p. 340.
64. Ibid., p. 334.
65. Marzano, *Visages de la peur*, p. 153.
66. Ronald Rogowski, "Institutions as constraints on strategic choice," in David A. Lake and Robert Powell (eds), *Strategic Choice and International Relations* (Princeton, NJ: Princeton University Press, 1999), p. 122.
67. Ibid., p. 133.
68. For a detailed study of fear in the United States, see Corey Robin, *Fear: The History of a Political Idea* (New York: Oxford University Press, 2006).
69. British Member of Parliament George Galloway uses the term and attributes it to Johnson though it is not clear that Johnson ever used it.
70. For an insightful interpretation see Cas Mudde, "The far right in the 2014 European

elections: Of earthquakes, cartels and designer fascists," *Washington Post* website, 30 May 2014), http://www.washingtonpost.com/blogs/monkey-cage/wp/2014/05/30/the-far-right-in-the-2014-european-elections-of-earthquakes-cartels-and-designer-fascists/

71. Fatima Mernissi, *Islam and Democracy: Fear of the Modern World* (New York: Addison-Wesley, 1992), p. 8.

CHAPTER TWO

Reconnecting culture with foreign policy

Fears affect the world view of individual foreign policy-makers. They shape domestic structures – both the institutions and culture they are made up of – out of which foreign policy emerges. They may spread across an international system creating an insecure and threatening environment. The focus of this chapter is on what international relations specialists call the domestic structures approach to foreign policy-making. Within this framework, I consider the cultural turn in international relations which assigns to culture greater influence among other domestic factors in affecting foreign policy.

FEAR, CULTURE, AND FOREIGN POLICY

A culture of fear has affected political societies for as long as they have existed. At certain times and places and under specific circumstances it has been more prominent than in other time- and place-specific conditions. In the scholarship on the origins and effects of fear, the primary focus has been on political rather than international society; Machiavelli's study of *The Prince* is a case in point.

But as with sentiments of glory and hubris, pride and shame, fear has always had salience for international politics. Indeed, Ken Booth and Nicholas Wheeler made a strong case for recognizing the impact of fear on international relations. They singled out the underestimated part played by human agency in determining international security and called for "security dilemma sensibility" – the empathy that allows an actor to perceive the motives and attitudes of others which are often stirred by fear.[1]

Rather than a focus on fear emerging out of the anarchy and threat perceptions inherent to the international system,[2] I look at fear emerging domestically and how it may be projected into the international arena. This can occur directly or indirectly, subtly or shamelessly, intentionally or unconsciously – but it needs to be studied.

I am concerned with the interplay of fear of the foreign arising at home and abroad. An obvious example is citizens' perceptions of the threat the "stranger" poses at home leading to fear of the far-off place the stranger comes from. In his description of xenophobia Bauman captured the interstices of domestic and international fears of migrants this way: "Xenophobia, the growing suspicion of a foreign plot and resentment of 'strangers' (mostly of emigrants, those vivid and highly visible reminders that walls can be pierced and borders effaced, natural effigies, asking to be burned, of mysterious globalizing forces running out of control)."[3]

Fears in the interstate system can be the products of domestic structures. Let me give four examples of home fears spreading to the international arena. First, fear of the growing presence of immigrants at home and that of impending international anarchy – a breakdown of the international system – can be interconnected. Second, securitization of migration policy, more precisely, framing immigration to be within the "domains of insecurity"[4] – combines the fear of foreigners allegedly stealing jobs, undermining social cohesion, and hybridizing national identity *with* a perception that government can no longer control immigration flows and national borders. Third, fears arise when measures to monitor foreigners threaten a backlash which may entail a spiral of violence and terrorism. Finally, the very process of policy-making on domestic and foreign issues may be viewed as having been hijacked by influential ethnic diasporas with transnational ties, thereby raising fears that a country's national action script (discussed below) is being undermined.

This chapter first reviews the different components making up domestic structures. It considers the influence of traditional institutional structures but also nonmaterial cultural ones;[5] one of these is citizens' expressions of fear and suspicion, particularly of strangers in their midst. I assess how the "black box" of decision-making may be affected by this array of domestic factors. Then I examine the cultural turn in the study of international politics at the end of the cold war and of the bipolar system. This shift from studying institutions to focusing on culture provided new tools and concepts to investigate linkages between domestic and foreign policies. Two cases of recent internationalized conflict – Libya and Ukraine – are presented to illustrate how the linkages function today. Finally, I look at the securitization of immigration and ways that it subsumes domestic and foreign policy issues. The "methods" question of whether culture generally, and fear specifically, "cause" particular types of foreign policy behavior, is addressed in Chapter 3.

FEAR AND DOMESTIC STRUCTURES

The making of foreign policy is a complex process whose dimensions international relations scholars traditionally divide into three levels of analysis: 1. the psychology, predispositions, and preferences of individual decision makers; 2. the domestic structures of a country including its institutions, actors, processes, values, and citizen attitudes; and 3. the structure of the global and regional systems, the balance of power in them, and the opportunities and constraints they provide an individual state to pursue its foreign policy objectives.[6]

A focus on domestic structures – sometimes termed state-level factors – is important because it "improves our understanding of policy. This level of analysis emphasizes the characteristics of states and how they make foreign policy choices and implement them."[7] Public fears, whether expressed in public opinion surveys or aggregated by populist parties and movements at election time, are a part of this "structure."

The term domestic structures is misleading. International relations scholars who adopt a structuralist approach prioritizing the domestic context of international politics do not limit their attention to domestic institutions and rules. They are also concerned with how structures of *constructed meaning* embodied in *norms or identities* affect what states do in the international arena.[8] In the recent past, the role of cultural factors affecting international politics has received greater attention. *Culture Matters*, Samuel Huntington titled a book published not long after his landmark *The Clash of Civilizations and the Remaking of World Order*.[9] The impact of culture on popular attitudes, populist movements, identity construction, and self-images has received considerable attention since.

More traditional domestic structures which have been studied are type of government (democratic or not), type of situation (crisis or not), and type of policy (immediate or longer-term effect). Principal actors and decision rules which affect foreign policy are central to state-level analysis, too. Members of a country's national security council are such principals: the state's chief executive (president); government head (prime minister); ministers of foreign policy, defense, national security, intelligence, and home affairs; chiefs of the general staff; and other actors such as area studies experts.

Participants in foreign policy-making are not only state officials with formal roles. The attentive public and opinion leaders are also engaged in many policy debates. Other actors are those with direct interests in how an issue is played out: for example, business lobbies, ethnic groups, epistemic communities, bureaucracies, transnational interest groups, single-issue groups, and public relations firms hired by foreign governments to promote their interests. Actors may also include groups that form part of civil society, nongovernmental organizations, and grassroots social, cultural, and ideological organizations. Most of these informal actors are motivated by advancing specific interests. Some of them use fear – of climate change, of an excessively over- (or under-) regulated business environment, of a threatening foreign power – as means of promoting their agenda.

The antecedent causes and influences on actors participating in foreign policy are important to identify because structures of meaning "affect the instrumental rationality of actors."[10] International relations specialist Peter Katzenstein believed that "security interests are defined by actors who respond to cultural factors." Among these cultural factors are norms: "collective expectations for the proper behavior of actors with a given identity."[11] For Katzenstein then, "The identities of states emerge from the interactions with different social environments, both domestic and international."[12]

By focusing primarily on the influence of citizens' fears and suspicions I am opening up a colorful Russian-style matryoshka doll called domestic structures. If the outer largest doll is the structure, the next largest one tucked inside it is named culture. Open that doll and we find a smaller doll representing citizens' values and attitudes. And the smallest doll of them all – the inner core or nucleus – is made up of fears.

Actors' rationality and emotions

Domestic political actors shape domestic structures and, in turn, foreign policy. The assumption that these decision-makers follow instrumental rationality when formulating foreign policy is an optimistic viewpoint. Is groupthink a rational form of behavior? And is it not usually influential? What of xenophobic demagoguery which produces irrational security fears and a corresponding hostile policy towards antipathetic nations? What is the role of human emotions ranging from insecurity to hubris? How far have we come from Swedish Count Oxiensterna's observation made in 1648? "You do not understand, my son, how small a part reason plays in governing the world."[13]

The appeal of demagoguery and xenophobia is precisely in its emotional, rather than rational, charge:

> Ordinary Jane and Ordinary Joe are quicker to feel than they are to think; they respond more readily to a message that touches their emotions than to one that requires them to attend to a carefully reasoned argument. Reason does not mobilize support; slogans do. Reasoning is demanding; slogans are comfortably compelling.[14]

Under such conditions gauging the effect of irrationality on foreign policy will be elusive.

One consequence of identifying the limits of rationality in shaping policy is to highlight the importance of other undervalued factors. Among these are human emotions. Today "'emotions-proof' research can no longer be sustained" as it is clear that an "instrumental and neutral-procedural conception of politics" has failed to capture important dimensions of politics. "The supremacy of 'interest' as opposed to 'passion' as an explaining factor of political action" has been discredited by international events occurring in the twenty-first century.[15]

Affect shapes not only politics at home but international relations. Scholar Pierre Hassner analyzed the impact of a range of emotions on politics but concentrated his attention on the question whether societies were returning to a fixation on "great fears." After World War II many societies were concerned with the "small fears" in life, such as those related to hygiene, food, and ecology. These were very different from the great fears which had haunted the Middle Ages, such as epidemics, hunger, and war. After the September 2001 terror attacks in the United States, however, great fears – of terrorism, foreigners, biological weapons – again became dominant.

For Hassner the spread of great fears involves a vicious circle. What he termed the barbarization of bourgeois societies occurred when, incited by the need for security, fear, and its twin passion hate, they barbarized themselves in order to confront their perceived enemies. Because of their fears, such liberal societies have begun to reject their own value system.[16]

Another French writer developed the idea of a globalization of emotions. Globalization includes a usually overlooked emotional dimension, Dominique Moïsi contended, which raises the question whether today we are caught up in a "clash of emotions." On one side are Europe and the United States affected by crises of identity engendering cultures of fear: fear of the rise of the other as rival or threat. On the other side stand China, India, and ASEAN member states characterized by a culture of hope. Confidence and optimism about their futures extend beyond just the sphere of economic growth.

Between is a culture of humiliation which affects the Arab and Muslim worlds; historic decline along with political, religious, and social frustrations leave them emotionally shattered. Then there are unclassifiable countries, such as: Russia, which combines all three emotions – fear, hope, and humiliation; Israeli society which has shifted from hope to anxiety; and African states which are drawn into a culture of hopelessness.[17] This analytical framework has been criticized for its reductionism and simplicity[18] but it succeeds in making a case for adopting a global map of emotions which can help explain the fractiousness of international politics.

If emotions are the antithesis of rationality, beliefs may also often be irrational. A recent study of US foreign policy highlighted how it is shaped by the beliefs of actors. "The key to understanding foreign policy failures, therefore, lies not in the actions themselves but in the beliefs that gave rise to them. Where do incorrect – pathologically incorrect – foreign policy beliefs come from?"[19]

Misguided belief systems, which corrupt foreign policy behavior, may be the product of fear or of some other human emotion. "The ancients would recognize these beliefs and place them into familiar categories: fear, honor, glory, and hubris. Modern leaders may be reluctant to acknowledge that they are susceptible to such basic, primal atavisms, but often their differences with the Caesars are more in style than substance."[20] Compared to other elements of domestic structures, political actors may suffer from the greatest aberrations of all.

Rules and institutions

Apart from political actors and the factors which affect them, decision rules and decision-making processes play crucial parts in foreign policy-making. At a general level, the democratic or authoritarian nature of the political system will affect foreign policy. The most cited example of the impact of type of government is the democratic peace theory which holds that democratic systems are more peaceful international actors than authoritarian ones. It has diverse implications.

> The democratic peace proposition is connected to many other propositions linking domestic politics and international relations, including that democracies are more likely to cooperate with each other, that democracies are more likely to win the wars they fight, that escalating military casualties degrade public support for war, that leaders initiate conflict to secure their domestic hold on power (the diversionary hypothesis), that democracies fight shorter wars, that different kinds of democracies experience different kinds of conflict behavior, that different kinds of authoritarian systems experience different kinds of conflict behavior, and others.[21]

An intriguing corollary is systemic democratic peace theory which claims that the more democracies there are in a region of the world or in the international system, the more peaceful it will become. This proposition offers a powerful argument in support of democracy promotion. Paradoxically, when pursued by President George W. Bush, democracy promotion was a policy identified by citizens around the world as exacerbating regional wars.[22]

Public opinion and foreign policy

Domestic structures shaping foreign policy include "We, the people." But citizens' agency in the making of foreign policy is notoriously inconsistent, fickle, and difficult to measure: "the public plays a highly variable role in foreign policy. Public opinion is generally of marginal importance in authoritarian governments while in democracies the role of the people is more complex."[23] Speculating about the policy influence of fearful publics can be a trying endeavor.

To add to the difficulties of assessing the public's influence on policy, it is on this subject that political science research has recorded little progress. We have not come far from the speculations of journalist Walter Lippmann nearly a century ago that public opinion suffers from low levels of political knowledge owing to lack of information and restricted access to facts. Anticipating social constructivist approaches of the turn of the twenty-first century, he also observed that the real world differed greatly from "the pictures in our heads."[24]

Mapping the effects of public opinion on the formulation of foreign policy appears to be a daunting task, then. Such findings as we have are frequently contradictory. On the one hand, "the conventional wisdom is that the public simply does not influence foreign policy . . . [and] it is not clear that leaders would follow the public's opinion." On the other is evidence that "there is some congruence between changes in public opinion and changes in foreign policy."[25] This intriguing latter possibility is what our three case studies explore.

One way to gauge the influence of public opinion on foreign policy is to review whether a government already had a propensity to pursue a particular foreign policy course. If this government decided not to act on its initial ideas and changed course, the role of public opinion may have proved decisive. As discussed in Chapter 3, the sequence of events can suggest whether a causal relationship exists.

Public opinion is often just an intervening, rather than independent, variable affecting policy-making. To pin down its causal role becomes elusive. Let me cite the example of public opinion and election outcomes. Why things happen the way they do in volatile elections and in messy electoral systems is not always easy to explain, particularly when irrational factors play a part. A focus on the influence of multiple or complex factors, many of which may not be rational, seems indispensable, therefore. One such factor is citizens' fears.

Public opinion may be embedded in a political culture. It is a resource waiting to be activated by entrepreneurial leaders but it can prove useful on certain occasions yet not on others. For example, in 2002 Gerhard Schroeder effectively played the anti-US card popular among the German public to be reelected as German chancellor. But that card proved ineffective when employed by candidates running against Angela Merkel in 2005, 2009, and 2013. Appealing to the state of public opinion does not guarantee success, therefore.

Moreover the rare, transformative leader such as French President Charles de Gaulle was able in large part to bend public opinion to his will. The more common type of transactional leader, such as Sweden's Fredrik Reinfeldt, calculates that he will gain more political influence by reflecting public opinion rather than transcending it.

Public opinion may at once be shifting, elusive, and indeterminate in its influence but the question of how attentive political leaders are to it on issues related to international politics is worth probing. Similarly the extent to which citizens in democracies – even if they are restricted to "attentive publics" – should be consulted and whether this helps improve the quality of both democracy and policy-making are key issues.[26]

Alex de Tocqueville believed it was undesirable for the public to influence leaders. In contrast to the aristocracy, that "firm and enlightened body," the public "may be led astray by ignorance and passion."[27] This view informed Machiavelli three centuries earlier and influences realist foreign policy-makers to this day.

Public opinion and international conflict

The impact of public opinion on going to war has been addressed in a number of American scholarly studies. One proposed that "The estimated effect of public opinion about foreign policy is particularly large and robust if a specific foreign policy issue is salient for foreign publics." Put differently, "foreign public opinion . . . has real policy consequences only when issues are highly controversial and discussed among foreign publics extensively and intensely."[28] The US image in the world in some measure does matter, then, in choosing among foreign policy alternatives.

Another US study compared public support for realist and liberal internationalist approaches to foreign policy. The proposition examined was that American public opinion is generally less sympathetic to realist balance-of-power views than to liberal internationalist ones. Two beliefs expressed by classical realists showed bias against taking public opinion seriously: "The first concern which stretches back to Thucydides was that democracies had a disadvantage in crafting foreign policy vis-à-vis authoritarian governments because of the need to appease a mass public that holds inchoate views about international relations." The second concern was that Americans filtered foreign policy decisions through a moralistic belief system. "This renders the mass public unable to digest the realist logic of a dispassionate, hard-headed national interest."[29]

Despite realists' skepticism about the limits of public opinion, the study pointed to a converse relationship: "surveys about foreign policy world views and priorities, the use of force, and foreign economic policies all reveal a strong realist bent among the mass American public. The overwhelming majority of Americans possess a Hobbesian world view of international relations."[30]

An analysis of the public discourse of American political leaders suggests that waning public support for wars in Vietnam in the 1960s and 1970s,

Iraq in the 2000s, and Afghanistan in the 2010s played a significant role in American exits from these conflicts. A similar shift in the public mood helped end Soviet military intervention in Afghanistan and other Third World conflicts in the 1980s. So political attitudes and national morale do appear to influence a state's international politics including its war proneness or conflict aversion. At the same time, we are drawn to the conclusion that public opinion largely judges actions after the event, not before. Rarely does it support military actions abroad that are going badly.

In theory, public opinion on foreign policy issues in established democracies will have greater impact than in newer democracies or nondemocratic systems. But in crisis-defined foreign policy issues having immediate effects, for example, Western European governments' willingness to join the US-led coalition of the willing in the invasion of Iraq in 2003 despite strong public opposition (whether expressed in surveys or through protests), the public's influence is highly circumscribed and usually indirect.[31]

The relatively limited influence of citizens on foreign policy has interested specialists studying politics in the new democracies of Eastern Europe. Some feel that secrecy is injurious to public policy-making and is "repugnant to the interests of liberty and those of peace."[32] The tradeoff is between prioritizing the essence of diplomacy – secrecy, flexibility, speed – which is hamstrung by an expanded public role – and singling out public participation as assuring governmental accountability and responsiveness.[33] It is telling then that the Maidan protests in Kiev in 2013–14 explicitly demanded more governmental responsibility towards citizens.

Let me turn to the findings of two studies of citizen attitudes and foreign policy in Ukraine. A 2003 analysis by Viktor Chudowsky and Taras Kuzio contended that Western assumptions about citizen–elite relations did not apply to Ukraine. That was because on policy issues Ukrainian public opinion was pragmatic rather than ideological. Not only that: Ukrainians expressed preferences for political parties and leaders on the basis of intuition, not reasoning. Finally the deep attitudinal divide between the country's regions undermined any attempt at generalizing.

Prescient findings, which anticipated Ukraine's political crisis of 2013–14, pointed to greater political activism in the western region – the "Ukrainian Piedmont" – than elsewhere. What is more, it had a disproportionate influence on national policy. In the west the public represented a diverse set of interests which took to politics whenever those interests were threatened.[34] These conclusions are as important to explaining the Euro-Maidan movement in Kiev as they are to understanding the anti-Maidan rebellion that broke out in the east in "Bolshevik Donbass."[35]

A second study concerned with public opinion and foreign policy in Ukraine as well as Poland focused on informed public opinion in the two countries' borderlands.[36] Nathaniel Copsey tested the hypothesis that, in western Ukraine (where we might expect the borderlands issue to have greater salience), elite public opinion (of professors and researchers in universities and think tanks) has the ability to communicate directly with the foreign policy community and impact decisions taken by foreign policy-makers. In contrast to the first study cited, this one did not find empirical support for the proposition that western Ukrainians had disproportionate influence in Kiev.

Another hypothesis concerned whether, in Ukraine and Poland, public attitudes towards the past are inflexible, not open to change, and not influenced by central government. The assumption is that in this region history matters and continues to affect Polish–Ukrainian relations. Here again there was no empirical support for such historical determinism.[37]

A conclusion Copsey reached that is of relevance to this study was that "no academic research within Ukraine or abroad has been carried out on the *making* of Ukrainian foreign policy." This has resulted in little political knowledge about "the most basic processes of Ukrainian foreign and security policy, such as the decision-making process."[38] Studying the making of foreign policy faces hurdles in many countries.

The black box of decision-making

Whichever the country selected, it is notoriously difficult to peer into the black box of foreign policy decision-making. What lies inside the black box is largely a subject of speculation based on inferences and leaks. Some informative data can emerge in subsequent autobiographies of participants or in current accounts published by well-connected journalists having "deep throat" sources. First-hand observation of the decision-making process is generally off limits to political outsiders.

Notwithstanding these limitations, other ways of probing into linkages between domestic actors and structures and foreign policy outcomes can be devised. The connection between these domestic factors and international politics can be imagined as inputs into, and outputs of, foreign policy encompassing a circular flow of ideas. External sources (other nations; the geopolitical climate), societal sources (the mood of the nation; national fears), government sources (type of government), role sources ("the office shapes its incumbent"), and individual-level sources (leadership values) combine to create foreign policy.[39]

Such complexity stemming from the domestic-foreign policy nexus makes it difficult to control for alternative causal variables and assess their weight. Political scientist Robert Putnam explained it this way:

37

Domestic politics and international relations are often somehow entangled, but our theories have not yet sorted out the puzzling tangle. It is fruitless to debate whether domestic politics really determine international relations, or the reverse. The answer to that question is clearly "Both, sometimes." The more interesting questions are "When?" and "How?"[40]

The idea of *la politique du dehors avec les raisons du dedans* – foreign policy formulated on the basis of domestic factors and reasoning – is worth unpacking. Public opinion, citizen values and behavior, and popular culture – all of which may reflect varying degrees and types of fear – have a place in foreign policy studies. Theorizing about the linkage between fears and foreign policy can provide analytic insight if it is operationalized through empirical research. In particular the proposition that heightened national fears at home, which target particular groups such as migrants or neighbors, can be projected to the international arena is plausible and worth testing.

In such research, causal connections, inferences, directions, and pathways may elude us. This may be precisely because international relations experts have viewed domestic and foreign influences as observationally separable levels of analysis.[41] The typology of distinct levels of analysis has become so reified that overlap between them is assumed to be impossible. But important associations can be established between exogenous and endogenous factors, especially if we specify the circumstances under which their symbiosis emerges.

DISTINGUISHING DOMESTIC FACTORS FROM THE FOREIGN

International relations scholars have been rethinking the linkage between the domestic and the international, helped along by the cultural turn beginning in the 1990s. Mainstream experts began to challenge the supposed separateness of domestic and foreign factors. For example, Georg Sørensen linked the domestic with the international in a holistic way by combining economic and normative relations with political and military ones.[42] A distinct analytical framework, known as foreign policy analysis, has also become influential:

> Foreign policy analysis as a distinct area of inquiry connects the study of international relations (the way states relate to each other in international politics) with the study of domestic politics (the functioning of governments and the relationships among individuals, groups, and governments).[43]

In the real world it is difficult to decouple domestic from foreign politics. Decision-makers often consider foreign policy options which they believe will be acceptable to their domestic audience. Such "two-level games" occur when leaders try to satisfy domestic constituencies and international imperatives simultaneously. Putnam provided the now-classic description of two-level games:

> Each national political leader appears at both game boards. Across the international table sit his foreign counterparts, and at his elbows sit diplomats and other international advisors. Around the domestic table behind him sit party and parliamentary figures, spokespersons for domestic agencies, representatives of key interest groups, and the leader's own political advisors.[44]

Putnam provided more than absorbing imagery of how decisions are taken in two different arenas. He also questioned whether rational choices could be made by one leader at the two: "The unusual complexity of this two-level game is that moves that are rational for a player at one board (such as raising energy prices, conceding territory, or limiting auto imports) may be impolitic for that same player at the other board." But Putnam added a caveat: " there are powerful incentives for consistency between the two games. Players (and kibitzers) will tolerate some differences in rhetoric between the two games, but in the end either energy prices rise or they don't."[45]

Two-level games are played in many messy issue arenas. One example is the study of the internationalization of domestic crises such as ethnic conflicts.[46]

The concept of nesting in multiple arenas – that is, two-level games – helps us parse the domestic–international linkage. A set of principles "A" – for example, restrictive immigration policy – may produce a set of principles "B" – a punitive foreign policy towards uncooperative sending countries – which is nested in "A". This creates a feedback loop that subsumes both "A's" influence on "B" as well as "B's" on "A". Thus, growing securitization concerns about international migration become a factor determining that "A" and "B" principles must both become harsher and more congruent with each other. Put differently, a reverse event occurs: *la politique du dedans avec les raisons du dehors*.

The premises of these nested games are familiar. Political actors do not act in a vacuum but under constraints. Even so they seek the best result possible under given conditions. The choices that these actors make from among a set of available actions are central to the analysis of nested games. Actors rank outcomes from best to worst and make their preferences based on this ranking. Outcomes with a higher utility are preferred to outcomes with a lower utility. Normative questions are left out: actors are concerned with a utilitarian pursuit of goals, not their moral value.

Games in multiple arenas, such as in domestic and external arenas, have variable payoffs: those in the principal arena (domestic) are influenced by the prevailing conditions in the other. Observing the game in just one arena – let's say restricting immigrant rights – may give the appearance that actors are choosing a suboptimal strategy. But when the nested game played in a second arena – pressuring external actors to control outmigration – is included in the analysis, the apparent suboptimal choice in the first game is balanced by the optimal choice made in the nested game.

Not all linkages between internal and external factors are determined by reciprocal influence. Some are primarily cumulative in nature. Since political leaders negotiate both in the international and domestic realms, a blurring of boundaries can result. External constraints may become transformed into domestic factors. Thus, being subjected to colonial rule can produce a culture of resistance, while exercising colonial dominion can propagate a culture of hierarchical relations.

James Rosenau outlined a model of linkage politics in which factors inside the state affected issues outside the state and vice versa.[47] Examples were the racist hierarchies prevalent in German and Japanese societies in the 1930s which served as enabling factors in their governments' unprovoked invasions and brutal occupations of neighboring states. Foreign policy is what states make of it and both liberal democratic and constructivist approaches to foreign policy predict that states' identities and domestic characteristics may influence their international roles and modes of operation.[48]

Analysis centered on how domestic factors condition international politics has been spotty. A study of Turkey emphasized how "Micro, or actor level variables, such as ethnic and religious differences among peoples, have profoundly shaped foreign policy patterns"[49] (Box 2.1). This is what

---

Box 2.1 Turkish leader's reaction to the passage of the Armenian Genocide Bill by the US House of Representatives in 2000

The United States is very unwary. If there is a country which cannot talk about genocide, it is the United States. The United States has laid its hands on an issue [that Turkey allegedly committed genocide of Armenians in 1915] which it should not be involved in at all. The genocide of American Indians is described in a book about to be published worldwide.

Besides, there are 30,000 Armenians doing business in Turkey, not counting those who are citizens of Turkey. We shall either mobilize these businessmen for their own interests and to lobby on behalf of Turkey, or we shall deport them immediately.

Source: Tansu Çiller, former Turkish Prime Minister (1993–96), Minister of Foreign Affairs (1996–97). Comments made at a press conference. Translated by Arda Akçiçek (Ankara). Available in Turkish on Turkiyegazetesi website, 8 October 2000, http://www.turkiyegazetesi.com.tr/Genel/a81427.aspx. The book she referred to is by controversial scholar-activist Ward Churchill, *A Little Matter of Genocide: Holocaust and Denial in the Americas 1492 to the Present* (San Francisco: City Lights, 2001).

Huntington's clash-of-civilizations thesis implied. Fears, hypopsia, and prejudices towards vulnerable groups at home can be transplanted to a regional, transnational, and even global arena.

Theories assigning primacy to external factors in the making of foreign policy hold that states are unitary actors behaving rationally and pursuing national interests. Internal theories, by contrast, point both to the existence of different actors within the state and to deviations from rationality as leaders attempt to satisfy domestic political goals by pursuing options not necessarily benefiting the state in international politics.[50]

Internal theories also expect differences to emerge across states' foreign policies despite the same international conditions they face. Such theories highlight the diversity of domestic political systems, cultures, and leaders who take states in different directions even as they confront the same external forces.[51] The exception to this rule is furnished by the democratic peace theory described earlier – such systems will not go to war with each other.

This may be as close as we can get to identifying regularities appearing in complex relationships – a principal objective of scientific research and beyond: "while we might have imagined that science would eventually show us how to rise above all our human details what we now see is that in fact these details are in effect the only important thing about us."[52]

Unraveling the domestic–foreign nexus represents a research challenge rather than disincentive, therefore. Three decades ago, Putnam noted that

> The most portentous development in the fields of comparative politics and international relations in recent years is the dawning recognition among practitioners in each field of the need to take into account entanglements between the two. Empirical illustrations of reciprocal influence between domestic and international affairs abound.[53]

Some analysts look back to the cold war era as one exhibiting greater transparency and clarity about what constituted home affairs and what were foreign matters. Thus "In the recent past, this distinction between foreign and domestic policy was easier to make, but contemporary politics and globalization have blurred the line between what is *foreign* and what is *domestic*."[54] Globalization and transnationalism appear to erase the significance of borders distinguishing domestic and foreign.

If we went even further back to the nineteenth century, we would find that domestic–international linkages were particularly entwined, not distinct, in the colonial era. Racial discrimination *was* the foreign policy of imperial European states. European political and economic power was interconnected with racist ideologies holding colonized peoples to be racially inferior. Civilizing and Christianizing missions went hand in hand with European colonial exploitation.

Today's debates on immigration and integration are sometimes racialized because of increased racial, ethnic, and religious diversity within European societies. But the field of international relations remains accused of being "deafeningly silent on race."[55] It appears unwilling to borrow and test key assumptions and concepts developed in postcolonial theory, for instance. This avoidance of normative reflexivity alone furnishes good reasons to investigate the influence of cultural biases on international politics.

The cultural turn in foreign policy studies

National culture and identity – domestic factors – serve as the repositories of state interests, making them salient, if not decisive, in the making of foreign policy. Consider this dynamic:

> As states face circumstances that emphasize certain interests (national survival, autonomy and independence, and so forth), a culture or identity may arise that internalizes those interests, and thus foreign policy may be constructed to serve the national identity, and thereby the state's interest.[56]

Culture provides the context for different lifestyles, linguistic diversity, value systems, social cohesion, and much else. Culture has recently even been put on a pedestal: South Korean President Park Geun-hye asserted that "In the twenty-first century, culture is power."[57]

Foreign policy theorist Valerie Hudson has provided one of the clearest and most persuasive expositions of culture's role in world politics.

> When we speak of culture and national identity as they relate to foreign policy, we are seeking the answers that the people of a nation-state would give to the following three questions: "Who are we?", "What do 'we' do?", and "Who are they?"[58]

Culture organizes meaning for a society: "culture tells us what to want, to prefer, to desire, and thus *to value*." It can suggest what to fear and what to trust. It also "provides scripts and personae that are re-enacted and subtly modified over time within a society."[59] It also ensures continuity in a state's foreign policy.

Hudson believes that cultural analysis can suggest which

> Well-known and well-practiced options, preferably tied in to the nation's heroic history, will be preferred over less well-known and less familiar options or options with traumatic track records – even if an objective cost-benefit analysis of the two options would suggest otherwise.[60]

Policy-makers will select the myths, narratives, and memes which validate their preferences.

To be sure, culture has no causal power. Even though shared systems of meaning are regularly refracted on to foreign policy-making "culture in and of itself is not a cause of anything in international relations [. . .] It is in the 'who draws what ideas' and the 'how the ideas are employed' aspects that causes of events can be found."[61] Already in 1996 Friedrich Kratochwil warned scholars not to submit to the temptation of inserting culture into international relations theories to explain everything we could not understand in the field. Something which supposedly explains everything in fact explains nothing, he contended.[62]

On the other hand, to leave out cultural explanations altogether is a mistake. The very choice of rulers is conditioned by cultural preferences: a "nation's leaders rise in part because they articulate a vision of the nation's role in world affairs that corresponds to deep cultural beliefs about the nation."[63] An established repertoire of templates and national action scripts is available to state leaders and may be revised and renewed by them.

Stirring up prejudices against minorities at home or neighboring nations in order to garner support for the adoption of hostile foreign policy is a time-honored tradition beginning with Sparta. When justifying interventions abroad many Western states contend, with no hint of irony, that liberal democratic values at home are informing their foreign policy behavior. What of the influence of culturally embedded fears, hypopsia, antipathies, and biases on foreign policy? Can they not be projected externally too? Moreover, if culture can serve as a guarantor of continuity in a state's foreign policy, is there not a risk that, for example, fears of Russia or of the Islamic world will be periodically recycled in foreign policy-making?

Paradigm shifts and caesuras do occur in foreign policy. To illustrate what the end of the cold war meant for scholars of international relations, Katzenstein invoked a dubious analogy – how the sinking of the *Titanic* affected shipbuilders.[64] New tools and frameworks of analysis were required to study the post-bipolar system. Among new ways to research the international system was to assign greater weight to the role of non-material factors, such as culture, and less to material ones, such as strategic balances of power. A key methods question arose then: can culture be used as a theoretical tool to make the analysis of international relations fuller?

The cultural turn in the study of international relations has resulted in "an anthropologization of international relations with a simultaneous assigning to the concept of culture a completely distinctive meaning congruent for this field."[65] But such a development is welcome if it distances us from stereotypical ways of looking at world politics.

One such way has rested on the assumption that all states have similar interests – power, prosperity, and prestige. Cultural differences among them are inconsequential for international politics if states share the same objectives.[66] After the cold war a state-centric approach to international politics had less appeal, and a case of extreme backlash against it was substituting civilizations for states as key actors. Barry Buzan and Richard Little ironized how this had the effect of pushing back the beginnings of the international system by over five thousand years – from the inception of the Westphalian order in 1648 back to the emergence of political order in Mesopotamia around 3500 BC.[67]

A more significant paradigm shift was the framework outlined by Alexander Wendt. Disagreeing with neorealists, such as Kenneth Waltz, who held that a state of anarchy was immanent in the international system, he claimed that the influence of anarchy is real to the extent that the identity of states is based on this belief. In other words, social constructions of reality should be the proper subject of analysis.[68] The intersubjectivity of actors defines social reality so that their preferences and understandings of their interests are the key factors to study. Cultural contexts shape these preferences and understandings.

Constructivist frameworks of this kind place less emphasis on material factors and, instead, "the most important aspect of international relations is social, not material." As a result, "the study of international relations must focus on the ideas and beliefs that inform the actors on the international scene as well as the shared understandings between them."[69]

As one example of how ideas can influence foreign policy-makers more than material or factual conditions, let me suggest how inaccurate popular perceptions of the "Muslim world" can be.

> India, a majority-Hindu country, has more Muslims than any country except for Indonesia and Pakistan, and more than twice as many as Egypt. China has more Muslims than Syria. Germany has more Muslims than Lebanon. And Russia has more Muslims than Jordan and Libya put together.[70]

To these demographic facts we can add policy-makers' distorted essentializing ideas about Muslims, their purported backwardness, and conservatism:

> With these notions in mind one crafts policy; he or she attempts to be inclusive rather than exclusive with his or her measures and must often find the lowest common denominator to implement policy. However, essentialist ideas are reductive and misrepresentative of the *actual* culture or people.[71]

On the other hand, adopting nonessentialist constructions can lead to the conclusion that cultural groups are too complex to study. They "focus on the complexity of culture as a fluid, creative social force which binds different groupings and aspects of behavior in different ways, both constructing and constructed by people in a piecemeal fashion to produce myriad combinations and configurations."[72] Getting culture right, this approach suggests, can be achieved only through ethnographic-type thick descriptions.

In turn Jeffrey Checkel reflected on the shift to structure and agency as units of analysis in foreign policy-making which implicated culture as well:

> The mutual constant interaction between structure and human agency . . . which is the basis for constructivist thinking about social reality, inherently inserts into theoretical reflection culture as an essential part of structure, on the one hand, and the human individual and its agency, actively creating culture and able to change its character, on the other.[73]

He added that "in the foreign policy arena, policy windows create a crucial link between the domestic and international settings."[74] External threats to the state and the need to defuse them open up such a window for the policy entrepreneur. But the latter is constrained by ideas that organizations and publics hold. A successful policy entrepreneur can project and empower these domestically generated ideas in the international arena.

Ned Lebow added further cultural components to the international relations agenda. Twentieth-century theories had neglected the importance of spirit and honor while exaggerating the role of reason. Realists were especially guilty because they were convinced that all human activities are the result of fear.[75] Culture for Lebow was, above all, that element of structure that reined in human passions stirred by fear and greed and gave human beings the chance to be guided by spirit, honor, and values. In short, it created norms that limited human aggression more effectively than reason or fear did.[76]

Lebow contended that both reason and risk-taking are culturally determined phenomena that differ across countries thereby making strategic logic situationally specific. The inference is that the choice whether out of fear a state bandwagons with a great power or decides to balance the powerful state is a strategic calculus more dependent on a country's cultural pathways than a rational choice.

A pioneer who highlighted culture's centrality to contemporary international relations was Joseph Nye. In 2002 he published a book developing the idea of two types of power in the international system. One is hard power which involves the use of military or economic force. The other is soft power which seeks to attract and co-opt.[77] In the second category lies culture which Nye understood as the aggregate of values and practices important to a society.

For Nye the "primary currencies" of soft power which attract or repel other states are culture, political values, policies, and institutions. These currencies – bearing an uncanny resemblance to the composite of domestic structures outlined above – persuade other actors to "want what you want."[78] Nye later

45

was to emphasize that just because soft power sought to persuade and not coerce did not mean it had to be benign; it could be used for disreputable purposes as well.[79]

A largely overlooked aspect of Nye's cultural approach is the part played by citizens' attitudes about foreign policy in countries targeted by soft power. These views are "crucial for the country attempting to use soft power to favorably affect policy outcomes." Using the American example, a key factor becomes "the importance of public opinion (about the U.S.) for policy outcomes *outside of the U.S.*, a question that has rarely been studied."[80] When the projection of soft power depends primarily on cultural features, external actors will be making judgments about the appeal of, or aversion to, the projecting state's cultural power. If judgments about the United States are already negative, anti-Americanism around the world may be difficult to dislodge no matter how much soft power the US mobilizes.

Both hard and soft power encompass a wide range of factors.[81] So Walter Russell Mead subdivided hard power into two categories, sharp and sticky power:

> Traditional military power can usefully be called sharp power; those resisting it will feel bayonets pushing and prodding them in the direction they must go. This power is the foundation of the U.S. system. Economic power can be thought of as sticky power, which comprises a set of economic institutions and policies that attracts others toward U.S. influence and then traps them in it.[82]

As for soft power, Mead introduced the subcategories of sweet and hegemonic power. The first singled out the cultural turn in international relations – the ideals, culture, and values of a country that appeal to others. Among ideals which American sweet power favored were democracy and women's rights. The second, hegemonic, was a synthesis of the others – "the interplay of sharp, sticky, and sweet power all working together."[83]

In the case of American grand strategy, effectively combining these different types of power had produced US global leadership: "Together with soft power (the values, ideas, habits, and politics inherent in the system), sharp and sticky power sustain U.S. hegemony and make something as artificial and historically arbitrary as the U.S.-led global system appear desirable, inevitable, and permanent."[84]

Elevating cultural factors to the status of determinants of domestic and foreign policies has further muddied the waters between what had for so long been compartmentalized into separate arenas. Cultures of fear developing within domestic and international societies and mutually supporting each other have broadened the scope of international relations studies. No better example of how this occurred can be cited than migration.

Securitizing immigration

In 1992, just months after the USSR had collapsed, political scientist Myron Weiner asserted that "Foreign policy and immigration policy is intertwined."[85] Not long after that a pioneering study of Sweden's immigration politics underscored how immigration and foreign policies were becoming conflated. Marie Demker and Cecilia Malmström contended that "Thanks to national borders, migration today involves foreign policy while receiving immigrants involves national policies." The foreign policy dimension emerges "because governments try to control immigration by making foreign policy decisions which entail cooperation and negotiations with other states in international fora."[86]

An imaginative observation drawn by Demker and Malmström was the existence of a "no man's land" between the two sets of policies: "Immigration policies find themselves trapped between on the one hand domestic political expectations about population control, cultural and social integration and economic growth; and on the other international expectations embedded in a normative system that expects other states to display generosity, solidarity and tolerance."[87]

Sweden has been more attentive to international norms than most countries in the world (a subject examined in Chapter 6). But the suggestion that a divide may emerge between citizens' attitudes and these international norms is an important corrective to the view that an isomorphic relationship exists between domestic and foreign policies.

The securitization of countries' immigration policies, which was spurred both by the ever-larger numbers of migrants arriving in Western states and the 2001 terrorist attacks in the United States, marked the end of a "no man's land" separating the domestic and the foreign:

> There has been a clear shift in emphasis in the perception of security away from what many would now see as the redundant nation-state to individuals and groups. Herein lies the paradox: how to reconcile the human right to move freely with the need to protect local cultures, economies, environments, health, and, in some cases, peace.[88]

Securitization has been conceptualized so as to reflect the dual threat coming from outside of and within a society:

> The term as it has been traditionally used in international relations literature is based on two major assumptions: one, that threat to a state's security principally arises from outside its borders, and two, that these threats are primarily, if not exclusively, military in nature.[89]

47

But the unprecedented level of human migration today requires revision of the traditional notion of securitization, and fear of migrating foreigners needs to be linked to foreign and security policy. Fears of the loss of national identity and of state sovereignty enter into a symbiotic relationship. Hypopsia of immigration becomes fused with threat perceptions in a master "fear narrative."[90]

Migration, defined as the cross-border movement of ethnically heterogeneous populations, is a process that makes different groups feel insecure, not because government authority declines but because strangers suddenly become locals:

> ... host populations are likely to develop a suspicion that their government becomes weaker, even though the opposite may be the case. The governments then face an immigrant policy dilemma in very much the same way they face the arms race dilemma. The appearance of being soft on immigration is likely to undermine domestic support for the government. But pursuing a tough restrictionist policy may result in economic costs, and it may criminalize immigration – exacerbating exactly the problems that need to be resolved.[91]

Other aspects of globalization, such as the free movement of capital, goods, entrepreneurship, and cultural production, also make governments look soft on protecting their borders. Yet, as Mikhail Alexseev concluded, "Migration (especially illegal migration across state borders) is often perceived as a sign of declining state sovereignty. The very fact that ethnic 'others' are capable to cross state borders and are hard to control once inside the host state sets the stage for increasing concerns of the host populations about security."[92]

Fear of anarchy threatening both the receiving society and the international system is heightened. The weaker the government looks on the task of gatekeeping its borders, the more probable it is that majority groups become uncertain and fearful about their future. Alekseev believed that "Immigration phobia in host societies is likely to be more intense, the more acute perceptions of emergent anarchy, the more ambiguous the sense of migrant intentions, and the more distinct and cohesive the perceived 'groupness' of migrants."[93] For anti-immigrant movements state adoption of a robust security policy becomes an urgent priority.

Fears and international fractiousness: Libya and Ukraine

To understand the changing character of domestic–foreign tangles, let me review two cases illustrating how domestic crises seem inevitably to become internationalized whenever major world powers make recourse to the security argument. Each case foreshadows the country studies presented in Chapters 4 and 5.

In early 2011 a rebellion broke out in Libya challenging the rule of long-time leader Moammar al-Qaddafi. It began as a domestic issue but quickly mobilized external actors to intervene. When antigovernment protestors in the eastern part of Libya first rose up against the entrenched political authorities in Tripoli, Qaddafi's forces responded with a harsh military crackdown. As reports of brutal attacks against the rebels and civilians began to circulate, however, Western governments reframed the internal conflict as a humanitarian crisis and demanded that an international response be given.

The first step was taken by the United Nations Security Council which voted to impose a no-fly zone over Libya as a way of protecting civilians. But, quickly, members of the North Atlantic Treaty Organization (NATO) recruited a number of Arab states and together they agreed to launch targeted airstrikes to protect the civilian population. By mid 2011, the United States and Germany began to deliver humanitarian supplies to rebel-held parts of Libya. France and Italy, in turn, sent military advisors to assist the rebels' fight against Qaddafi's military forces.

What began as a domestic uprising had become an item on the foreign policy agenda of many Western states (Chapter 4 will examine France's international engagements in greater detail). Overthrow of the dictatorship, a change of government, and a more democratic regime – all domestic Libyan matters – became goals pursued by a combination of Libyan actors and foreign governments. It soon became clear, however, that the post-Qaddafi government had its own legitimacy problems which complicated external actors' exit strategies. For Libyans the domestic–foreign linkage was there to stay for the foreseeable future.

Europeans were not insulated from the Libyan crisis, however. For many years Qaddafi had skillfully played on Europe's fears of in-migration from Africa including its racist component. As head of a leading migration transit country across which large numbers of sub-Saharan Africans reached the Mediterranean with hopes to sail across to Italy and reach the rest of the European Union, Qaddafi had announced that he was the only man who had the power to keep Europe from becoming black. To varying degrees, a number of European states made bilateral deals with him to reward him for keeping African migrants from reaching Europe's shores.

With Qaddafi dead in the revolt, the smuggling of refugees across the Mediterranean increased significantly. By 2014 Italy appealed for EU help as it did not have the resources to manage a refugee crisis on the scale it had reached. At this time elections to the European Parliament produced an unprecedented shift to anti-immigrant parties, from Mediterranean to Nordic states. The initially isolated 2011 rebellion in eastern Libya, which

---

Box 2.2 Vladimir Putin's two-level games

Russia's decision to fire artillery from within Russia on to Ukrainian military positions transforms the security environment throughout Eastern Europe, the chairman of the Joint Chiefs of Staff said. "You've got a Russian government that has made the conscious decision to use its military force inside of another sovereign nation to achieve its objectives," Army General Martin E. Dempsey said at the Aspen Security Forum:

> I think this is very clearly Putin, the man himself, with a vision for Europe, as he sees it, to what he considers to be an effort to redress grievances that were burdened upon Russia after the fall of the Soviet Union, and also to appeal to ethnic Russian enclaves across Eastern Europe with . . . a foreign policy objective, but also a domestic policy objective. And he's very aggressive about it, and he's got a playbook that has worked for him now two or three times.

"If I have a fear about this, it's that Putin may actually light a fire that he loses control of." Dempsey's real concern is that having this fire in an isolated part of Eastern Europe may not stay in Eastern Europe.

Source: Claudette Roulo, "Dempsey: Russian Attacks Change Europe's Security Landscape," DoD News website, 25 July 2014, http://www.defense.gov/news/newsarticle.aspx?id=122751

---

had become internationalized, had had the unexpected effect of conjuring up among many of Europe's citizens the specter of a black, Arab, and Muslim Europe. The politics of fear from below forced politicians to play two-level games aimed at punishing irregular immigrants *and* the sending and transit countries they had come from and through.

The 2014 crisis over Ukraine's government and territorial integrity provided more compelling evidence of how domestic and international politics cannot easily be decoupled (Box 2.2). Depending on an observer's preference, its origins were deep seated: a six-hundred-year history of Ukrainian–Russian relations but also a crisis of state identity since Ukraine's independence in 1991. The crisis came to a head when, at the eleventh hour in late 2013, Ukraine's leaders went back on a commitment to sign an association agreement with the European Union. It immediately triggered citizens' occupation of central parts of the capital for months to come.

From the Kremlin's perspective a red line had been crossed when the democratically elected administration of President Viktor Yanukovych was overthrown after a winter of popular protests on what was called the Euro-Maidan in Kiev. This administration was ousted by a hastily called parliamentary vote which also ordered the reintroduction of a previous constitution transferring power from the executive to the legislative branch; the appointment of an acting president until an election could be held; and a new prime minister and cabinet enjoying the strong backing of the United States and European Union. For the Kremlin, these events were a putsch.

An integral theme of the Kremlin narrative was that the Maidan protests had been inspired and organized by other countries; neighboring Poland and Lithuania were named as training sites for protesters but the United States was regarded as the mastermind. The violent overthrow of Yanukovych and his replacement with pro-Western politicians seemingly handpicked by a US State Department official involved Western interference in Ukrainian domestic politics. For the Kremlin, anti-government protests had borne a foreign brand from the outset.

Russia's leaders repeated that the geopolitical crisis in winter of 2013–14 was Western inspired and required their response in order to protect the significant Russian population living in southern and eastern Ukraine. Largely through osmosis – a takeover from within – pro-Russian forces gained control of Crimea and, in a matter of weeks, annexed it to the Russian Federation. Next, primarily through military assistance flowing across parts of the uncontrolled Ukrainian–Russian border, they destabilized much of eastern Ukraine forming paramilitary units, self-government administrations, and separatist movements. In contrast to the Libyan events, Ukraine's crisis was international, even geostrategic, from the beginning, whether from Moscow's or Kiev's perspective.

A mirror image of these events shaped the Ukrainian government's narrative on Crimea's breakaway from the unitary Ukrainian state. Dismissing the legitimacy of supposed self-defense units taking over Crimea, this narrative emphasized how the deployment of outside military forces – Russia's – had led to the quick occupation of the peninsula and a quickly organized referendum on Crimea's future. For Kiev Crimea's future was exclusively a domestic issue to be resolved by the government and citizens of Ukraine. Armed conflict between pro-Kiev and separatist militaries in the Donbass region in 2014 was an even clearer case of an internal Ukrainian affair. But the presence of outside observers in eastern Ukraine from the Organization for Security and Cooperation in Europe (OSCE), as well as agreements reached in Minsk, Belarus, between the different parties to the conflict for a permanent ceasefire were evidence that the separatist issue had become internationalized.

Was the Russian Federation's annexation of Crimea a violation of international law as Kiev claimed? The International Court of Justice's 2010 ruling on the legitimacy of Kosovo's plebiscite to separate from Serbia had stressed that no international law existed preventing a region from holding a referendum on independence. It therefore left the legality of the breakaway state an open question. The issue in Crimea revolved then around whether its plebiscite on independence was fair and representative of public opinion; evidence does point to strong local support for annexation by the Russian Federation, minority Crimean Tatar opposition notwithstanding. Indeed, President Putin confirmed that Russia had conducted informal public opinion polls in Crimea before its takeover had begun. The results strongly supported annexation thereby supposedly forcing Putin's hand.

Both Ukrainian and Russian narratives agreed that a domestic conflict over political power and territorial integrity had become internationalized from the beginning, and perhaps also because of historical path dependence. Kiev blamed Russia and its history of expansion for this, thereby following a standard russo-hypopsic script. Moscow pointed the finger at the West and its institutions ever bent on enlargement – the European Union and NATO In this way it was returning to centuries of a master narrative raising Russian fears of Occidentalism.

Instead of fear stimulated by migration trends, in Ukraine we observe the insidious consequences of an interlocked history, particularly in its eastern and southern regions. The post-1991 effort to compartmentalize the domestic and the foreign has proved to be inescapably crisis-generating. Chudowsky and Kuzio's findings (reported above), calling attention to the deep attitudinal divide between Ukraine's west and east, are substantiated.

Conclusions

The power of culture in international relations may be called soft or sweet, even sticky. What is incontrovertible is the widespread recognition today of its importance in analyzing politics among nations.[94] Fears can pervade a culture. That culture in turn can tell foreign policy-makers who they are and what their interests should be. We have arrived at the point where discussion of a research design which may connect fear, culture, and foreign policy is needed. This is the subject of Chapter 3.

Notes

1. Ken Booth and Nicholas J. Wheeler, *The Security Dilemma: Fear, Cooperation, and Trust in World Politics* (New York: Palgrave Macmillan, 2008).
2. For a detailed literature review see Shiping Tang, "Fear in International Politics: Two Positions," *International Studies Review*, 10:3 (September 2008), pp. 451–71.
3. Zygmunt Bauman, *Europe: An Unfinished Adventure* (New York: Polity Press, 2004), p. 99.
4. Jef Huysmans, *The Politics of Insecurity: Fear, Migration and Asylum in the EU* (London: Routledge, 2006), p. 4.
5. In this study I do not include political culture as an independent variable because of its possible tautological nature: that part of culture defined as political will *eo ipso*

affect domestic and international politics. For an early study of the linkage between political culture and international politics see Roland H. Ebel, Raymond Taras, and James D. Cochrane, *Political Culture and Foreign Policy in Latin America: Case Studies from the Circum-Caribbean* (Albany, NY: SUNY Press, 1991).

6. Two common assumptions in the study of international relations discarded here are that: 1. foreign policy analysis constitutes a distinct subfield of international relations; and 2. domestic and foreign policies are heuristically distinguishable.

7. John T. Rourke, *International Politics on the World Stage*, 10th edn (New York: McGraw Hill, 2005), p. 78.

8. Peter J. Katzenstein, "Introduction: Alternative Perspectives on National Security," in Katzenstein (ed.), *The Culture of National Security: Norms and Identity in World Politics* (New York: Columbia University Press, 1996), p. 66. Italics mine.

9. Lawrence E. Harrison and Samuel P. Huntington (eds), *Culture Matters: How Values Shape Human Progress* (New York: Basic Books, 2001); Samuel Huntington, *The Clash of Civilizations and the Remaking of World Order* (New York: Simon & Schuster, 2011; first published 1996).

10. Katzenstein, "Introduction," p. 12.

11. Ibid., pp. 2, 5.

12. Ibid., pp. 23–4.

13. F. G. Bailey, *Treasons, Strategems, and Spoils: How Leaders Make Practical Use of Beliefs and Values* (Boulder, CO: Westview Press, 2001), p. 9.

14. Ibid., p. 8.

15. Nicolas Demertzis, "Introduction: Theorizing the Emotions-Politics Nexus," in Demertzis (ed.), *Emotions in Politics: The Affect Dimension in Political Tension* (Basingstoke: Palgrave Macmillan, 2013), p. 2.

16. Pierre Hassner, "La revanche des passions," *Commentaire*, 110 (Été 2005), pp. 299–312. See his references for an erudite bibliography of works on fear. A pioneering study on the influence of the two "master emotions" – pride and shame – that affect foreign policy is Thomas J. Scheff, *Bloody Revenge: Emotions, Nationalism and War* (Lincoln, NE: iUniverse.com, 2000).

17. Dominique Moïsi, *La géopolitique de l'émotion: comment les cultures de peur, d'humiliation et d'espoir façonnent le monde* (Paris: Flammarion, 2008).

18. See Daniel Vernet, "'La Géopolitique de l'émotion,' de Dominique Moïsi: le monde dans tous ses états," *Le monde* website, 26 November 2008, http://www.lemonde.fr/livres/article/2008/11/26/la-geopolitique-de-l-emotion-de-dominique-moisi_1123339_3260.html

19. Christopher J. Fettweis, *The Pathologies of Power: Fear, Honor, Glory, and Hubris in U.S. Foreign Policy* (New York: Cambridge University Press, 2013), p. 2.

20. Ibid., pp. 2–3.

21. Dan Reiter, "Democratic Peace Theory," *Oxford Bibliographies*, http://www.oxford-bibliographies.com/view/document/obo-9780199756223/obo-9780199756223-0014.xml See also Michael W. Doyle, *Liberal Peace: Selected Essays* (New York: Routledge, 2011).

22. David M. DeBartolo, "Perceptions of U.S. Democracy Promotion" (Heinrich Boll Stiftung May 2008), http://pomed.org/wp-content/uploads/2008/05/pomed-perceptions-i-middle-east.pdf

23. Rourke, *International Politics*, p. 88.

24. Walter Lippmann, *Public Opinion* (New York: Macmillan, 1922), p. 32.
25. Juliet Kaarbo, Jeffrey S. Lantis, and Ryan K. Beasley, "The Analysis of Foreign Policy in Comparative Perspective," in Beasley, Kaarbo, Lantis, and Michael T. Snarr (eds), *Foreign Policy in Comparative Perspective: Domestic and International Influences on State Behavior* (Thousand Oaks, CA: CQ Press, 2012), 2nd ed., p. 14.
26. See James Rosenau, *Public Opinion and Foreign Policy: An Operational Formulation* (New York: Random House, 1961); also Ole R. Holsti, *Public Opinion and American Foreign Policy* (Ann Arbor, MI: University of Michigan Press, 1999), pp. 1–21.
27. Alexis de Tocqueville, *Democracy in America*, vol. 1 (New York: Vintage, 1958), pp. 243 5.
28. Richard Sobel, *The Impact of Public Opinion on U.S. Foreign Policy Since Vietnam: Constraining the Colossus* (Oxford: Oxford University Press, 2001), p. 582. See also Lawrence R. Jacobs and Benjamin I. Page, "Who Influences U.S. Foreign Policy?" *American Political Science Review*, 99.1 (2005), pp. 107–23.
29. Daniel W. Drezner, "The Realist Tradition in American Public Opinion," *Perspectives on Politics*, 6:1 (March 2008), p. 52. The contrast between realist versus liberal internationalist foreign policy priorities and world views is provided in Table 1, p. 54.
30. Ibid., p. 63.
31. Rourke, *International Politics*, p. 90, Table 3.2 for a list of issues where political leaders and the public in the United States agree or disagree. There is more agreement than not but, where there is disagreement, it is often because leaders are more internationalist, forming part of cosmopolitan elites, than citizens. This was true of President George W. Bush, often misidentified as prioritizing the United States's national interests.
32. Jeremy Bentham, *Works of Jeremy Bentham* (London: Longman, 1968), vol. 8, p. 561; quotation from vol. 2, p. 547.
33. Holsti, *Public Opinion*, p. 192.
34. Viktor Chudowsky and Taras Kuzio, "Does Public Opinion Matter? The Case of Foreign Policy in Ukraine," *Communist and Post-Communist Studies*, 35:3 (September 2003), pp. 273–90.
35. The term was used by Leonid Kravchuk, first president of independent Ukraine, in my interview with him in Warsaw, 8 July 2014.
36. Nathaniel Copsey, *Public Opinion and the Making of Foreign Policy in the "New Europe": A Comparative Study of Poland and Ukraine* (Farnham, Surrey: Ashgate, 2009), p. 11.
37. Ibid., pp. 16–17.
38. Ibid., p. 16.
39. Charles W. Kegley, Christopher M. Jones, Eugene R. Wittkopf, and Mark A. Boyer, *American Foreign Policy: Pattern and Progress* (New York: Wadsworth Publication Company, 2007).
40. Robert D. Putnam, "Diplomacy and domestic politics: the logic of two-level games," *International Organization*, 42:3 (summer 1988), p. 427. For a review of earlier studies of "linkage politics" see pp. 430–3.
41. Milja Kurki, *Causation in International Relations: Reclaiming Causal Analysis* (Cambridge: Cambridge University Press, 2008), p. 250.
42. Georg Sørensen, *Changes in Statehood: the Transformation of International Relations* (Basingstoke: Palgrave, 2001), p. 5.
43. Kaarbo, Lantis, and Beasley, "The Analysis," pp. 1–2.

44. Putnam, "Diplomacy," p. 434.
45. Ibid.
46. See the select bibliography in Ray Taras and Rajat Ganguly, *Understanding Ethnic Conflict: The International Dimension*. 4th edn (New York: Pearson, 2010).
47. James Rosenau, "Towards the Study of National–International Linkages," in Rosenau (ed.), *Linkage Politics: Essays on the Convergence of National and International Systems* (New York: Free Press, 1969), p. 44.
48. Ted Hopf, *Social Construction of International Politics: Identities and Foreign Policies* (Ithaca, NY: Cornell University Press, 2002); also Steve Smith, "Foreign policy is what states make of it," in Vendulka Kubálková (ed.), *Foreign Policy in a Constructed World* (Armonk, NY: M. E. Sharpe, 2001), pp. 38–55.
49. Carolyn C. James and Özgür Özdamar, "Modeling Foreign Policy and Ethnic Conflict: Turkey's Policies towards Syria," *Foreign Policy Analysis* 5:1 (January 2009), p. 34.
50. Kaarbo, Lantis, and Beasley, "The Analysis," p. 13.
51. Ibid.
52. Stephen Wolfram, *A New Kind of Science* (Champaign, IL: Wolfram Media, 2002), p. 846, http://www.wolframscience.com/nksonline/page-846-text?firstview=1
53. Putnam, "Diplomacy," p. 459.
54. Kaarbo, Lantis, and Beasley, "The Analysis," p. 4.
55. Christine B. N. Chin, "Claiming Race and Racelessness in International Studies," *International Studies Perspectives*, 10:1 (February 2009), p. 93. See the other chapters in this issue making up the "ISP Forum: Race and International Relations."
56. Ryan K. Beasley and Michael T. Snarr, "Domestic and International Influences on Foreign Policy: A Comparative Perspective," in Beasley, Kaarbo, Lantis, and Snarr, *Foreign Policy in Comparative Perspective*, p. 331.
57. Quoted in http://english.yonhapnews.co.kr/national/2013/02/25/95/0301000000AE N20130225001500315F.HTML
58. Valerie M. Hudson, *Foreign Policy Analysis: Classic and Contemporary Theory*, 2nd edn (Lanham, MD: Rowman and Littlefield, 2014), p. 118.
59. Ibid., pp. 123–4.
60. Ibid., p. 136.
61. K. F. Wilkening, "Culture and Japanese Citizen Influence on the Transboundary Air Pollution Issue in Northeast Asia," *Political Psychology*, 20:4 (1999), p. 8.
62. Yosef Lapid and Friedrich Kratochwil, "Is the ship of culture at sea or returning?" in Lapid and Kratochwil (eds.), *The Return of Culture and Identity in IR Theory* (Boulder, CO: Lynne Riener, 1996), p. 205.
63. Hudson, *Foreign Policy Analysis*, p. 130.
64. Peter Katzenstein (ed.), *The Culture of National Security: Norms and Identity in World Politics* (New York: Columbia University Press, 1996), p. xi.
65. Hanna Schreiber and Grażyna Michałowska, "Wprowadzenie: zwrot kulturowy w stosunkach międzynarodowych," in Schreiber and Michałowska (eds), *Kultura w stosunkach międzynarodowych: zwrot kulturowy* (Warsaw: Wydawnictwa Uniwersytetu Warszawskiego, 2013), pp. 8–9.
66. See the neorealist argument made by Kenneth Waltz, *Theory of International Politics* (New York: McGraw-Hill, 1979).
67. See Barry Buzan and Richard Little, *International Systems in World History: Remaking the Study of International Relations* (New York: Oxford University Press, 2000).

68. Alexander Wendt, "Anarchy is what states make of it: the social construction of power politics," *International Organization*, 46:2 (spring 1992), pp. 391–425.
69. Robert Jackson and Georg Sørensen, *Introduction to International Relations: Theories and Approaches* (New York: Oxford University Press, 2013), p. 162.
70. Pew Forum on Religion & Public Life Project, "Mapping the Global Muslim Population," 7 October 2009, Pew Research website, http://www.pewforum.org/2009/10/07/mapping-the-global-muslim-population/
71. Ibid.
72. Ibid.
73. Anna Wojciuk, "Kultura w teoriach stosunków międzynarodowych," in Schreiber und Michałowska (eds), *Kultura w stosunkach międzynarodowych*, p. 37.
74. Jeffrey T. Checkel, "International Norms and Domestic Politics: Bridging the Rationalist–Constructivist Divide," *European Journal of International Relations*, 3:4 (December 1997), p. 473.
75. Richard Ned Lebow, *A Cultural Theory of International Relations* (Cambridge: Cambridge University Press, 2008), pp. 26–8.
76. Ibid., p. 557.
77. Joseph S. Nye Jr, *The Paradox of American Power: Why the World's Only Superpower Can't Go It Alone* (New York: Oxford University Press, 2003). Nye referred to soft power as early as 1990 in his book *Bound to Lead: The Changing Nature of American Power* (New York: Basic Books, 1991). He elaborated on the concept in his *Soft Power: The Means to Success in World Politics* (New York: Public Affairs, 2005). In 2008 US Secretary of State Hillary Clinton referred to smart power which borrowed from Nye's idea of soft power.
78. Nye, *Soft Power*, p. 31.
79. Nye, *The Future of Power* (New York: Public Affairs, 2011).
80. Benjamin E. Goldsmith and Yusaku Horiuchi, "In Search of Soft Power: Does Foreign Public Opinion Matter for US Foreign Policy?" *World Politics*, 64:3 (July 2012), pp. 556–7.
81. For example, the Monocle Soft Power Survey includes over a hundred factors determining rankings including Olympic medal totals. In 2013, Germany ranked highest in soft power followed by the United Kingdom, the United States, France, Japan, Sweden, Australia, Switzerland, Canada and Italy. Thus, G-7 members were all in the top ten.
82. Walter Russell Mead, "America's Sticky Power," Foreign Policy website, 1 March 2004, http://www.foreignpolicy.com/articles/2004/03/01/americas_sticky_power
83. Walter Russell Mead, *Power, Terror, Peace and War: America's Grand Strategy in a World at Risk* (New York: Knopf, 2004) pp. 36–40, 25.
84. Mead, "America's Sticky Power."
85. Myron Weiner, "International Population Movements: Implications for foreign policies and migration policies," in Donald L. Horowitz and Gerard Noiriel (eds), *Immigrants in Two Democracies: French and American Experience* (New York: New York University Press, 1992), p. 439.
86. Marie Demker and Cecilia Malmström, *Ingenmansland? Svensk immigrationspolitik i utrikespolitisk belysning* (Lund: Studentlitteratur, 1999), p. 145.
87. Ibid., p. 154.
88. Nana Poku and David T. Graham (eds), *Redefining Security: Population Movements and National Security* (Westport, CT: Praeger, 1998), p. xv.

89. Mohammed Ayoob, "The International Security System and the Third World," in William C. Olson (ed.), *Theory and Practice of International Relations*, 9th edn (Englewood Cliffs, NJ: Prentice Hall, 1994), p. 225.
90. Roger D. Petersen, *Understanding Ethnic Violence: Fear, Hatred, and Resentment in Twentieth Century Eastern Europe* (Cambridge: Cambridge University Press, 2002).
91. Mikhail A. Alexseev, *Immigration Phobia and the Security Dilemma: Russia, Europe, and the United States* (Cambridge: Cambridge University Press, 2006), p. 38.
92. Ibid., p. 40.
93. Ibid., p. 69.
94. For Hans Morgenthau, author of *Politics among Nations: The Struggle for Power and Peace* (New York: Alfred A. Knopf, 1948), it was hard power that had been decisive throughout history.

Chapter three

Reflections on designing research for the study of fear and foreign policy

In this chapter I review the types of theories, concepts, methods, and measures that may prove useful when designing research to assess the impact of citizens' fears on foreign policy. It is divided into three sections: building theory; telling causal stories; and conducting interpretive research.

The chapter has a second objective: to offer reflection and introspection on the character of social science research. Such "reflexivity" about methods is an injunction that has been made by many leading social theorists.

Alvin Gouldner's reflexive sociology proposed an interrogation of the discipline itself alongside that of a chosen problematic. Pierre Bourdieu called for demystification of the tools of sociology in order to expose the cognitive power it wielded. Anthony Giddens believed that constant revision and updating of our knowledge of the social world demands greater reflexivity. Zygmunt Bauman suggested that the way to capture constant social change is to examine liquefied modernity understood as acceleration of social processes. It would result in a reflexivity based on directing the principles of modernity towards modernity.[1]

This chapter in part aims to turn the attention of consciousness back upon itself, therefore, to cause us to be thinking about thinking.

Building theories

It is difficult empirically to test the proposition that, among the many factors embedded in domestic structures, it is the culture of fear which will be the most influential. But this is the purpose of employing a concept such as fear to explain a society's dynamics: ". . . even a theoretical concept, one which claims utility in helping to explain the social world, must bear some relationship to empirical phenomena."[2] There is a standing invitation, then, to adopt fear as an explanatory variable for foreign policy-making.

A research design needs to take into account the influence exerted by many different factors if only then to rule out ones that cause little variance in the variable to be explained. The study of foreign policy is made more robust by including a "geopolitics of emotions" including fear in the research design. It can explain why political leaders regularly play two-level games in which they try to satisfy domestic constituencies and international imperatives simultaneously. A non-interests-based approach to policy-making can exist. Major policy courses may sometimes be triggered by moral panics, not rational interests. Evaluating the extent to which fear as an independent variable can cause variations in foreign policy is a way to approach such research problems.

Are theories necessary to understand social phenomena? After all, "Without theories, we are faced with the unreadable chaos of reality."[3] Two of the best-known international relations theorists, John Mearsheimer and Stephen Walt, have claimed that "Theory is the lodestone in the field of International Relations (IR). Its theorists are the field's most famous and prestigious scholars."[4] They outline the indispensability of theories in research:

> Theory is invaluable for many reasons. Because the world is infinitely complex, we need mental maps to identify what is important in different domains of human activity. In particular, we need theories to identify the causal mechanisms that explain recurring behavior and how they relate to each other. Finally, well-crafted theories are essential for testing hypotheses properly.[5]

Let me review what a theory is. It is an explanation which organizes separate pieces of information in a coherent way. Researchers typically develop a theory once they have collected empirical evidence. Theories provide not just maps about a complex world but also tell a causal story about events: they specify how one or more factors affect a particular phenomenon. They sometimes take into account mechanisms which may not otherwise be observable in analyses of how the world functions.

Theorists are conscious and reflexive about how they simplify assumptions about which factors matter most to a particular outcome. That is, they prioritize parsimonious forms of explanation providing the most economical way of reporting a set of observations. Parsimony's opposite may be thick description associated with classic methods of research in human anthropology and ethnography. A final criterion for good theory is that it allows for research results to be tested and reproduced by others.

Good theories can provide multiple benefits. They can revolutionize thinking about the world. They may allow us to make predictions about the future. Mearsheimer and Walt note that theories are crucial to diagnosing policy problems, taking policy decisions, and evaluating policy outcomes. That is because "A good theory identifies indicators we can use to determine whether a particular initiative is working, because criteria for evaluation are embedded within it."[6]

59

Theories are particularly important as a guide to analysis in novel situations and where information is sparse or unreliable. Of course, the researcher must be conscious of the dangers of reaching for a familiar theory to advance explanations about uncharted, unfamiliar, or unique circumstances. Conceptual stretching, involving the application of ideas salient for one culture to a foreign setting, is a fallacy that must be avoided. The canons of social science inquiry in the West have been attacked for incorporating Western forms of knowledge, of rationality, and of values while excluding other kinds – traditional (animist), philosophic (Buddhism, Hinduism), analytic (Confucianism), and others. Instances of Eurocentric paradigms about the world were critiqued in the previous chapter.

Given how developing and employing theory provide so many advantages, Mearsheimer and Walt lament the atheoretical trend in international relations which they believe leads to a dead end in both innovative research and theory building (Box 3.1). Unlike many critics of contemporary political science, they do not single out the two standard lightning rods – rational choice and quantitative methods – for embodying the shortcomings of the discipline. Rather, it is the steady disregard for theory's utility that concern these authors.

> . . . paradoxically, the amount of serious attention IR scholars in the United States pay to theory is declining and seems likely to drop further in the years ahead. Specifically, the field is moving away from developing or carefully employing theories and instead emphasizing what we call simplistic hypothesis testing. Theory usually plays a minor role in this enterprise, with most of the effort devoted to collecting data and testing empirical hypotheses.[7]

Box 3.1 The road to ruin according to Mearsheimer and Walt

We believe downgrading theory and elevating hypothesis testing is a mistake. This is not to say that generating and testing hypotheses is unimportant. Done properly, it is one of the core activities of social science. Nevertheless, the creation and refinement of theory is the most important activity in this enterprise. This is especially true in IR, due to the inherent complexity and diversity of the international system and the problematic nature of much of the available data. Scholars do not have to invent their own theory, of course, or even refine an existing theory, although these endeavors are highly prized. It is necessary, however, that social scientists have a solid grasp of theory and use it intelligently to guide their research.

Source: John J. Mearsheimer and Stephen M. Walt, "Leaving theory behind: Why simplistic hypothesis testing is bad for International Relations," *European Journal of International Relations*, 19:3, p. 429.

A riposte to these authors' views is that theory is more alive and well than they assume. By its nature hypothesis testing is not a separate enterprise from theory development. Hypotheses are derived from theories in order to test and refine them. They predict (whether accurately or not is to be discovered) that more of X will lead to more of Y. By contrast theories are causal and assert that X influences Y. Simplistic hypothesis testing uninformed by theory is, therefore, not hypothesis testing at all.

Counterfactual analysis

In defense of less theory-driven forms of explanation stands political scientist Ned Lebow. He observes how theories have psychological importance for social scientists. By reducing complexity and suggesting simple explanations, they give closure – and the appearance of success – to scientists embarked on large research projects. Theories create the myth that a rigorous construction of the past can serve as an accurate guide to anticipating the future. The loss of this predictive capacity would be devastating to practitioners. Accordingly, "Social scientists committed to theory building of this kind are correspondingly reluctant to admit the failings of their theories, let alone the overall difficulties encountered by the predictive enterprise."[8]

For Lebow, international relations specialists like himself can be overly protective about their theorizing enterprises. An inference arising from his critique is that IR theorizing is not especially sophisticated or robust, thereby putting its practitioners on the defensive. One common defense mechanism they resort to is to dismiss the influence of chance in shaping history. Lebow adds that how historical research questions are posed shapes how they are answered, a line of critique exposing tautological framing. The antidote to these defense mechanisms is to engage in counterfactual analysis. Understood literally, a counterfactual is something contrary to established fact. But it also can constitute a causal assertion allowing us to probe the causes and contingency of the social world.

The proposition that citizens' fears of "strangers" who live in their "own" society or perhaps in a nearby country may shape a country's foreign policy represents a "long-shot counterfactual." That is, fears may constitute a factor at a certain temporal or spatial remove from an event which nevertheless suggests the possibility of an alternative scenario to the one which did unfold.[9] Citizens' fears are a phenomenon appearing at some distance from the black box of foreign policy-making but they can still have impact on outcomes.

Conducting "counterfactual unpacking", which can explain the connection between antecedent factors (such as domestic fears) and consequents (such as hostile foreign policies), is an essential component of designing research. Sometimes, counterfactual analysis may be founded on mere speculation ("what-ifs") about causal chains but, at other times, it is guided by empirical evidence supporting the linkage.

Contingent factors are central to causal chains. Because they are defined by the uncertainty whether they will appear, they can be regarded as chance events. One chance event entering a causal chain can have an enormous impact on history; the assassination of Grand Duke Franz Ferdinand in Sarajevo in 1914 setting off World War I was chance (he returned to his route and passed in front of his assassin after already surviving an earlier attempt on his life that day). Similarly, one chance development or the appearance of an unknown "X factor" shaping a country's foreign policy (such as the 2010 air crash in Smolensk killing the Polish president and dozens of his senior advisors) can – though does not have to (as was the case with the Smolensk event, see Chapter 5) – have serious and long-term consequences. Singling out long-shot counterfactuals reveals how unlikely any outcome, including the one that took place, really was from the perspective of a later time and place.

Lebow's golden mean is a "reflective equilibrium" between theory- and imagination-driven modes of analyzing the past. In answer to the question "how can we avoid becoming prisoners of our preconceptions?"[10] his advice is to let our imagination run riot. This is an appealing idea but it draws us away not just from established canons of social science inquiry, whatever their weaknesses, but also rigorous, systematic, fact-based analysis. A search for causality and linkage also may become a casualty of atheoretical research.

Telling causal stories

Many kinds of causal connections, linkages, associations, and correlations between variables can exist. The presumption of causality, that an independent variable affects a dependent one, is notoriously difficult to prove in the social sciences, not least when qualitative data are used. Yet it represents the holy grail of many researchers' goals. As discussed below, causation is not all that it is sometimes cracked up to be and leaves many questions unanswered.

Social scientists have wisely shifted emphasis to the identification of causal inferences. Given the probability of discovering no incontrovertible proof of a causal event, making inferences is an appealing, modest alternative. It uses a process of reasoning to reach the conclusion that something may be the cause of something else. Reaching this threshold is important if theory is to tell a causal story, no matter whether parts of it appear to be the stuff of fiction.

The causal story told in this book is how citizens' fears and suspicions of others may have consequences for policy. There appears to be a connection between antecedent and consequent which merits closer examination. That appearance suffices to begin to narrate a causal story that will suggest how strong the linkage really is.

To infer whether citizens' fears and suspicions may cause foreign policy shifts, it is first necessary to establish that fears and foreign policy change in a particular sequence. That is the purpose of examining delineated time periods following political turning points (they occur in 2006–07 and end in 2014 in the three case studies). Instead of generating a set of hypotheses to be tested, I follow Mearsheimer and Walt's call to give primary importance to a theory that provides maps of the world and tells plausible causal stories.

Let me call the causal story of public fears' impact on foreign policy the "Thucydides' Theorem." The Greek historian underscored the part played by fear in shaping the *interpolis*, that is, relations between city-states. Sparta came to fear Athens because of the quick growth of Athenian power; "the Spartans did not, of their own accord, come to fear the Athenians." As Calabrese puts it, "The Spartans' concern is not that Athens is about to sack the city, but that it will, at some future time, cause Sparta grave harm."[11]

Thucydides solidifies the theorem's validity by citing Athens's open apology for its empire before the Spartan assembly. Referring to an antecedent stimulus–response phase, Athens claimed that it, in turn, had come to fear Persia's long-term expansionist threat. This fear grew more acute when Sparta decided to abandon the Greeks' common struggle against Persia. So fear of Persia drove the Athenians to build their military strength which, in turn, evoked Spartans' fear of Athens. This circular process is what a security dilemma signifies. Thucydides theorizes, then, that "the Athenians becoming great and furnishing fear to the Spartans drove them to war."[12]

Let me retell this causal story using the research framework of this book. Perceptions of a longer-term threat posed by the growing presence of foreigners in a society, thereby eroding its cohesion and identity, prompt citizens' fears. In similar fashion, perceptions within a society of a powerful and threatening neighboring nation may induce fear and hypopsia of it. These fears do not necessarily drive these societies to war against these foreigners, as Thucydides reported was the case of Sparta and Athens. But they may fashion, directly or indirectly, a more hostile foreign policy towards the sources of these threats. Inferring a causal connection between the two factors allows a story to be told regardless of whether it proves conclusive about the linkage or not.

Causality and correlations

Perhaps the most memorable methods-related quotation of all time is one attributed to ancient Greek philosopher and scientist Democritus: "I would rather discover one causal law than be King of Persia." In a way as unrelated to

Democritus as is imaginable, contemporary Zimbabwean novelist Dambudzo Marechera speaks of "The chaos between causes and effects" in his shamanistic parody of African identity.[13] Given such trepidations about causality, what can this study demonstrate in seeking to tie fear to foreign policy?

A point of departure is to accept that "All sciences are set up in such a way as to avoid, elude, and overlook complexity as much as possible. Complexity is the bane of the would-be scientist, and yet complexity is a characteristic of much, if not most, of the world around us."[14]

The challenge is how to parse complexity while accepting its elusiveness. Choosing cases, not for their representativeness but for the presence or absence of particular factors which a theory claims are important, limits the number of variables to be studied. Establishing causality is a luxury in this exercise, not a necessity. As Katzenstein put it, the goal of comparative research is to develop "explanatory arguments, not causal imagery."[15]

In his *Metaphysics*, Aristotle identified four general types of causes: 1. the material cause, that is, what a being's matter consists of; 2. the formal cause, what a being's essence is; 3. the efficient cause, what brings about the beginning of or change to a being; 4. the final cause, what a being's purpose is.[16] For theologians a first cause is also of crucial importance.

Like Aristotle, Thomas Aquinas believed that an uncaused primary mover must exist because an infinite regression of causality is logically impossible. Searching for causal relationships can serve not just as Thomistic proof of God's existence but, more unassumingly, as the starting point for empirical research. Accordingly "Modern political science fundamentally revolves around establishing whether there are *causal relationships* between important concepts."

This sounds simple: for causality to exist cause must be shown to precede effect. But there are obstacles standing in the way:

> If we wish to know whether some X causes Y, we need to cross four causal hurdles: (1) Is there a credible causal mechanism that connects X to Y? (2) Can we eliminate the possibility that Y causes X? (3) Is there covariation between X and Y? (4) Is there some Z related to both X and Y that makes the observed relationship between X and Y spurious?[17]

Observational studies like this one are concerned with causal sequences and variations. Drawing possible causal connections between citizens' fears and foreign policy outcomes was the first step in designing this research. But causality means many things to many people and let me unpack different meanings of the term.

A connection often mistaken for causality is *correlation* – a statement that two factors are related independent of their sequence. A true correlation is when two variables are related because certain values of one variable coincide with certain values of another variable. But it is only if the values of one variable produce those of another that there is a causal relationship. Ascribing causality to the coincidence of variations in two factors is premature; the influence of outside factors causing the two phenomena to covary must first be ruled out.

It is axiomatic that establishing a correlation between two variables does not signify establishing a causal relationship between them in either direction. Especially in the absence of numeric data, the precise nature of the relationship is likely to remain unknowable. The illusion of causality (discussed further below) created by the existence of a correlation needs to be shunned.

The related concept of covariation indicating that an alleged cause simply covaries with its supposed effect has many analytical advantages. Key to measuring covariation is the temporality separating cause from effect. It highlights how one event precedes another. Covariations provide the basis for inferring causality. Much of interpretive research draws causal inferences from a sequence of events. It entails identifying a possible causal connection based on the conditions in which an effect occurred. Causal inference analyzes the response of the effect variable when the suspected cause is changed. In medicine, for example, the aim of causal inference research is to identify the different impacts of exposure to a particular treatment.

Causal sequencing

For political scientist Anna Grzymala-Busse timing and sequencing need to be distinguished from each other: "Timing exhibits dependence on the changes in the external context; sequencing exhibits dependence among its constituent states."[18] It is sequencing that underpins causation and reveals the stages of historical processes. Grzymala-Busse believes that the dynamics of sequences have remained underspecified, a criticism important to ordering this study.[19]

Causal sequences entail state dependence, that is, the state of a phenomenon at a particular point in time is dependent on its earlier states. State dependence can vary from the simple, where it is a function of the immediately preceding state, to path dependent, where successive states are increasingly dependent on all previous states. Some sequences contain only a simple ordering of causes and outcomes. For example, in additive causal relations $(A + B = C)$, a combination of events produces the outcome of interest. By contrast with conditional interactive causes A produces C only in the presence of B. A and B do not affect each other but, when combined, they produce C.

The author cites the example of modernization theory where political participation followed contestation and both were considered responsible for democratic development. But contestation did not itself cause participation.[20] Similarly, in this book it may be that citizens' fears of foreigners and an economy in recession together produce hostile foreign policy towards Muslim-majority states, Russia, or some different chosen Other. But a weak economy may not itself evoke public fears.

Mechanisms are pivotal to causality, too. These are:

> ... recurrent causal links between specified initial conditions and outcomes. Specific *sequences* (orderings) of mechanisms and events then constitute *processes*. The analysis of mechanisms and processes invokes temporality since mechanisms specify *change*: how and why shifts, trends, and developments occur. Whether belief formation, policy transformation, or the reproduction of power, mechanisms take place in time.[21]

Certain causal mechanisms take place under specific temporal configurations. For example, singling out the mechanism of a political party which aggregates xenophobic opinion is central to a study of the political impact of fear. It can tease out public opinion as an exogenous variable affecting foreign policy.

This study's focus on temporal configurations seeks to disentangle causal mechanisms. The three case studies describe the state of citizens' fears of foreigners and the state of foreign policy towards particular countries at the outset of a delineated six- to seven-year period. This point in time is treated as a caesura (the French term *rupture* may capture the idea better) – the start of a new government coalition taking power. Then shifts in public opinion about immigrant groups or foreign countries are traced and compared to changes (if any) in a foreign policy course. Does evidence indicate that the two covary? If they do, then the theory that a domestic factor, such as fears, has an effect on foreign policy receives support. If the result is null then a significant inference can be drawn: foreign policy has a life of its own largely independent of public fears and distrust.

Causal dilettantism

Cause and effect have sometimes been depicted as the process of a billiard ball striking another one and setting it in motion. Already in 1748 philosopher David Hume introduced this analogy to advance his concept of causation and of causal relations.[22]

But "new causality" takes issue with such an understanding of cause and effect. It might impute quasi or fake causation in the billiard ball example.[23] For instance, (probable) cause is central to legal argument including today in international law. Legal specialists would say that the cause of the second billiard ball's motion depends on whether the perspective is of someone defending or prosecuting the first cue ball. A defense of the cue ball may claim that the movement of the struck billiard ball might have been an unrelated coincidence – chance – having nothing to do with being struck. But prosecuting the first billiard ball might lead to charges against it that the struck second billiard ball lost its chance of becoming a higher-status bowling ball by being hit by the first ball.[24] Probable cause to harm or injure would be the prosecution's argument.

Another revisionist approach to causation is taken by advocates of counterfactual analysis of causation. They reject broadly accepted regularity analysis in favor of the "promising alternative" of counterfactual analysis.[25] They accept that event A (the cause) and C (the effect) can both occur but add the counterfactual conditional that, had A not occurred, neither would C have.

Applied to this study, a counterfactual proposition would be that a country's government seeks to compensate for xenophobia at home by spreading goodwill abroad. This "reaction effect" is precisely the contrary of the anticipated outcome – that fears at home will produce fear aggression abroad. In the case of France, presented in the next chapter, the creation of a Mediterranean Union in 2008 may furnish evidence of a counterfactual proposition: at precisely a time when Islamophobic attitudes in France were growing, President Sarkozy reached out to many Muslim-majority states by associating them with an organization also comprising European Union member states. This compensatory mechanism was introduced and French foreign policy set in a different direction because of the counterfactual conditional that, without Islamophobia at home (A), Islamophile foreign policy (C) could not have been adopted.

Counterfactual analyses focus on singular- or token-causal claims.[26] But the value of simple analysis of singular causation in terms of counterfactuals is dubious. Valerie Hudson and her co-authors propose a different revisionist view of causality which lowers the threshold for causal inference: "The act of imputing causality *is the act of identifying rule-based patterns in the phenomena we study*, with the caveat that the complete consequences of the rules specified are probably not going to be knowable in advance."[27] The research objective becomes to identify the rules that human agents use to produce patterns even though there is no guarantee that either the patterns or the rules will be easily discovered.

Causal illusions

A promising lead for a causal connection between variables may be a case of an *illusion of causality* following the appearance of a correlation. An illusory correlation is to see the relationship one expects in a set of data when no such relationship may exist. The circulation of stereotypes offers an example. People often overestimate the association between stereotyped groups and stereotypic behavior. They exaggerate the frequency of these events even when only a few such correlations are actually observed.[28] A common case is when people form spurious associations between membership in a statistically defined minority group and rare, usually negative, behavior. This occurs because both independent and dependent variables capture the observer's attention since they are novel or deviant. It is one way that stereotypes form in the first place, then endure.

Illusory correlations involve information-processing shortcuts shaping human judgments. One of these shortcuts is the ease with which an idea comes to mind: "availability" of a scenario is often used to estimate how likely an event is or how often it occurs. This can result in illusory correlation because some pairings come easily and vividly to mind even though they occur infrequently. The contrast is with representativeness – the degree of similarity between an individual and the most typical example of a category.

Measurement is essential. When an independent variable is characterized by multidimensionality – citizens' fears and suspicions in this study are treated as a multidimensional phenomenon – they must be measured multidimensionally. The multidimensional measures observed here do not lend themselves to quantifiable measurement.

More often than not comparative research, such as this study, is characterized by the importance of factors impossible to control which intervene in causal relationships. Instead of seeking deterministic matches, then, the objective, as in most interpretive research of this kind, is to suggest probabilistic causal relationships. A probabilistic causation is the statement that if X appears Y probably follows, not that it must follow.

Another problem in looking for causal relationships and causal direction is that my theory about the connection between fear and foreign policy is bivariate even though social reality is inherently multivariate. Nevertheless this theory, like most bivariate theories about social phenomena, does not assume a single cause which has a single effect. To be sure, a variable defined in a multidimensional way, and having an effect on a dependent one, still furnishes a bivariate case. An example is the statement that a spike in public fears (a composite of indicators) of a selected group causes a hostile foreign policy towards the countries of origin of that group. The many other factors making up a domestic structure are ignored.

Instead of focusing on the fears–foreign policy causal linkage, it is possible to treat the observable effects of cultural phenomena, such as fear, on foreign policy as a heuristically useful metaphorical assumption rather than as an explanation. It may even be the case that a factor may possess explanatory power *and* serve as a powerful metaphor of a connection between political phenomena. Right-wing rallies around the statues of World War II Fascists can be an example.

Quantitative researchers may argue that connections between events can be captured through use of multivariate statistical analysis. A world of metaphors is far removed from such methods. In the specific case of measuring factors shaping a country's foreign policy, multivariate analysis is unlikely to pin down causal factors and outcomes with greater exactitude than an interpretive approach.

Six decades ago David Easton expressed dissatisfaction with a political science that was concerned with developing normative, as well as partial, causal theories but was wary of advancing general systemic theory.[29] In Easton's spirit it is valuable to imagine continuous feedback loops incorporating the reciprocal influence on one another of domestic and international factors.

CONDUCTING INTERPRETIVE RESEARCH

The connection between two events, whether we think of it as cause and effect or covariation, requires accurate measurement because with it emerges a more vivid and powerful causal story. Coding variables in binary terms, such as strong or weak, encounters problems of its own, such as the validity question – is the measure really measuring what it is supposed to?[30] Critiques of exercises in metrics have contended that they code and measure only what is trivial and do not code and measure what is important. Because of the complexity and multidimensionality of this topic, arriving at valid measures is challenging.

Demonstrating causality is at the far end of a methods continuum from a plausibility probe. In contrast to Pythagoras, Greek mathematician and mystic, today's social science does not explicitly aspire to the standard of *quod erat demonstrandum* (QED) – "which was to be demonstrated" – incontrovertible proof of a prior mathematical statement or philosophical argument. But the search for concrete, context-dependent knowledge is as intense as ever.[31]

Plausibility probes, also known as exploratory studies, comprise one such type of search. They are attempts to do something modest: to determine whether the theory's potential is sufficient to warrant testing. At a minimum, a plausibility probe of a theory tries to confirm that a theoretical construct is worth considering at all, that an empirical instance of it can be found.[32] It can furnish the initial cases towards developing a theory which can then be further tested empirically. This does not imply lowering social science standards of evidence or inference.

Most social science research is located somewhere between studies of causality and test probes. On the one hand are quantitative studies measuring the covariation of an independent variable with a dependent variable.

Box 3.2 Replacing solid with liquid thinking

[Bauman's] later writings, that is, the work he writes after his academic retirement, increasingly takes on the liquidity he wants to explain on a sociological level: the solid principles of scientific research or the rigorous argumentative writing he produced earlier give way to liquid forms of thinking and writing. His work becomes highly fragmented, descriptive, and he rejects the quantitative research that increasingly dominates sociology. His writings display a moral appeal that is often disturbing. His work raises doubts about Western culture, and that is not always appreciated.

Source: Anonymous author, "Hospitality and its Ambivalences: on Zygmunt Bauman," *Hospitality and Society*, forthcoming (2015).

At the other end of the spectrum are postmodernist, axiological, "liquid" approaches to interpreting observable phenomena, such as that found in the "late" sociology of Bauman (Box 3.2).

Making methods explicit is important for legitimizing subsequent empirical findings even of the liquid kind Bauman generates. It is particularly important for interpretive meaning-based studies to identify their research design and method. That is because "Most researchers using interpretive methods have just set about doing the work, telling the tale, without explicit reflection on their methodological considerations, choices, and decisions."[33]

Sometimes method disclosure is not needed when a community of scholars shares the same epistemological assumptions as the researchers. But, generally, method transparency in meaning-based studies strengthens validity and objectivity claims. It can enhance understanding across disciplinary divides and promote additional theorizing. Not assuring transparency leads to many shortcomings:

> The lack of such explicitness about their systematicity and the disinclination to situate methods discussions in their philosophical grounding has contributed to the (false) impression that interpretive methods are not serious scholarship; that their procedures are not rigorous or systematic and that their findings are not trustworthy, being little more than "opinion."[34]

Cases and comparisons

Interpretive researchers value flexibility which allows concepts and understandings to emerge from the qualitative data collected. "Researchers in interpretive modes more commonly begin their work in an abductive logic of inquiry, with puzzles or a sense of tension between expectations and prior observations, grounded in the research literature and, not atypically, in some prior knowledge of the study setting."[35]

But empiricism alone is insufficient: "facts alone are not enough to yield scientific explanations. What is missing is a relationship – that is, the association, dependence, or covariance of the values of one variable with the values of another."[36] That is the purpose of Thucydides' Theorem for organizing this research investigation of fear and its policy consequences.

The objectives of interpretive research guiding this study include the following: 1. establishing a relationship between variables; 2. demonstrating that the results are true under specific conditions; 3. identifying whether one phenomenon precedes another; and 4. eliminating as many explanations (confounding factors) for the observed finding as possible.[37] The aim is to develop an explanatory model of how citizens' fears shape foreign policy.

Much of comparative research, including in migration studies, is distinctive in terms of the conceptual focus given to cases rather than types of data.[38] That is because the goal of such research is to examine how structures, cultures, processes, norms, and institutions affect outcomes through the combination and intersection of causal mechanisms. Decisions about case selection and comparison are integral to theory- and concept- building. Should cases be cherry picked, for example? In this study cases were chosen in part where there was a possibility that public opinion could affect foreign policy – that is, choice of a democratic system was essential.

Comparative research explores a gamut of evidence ranging from interview data and public opinion surveys to documentary materials and observations in the field. Selected groups can be compared in terms of such categories as race, national origins, and ethnicity; this has long been the case in the United States. In France and Sweden, by contrast, researchers have been compelled by state policies to reject such social categories as explaining anything. Instead, other categories are highlighted: socio-economic class; educational achievement; and, increasingly, religious values.

The method of structured, focused comparison is applied in this study. Structured, because the same research questions are asked of each case to standardize data collection. Focused, because only certain aspects of each country's politics are investigated.[39] Case selection is guided by the aim of holding certain factors constant. In this study, the factor that must be kept constant as much as possible is the international environment. Thus, I have chosen a common time period, 2006 to 2014, and three European democracies all of which experienced a government change in 2006–07. This allows us to see more clearly the impact of other independent variables, such as elite and citizen fears, the conditions in which they emerge in each country, how state policies and politicians encourage or suppress them, whether these fears are inwardly or outwardly directed.

71

Other selection criteria are the contrasting types and targets of fear, the fieldwork experience and language skills of the researcher, and the different parts of Europe represented by the three countries. To be sure, France was not chosen because it is representative of Spain or Italy; Poland of Lithuania or Slovakia; and Sweden of Denmark or Norway.

The outcomes – different foreign policies towards particular "problem" countries – are shaped by these characteristics. Do having five million Muslims in a country's population, as is the case of France, having Russia as a neighboring country like Poland, or having communitarian values, as has Sweden, make a difference to the salience of fear in driving foreign policy? It may be that the research produces null results – little substantiated linkage between selected independent variables and outcomes. But, even if frustrating, such a finding is itself important in helping disregard certain factors, concepts, and even theories.

Data debates

Causality questions aside, data and their quality can be as significant to research outcomes as the mix of methods used. The effort to acquire knowledge about the factors affecting foreign policy involves the collection and interpretation of different types of data, such as relevant historical facts, survey results, case study analyses, and observed behavior.

Methods and design which generate empirical data relevant to answering research questions and helping build theory are of special importance. There are pitfalls with data-driven and data-dumping research: as one follower of Easton warned, in his time "A multitude of 'facts' about political life had been collected but the principles of selection had been inconsistent, incoherent, and often unconscious." Following Easton, the corrective has been to develop a "conscious, logically articulated conceptual framework, one which provide both a check-list of the relevant questions to be asked about the various aspects of political life, and a set of concepts in terms of which a researcher could systematically set down his answers." [40] It is in this spirit that this study is framed.

Since at least the 1960s, event data have been employed in the analysis of not just bounded domestic political systems but states' international behavior, too. Hudson and her co-authors raise the problematic posed by Easton over half a century ago: ". . . we are still trying to learn how to use them [event data] effectively." In referring to international relations they add: ". . . since no one had looked for patterns in this fashion before, we first needed to demonstrate that we could find them, and that the patterns had some plausible correspondence to our underlying qualitative understanding of the situation we were analyzing."[41]

72

The way to sidestep this problem may be to subscribe to a new, less demanding understanding of causality. The "new view of causality imposes a temporal boundedness to our ability to falsify," that is, it becomes "possible to determine for a given period of time whether one specific set of rules is more or less satisfactory than another specific set of rules in accounting for the behavior during that period."[42] To reach such a methods threshold is already to achieve much. Specifying conditions under which a causal connection emerges is to advance our knowledge of political phenomena. And it is the starting point for relating a causal story.

CONCEPTS AND CONSEQUENCES

Reflexivity and introspection about research design, concepts, and methods are particularly important when the research problem concerns the relationship between values and culture on the one hand and foreign policy shifts on the other. Using exclusively qualitative data to elucidate the relationship makes the need for taking stock about methods more pressing; hence this chapter's exposition.

But being reflective about concepts and methods should not stand in the way of asking bold and significant questions. How responsive are leaders to public opinion, to citizens' fears, to deviations from a nation's cultural pathways, especially when they may have an impact on international politics? Finding evidence of covariation between the two factors is illuminating in itself.

Foreign policy outcomes described in this book are based on a conventional approach tracing political and security relations between states and what they perceive as their significant Others. It is important to distinguish between foreign policy *discourses* – debates about different policy objectives and courses of action – and foreign policy *outputs* – the actual course of action taken by policy-makers. To be sure, discourse analysis can provide clear and persuasive narratives of why a particular foreign policy course was taken.

A focus on endogenous factors shaping a particular foreign policy approach subsumes analysis of partisan politics, the politics of fear, public opinion, conceptions of the national interest, a sense of rationality. But cultural factors need to be included, as noted in Chapter 2; ideational ones, such as citizens' values, national action scripts and role conceptions, and ideologies shape foreign policy, too.

The next chapter presents the first case study – an analysis of Islamo-hypopsia in France and its possible spillover effects on the country's foreign policy towards immigrant-sending, francophone, African states.

Notes

1. "Reflexivity in Sociology," Science Encyclopedia website, <a href="http://science.jrank.org/pages/11000/Reflexivity-Reflexivity-in-Sociology.html"> Reflexivity-Reflexivity In Sociology

2. Nasar Meer, *Key Concepts in Race and Ethnicity* (Thousand Oaks, CA: Sage, 2014), p. 3.

3. W. Phillips Shively, *The Craft of Political Research* (New York: Longman, 2013), 9th edn, p. 4.

4. John J. Mearsheimer and Stephen M. Walt, "Leaving theory behind: Why simplistic hypothesis testing is bad for International Relations," *European Journal of International Relations*, 19:3 (September 2013), p. 428.

5. Ibid., p. 430.

6. Ibid., p. 436.

7. Ibid., p. 428. The authors take special aim at doctoral studies in the United States. On the shortcomings of hypothesis testing see my book review in *Perspectives on Politics*, 12:1 (March 2014), pp. 252–4. The book in question is by Şener Aktürk, *Regimes of Ethnicity and Nationhood in Germany, Russia, and Turkey* (Cambridge: Cambridge University Press, 2012).

8. Richard Ned Lebow, *Forbidden Fruit: Counterfactuals and International Relations* (Princeton, NJ: Princeton University Press, 2010), p. 14.

9. Ibid., Chapter 6. See also my "Counterfactual Thought Experiments and Scholars' Compulsion for Closure," *European Political Science*, 9:4 (December 2010), pp. 524–32.

10. Lebow, *Forbidden Fruit*, p. 147.

11. Brian E. Calabrese, *Fear in Democracy: A Study of Thucydides' Political Thought* (Ann Arbor, MI: ProQuest, UMI Dissertations Publishing, 2008), p. 23, note 35; p. 24.

12. Thucydides, *History of the Peloponnesian War* (Harmonsworth: Penguin, 1954), Book I, Chapter 23, p. 6.

13. Dambudzo Marechera, *Black Sunlight* (New York: Penguin, 2012), p. 97.

14. Valerie M. Hudson, Philip A. Schrodt, and Ray D. Whitmer, "A New Kind of Social Science: The Path beyond Current (IR) Methodologies May Lie Beneath Them." Paper prepared for the Annual Meeting of the International Studies Association, Montreal, Quebec (March 2004), p. 3.

15. Ronald L. Jepperson, Alexander Wendt, and Peter J. Katzenstein, "Norms, Identity, and Culture in National Security," in Katzenstein (ed.), *The Culture of National Security: Norms and Identity in World Politics* (New York: Columbia University Press, 1996), p. 66.

16. Aristotle, *Metaphysics* (Cambridge, MA: Harvard University Press, 1989), Book 5, p. 1013a.

17. Paul M. Kellstedt and Guy Whitten, *The Fundamentals of Political Science Research* (New York: Cambridge University Press, 2013), p. 45.

18. Anna Grzymala-Busse, "Time Will Tell? Temporality and the Analysis of Causal Mechanisms and Processes," *Comparative Political Studies*, 44:9 (December 2010), p. 1289.

19. Ibid., pp. 1267–97.

20. Ibid., p. 1275.
21. Ibid., p. 1268.
22. David Hume, *Enquiry concerning Human Understanding*, 3rd edn (Oxford: Oxford University Press, 1975).
23. On causation involving billiard, tennis, and other balls see "Causal Processes," *Stanford Encyclopedia of Philosophy* website, 10 September 2007, http://plato.stanford.edu/entries/causation-process/
24. I am grateful to Nikolas Rajkovic of the European University Institute for suggesting to me this analogy from international law.
25. David Lewis, "Causation as Influence," in John Collins, Ned Hall and L. A. Paul (eds), *Causation and Counterfactuals* (Cambridge, MA: MIT Press, 2004), pp. 75–106.
26. An example of token causation is this: "Suzy throws a rock which causes a window to break. That is token causation: a particular event 'c' causes another particular event 'e.'" See Ned Hall and L. A. Paul on causation on the Philosophy TV website, http://www.philostv.com/ned-hall-and-l-a-paul/
27. Valerie M. Hudson, Philip A. Schrodt, Ray D. Whitmer, and Adam Shanko, "A New Kind of Social Science: Analyzing Israeli–Palestinian Event Data Using Reverse Wolfram Models," BYU website, http://nkss.byu.edu/FPAWolfram3.14.06.isa.pdf," p. 18. Italics in original.
28. I am grateful to Peter Olofsson, Trinity University, San Antonio for developing this idea. See his *Probabilities: The Little Numbers that Rule our Lives* (Hoboken, NJ: John Wiley, 2010). See also Steven J. Stroessner and Jason E. Plaks, "Illusory Correlation and Stereotype Formation: Tracing the Arc of Research over a Quarter Century," in Gordon B. Moskowitz (ed.), *Cognitive Social Psychology: The Princeton Symposium on the Legacy and Future of Social Cognition* (Mahwah, N.J.: Lawrence Erlbaum Associates, 2001), pp. 247–59.
29. David Easton, *A Systems Analysis of Political Life* (New York: Wiley, 1965).
30. See my Boolean statement based on coding about the collapse of the USSR in "From Matrioshka Nationalism to National Interests," in Ian Bremmer and Ray Taras (eds), *New States, New Politics: Building the Post-Soviet Nations* (Cambridge: Cambridge University Press, 1997), pp. 688–93.
31. Bent Flyvbjerg, "Five Misunderstandings About Case-Study Research, " in Clive Seale, Giampietro Gobo, Jaber F. Gubrium, and David Silverman (eds), *Qualitative Research Practice* (Thousand Oaks, CA: Sage, 2004), pp. 420–34.
32. Harry Eckstein, "Plausibility probes," in Eckstein, *Regarding Politics: Essays on Political Theory, Stability, and Change* (Berkeley, CA: University of California Press, 1991), p. 148.
33. Dvora Yanov and Peregrine Schwartz-Shea, "Wherefore 'Interpretive?' An Introduction," in Yanov and Schwartz-Shea (eds), *Interpretation and Method: Empirical Research Methods and the Empirical Turn*, 2nd edn (Armonk, NY: M. E. Sharpe, 2014), p. xv.
34. Ibid., p. xvi. For a list of the varieties of interpretive research methods including case and constructivist studies analysis see Table I.1, p. xxiii.
35. Ibid., p. xviii.
36. Janet Buttolph Johnson and H. (Henry) Reynolds, *Political Science Research Methods*, 7th edn (Thousand Oaks, CA: Sage, 2012), p. 76.
37. Ibid., p. 166.

38. Irene Bloemraad, "The promise and pitfalls of comparative research design in the study of migration," *Migration Studies*, 1:1 (2013), p. 27.
39. Alexander L. George and Andrew Bennett, *Case Studies and Theory Development in the Social Sciences* (Cambridge, MA: MIT Press, 2005), p. 67.
40. Michael Evans, "Notes on David Easton's Model of the Political System," *Journal of Commonwealth Political Studies*, 8:2 (1970), pp. 117–18.
41. Hudson et al., "A New Kind," pp. 36–7.
42. Ibid., p. 19.

CHAPTER FOUR

French Muslims and France's foreign policy

Is it the case that European states having significant Muslim minorities are inclined to pursue *la politique du dehors avec les raisons du dedans?*[1] That is, is foreign policy dictated by domestic issues? For Jocelyn Evans, who employed this phrase in his study of the influence of the *Front National* on France's foreign policy, right-wing parties may target scapegoats for domestic problems who can be simultaneously found abroad as well as at home. Muslim migrants and minorities within the country are viewed as extensions of Muslim-majority states located in the international arena. They pose an equal threat to national cohesion, national security, and the national interest, anti-immigrant parties claim.

A reverse relationship may also be conceivable. To hate the external foe allows us to reconcile and bond with the internal one. Sociologist Georg Simmel claimed a century ago that antagonism towards a foreign enemy had a positive integrative effect on internal group cohesion: "Conflict may not only heighten the concentration of an existing unit, radically eliminating all elements which might blur the distinctions of its boundaries against the enemy, it may also bring persons together which have otherwise nothing to do with each other."[2]

Over two centuries ago, on 27 January 1794, Barère de Vieuzac presented a report to *La Convention* (or Constituent Assembly) on behalf of Robespierre's Committee of Public Safety. It painted a fear of the foreign with extraordinarily broad strokes: "Federalism and superstition speak Breton; emigration and hatred of the Republic speak German; the counter-revolution speaks Italian; and fanaticism speaks Basque. Let us smash these harmful and faulty instruments." Historically, then, as one specialist on language politics concluded, in France "the Other is located most fundamentally in language."[3]

Defining Republican identity

France has long considered itself to be an egalitarian, color-blind, secular republic. Setting aside recent in-migration flows, state policy has been not to recognize the existence of minorities on its territory. This principle is illustrated in the unrecognized minority status of Bretons, Occitanes, or Picardiens. The logic is that *une discrimination positive* – a form of affirmative action – cannot occur if there are no officially recognized diverse groups to apply it to. To be sure, "the parameters of French policies toward the country's minorities have changed drastically in the past decades, from a classically Republican and 'color-blind' approach to something more nuanced." [4] But, if there is only a gradual and grudging acceptance of national minorities, what must be the situation for recent immigrant communities that have established themselves in the country?

French republican identity has been understood primarily as organic, civic, and linguistic. No wonder that President Sarkozy's initiative in 2008 to create a Ministry of Immigration, Integration, National Identity, and Co-Development was so revolutionary in its assumptions even if nearly three-quarters of French respondents to a survey approved of this institution.[5] In a 2007 campaign video he had rhetorically asked about what French identity entailed:

> If we do not tell newcomers and people who want to become French what France is, how can they be integrated? The failure of the French integration system is due to the fact that we have forgotten to talk about France. Myself, I do not want to forget France, because France is at the heart of my program.[6]

In 2009 Sarkozy launched a national discussion on what it meant to be French, expecting it would lead to a broad consensus. Instead it was transformed into a platform from which many anti-immigration groups expressed their fears of growing diversity in the country. The law banning public wearing of the burka coincided with this debate and further polarized it. In 2010 the president ended the discussion while the ministry he had created was reintegrated with the Interior Ministry.

Once raised, the national identity question would not go away, however. In 2011, during a talk show, Sarkozy bandwagoned with other Western European leaders, including Angela Merkel, in emphasizing the failure of multicultural policies:

> The truth is that in all our democracies we have been too concerned about the identity of those who come and not enough about the identity of those who welcome. A person coming to France must be ready to melt into one single community, which is the national community.[7]

Sarkozy's statement hinted at the reappearance of an assimilationist discourse seeking a monocultural redefinition of national identity. It was not to be limited to nationality or citizenship: becoming French entailed a process of acculturation, that is, "melting into" the French community.[8] But on the basis of interviews with about a quarter of the more than four hundred candidates of Arab and Muslim origin who had run in the 2012 legislative elections, Gilles Kepel, political scientist and long-time observer of the Muslim fact in France, discovered views on French and Muslim identity diverging greatly from the monocultural model. His research also revealed significant changes within Muslim communities over the past twenty-five years: in particular, the presence of more violence, drugs, and Salafism (a conservative Islam).[9] Kepel's research revealed how explosive the identity debate could be.

Playing the French identity card had helped Sarkozy win the presidency, and he resorted to it again five years later in his bid for reelection. At his first campaign meeting as reelection candidate, he began: "Today I have come to talk about France. We don't talk enough about France, as if it were old-fashioned to talk about France." But, in 2012, the French identity gambit electorally boomeranged, just as his identity debate had.[10]

Sarkozy was not the only governmental voice elaborating on French identity. His interior ministers, including Claude Guéant who took the helm of the reintegrated department in 2010, debated the topic. Two years into his tenure, he singled out how the numbers of legal migrants had fallen following passage of a more restrictive law on immigration in June 2011. In explaining this "achievement" he invoked many of his predecessors' arguments while framing the policy as an integral part of the republican tradition:

> The sense of our policy is a certain conception of France and of French society. We want France to remain faithful to its values, its great Republican principles, such as *laïcité* and equality between men and women. We refuse communitarianisms and the secluded life of ethnic or religious communities which follow their own rules, which are neither the rules of the Republic nor of France. It is for that reason that the foreigners we welcome must integrate. It is they who must integrate and not the other way round.[11]

In 2011 Sarkozy's ruling party *Union pour la majorité présidentielle* (UMP) had convened a debate on Islam. It put forward a twenty-six-point secularism charter that would, among other things, forbid citizens from invoking religious beliefs and practices as a basis for disobeying laws regulating use of public spaces. The target was overt displays of Islamic faith, such as the wearing of veils and saying of prayers on the streets which Sarkozy claimed weakened the country's secular identity. Any agreed-upon charter was to serve as the basis for legislation, edicts, and police orders promoting *laïcité*.

Muslim groups objected to the proposed restrictions on their religious freedoms.[12] The UMP charter on secularism was seen as leading to anti-Muslim public policies. Some Muslims had already been blindsided by opening up discussion of what it meant to be French. Their suspicions of Sarkozy were reinforced by what they saw as his more considerate treatment of France's Jewish community. They cited his 2008 proposal that every ten-year-old French school pupil should be entrusted with the memory of one of the eleven thousand French child victims of the Holocaust. Sarkozy had dropped this idea after a committee in the Ministry of Education recommended instead that pupils *learn* about the fate of French Jewish children who were victims of the Holocaust rather than *adopting* the identity of a victim.[13] For many French Muslims, the national identity debate was a product of increasing fears about Islam in France and the government brainstorming about a way to allay them.

THE MUSLIM FACT IN FRANCE

Initially Muslims coming from North Africa and other states to France were viewed as sojourners rather than permanent settlers. Given dreadful conditions obtaining across North Africa during, but even after, the 1954–62 Algerian war of independence, this was a naive perspective. But it also had real policy consequences for France. As William Safran noted already in 1986, French leaders assumed that "Islamic or any other religious consciousness is artificial, temporary, and in the long run irrelevant, and that the Arab identity of Maghrebi immigrants can somehow be politically and analytically divorced from their Islamic identity." In short, "the Islamic aspect of these immigrants has been widely ignored." This may have been in keeping with the civic republican ideal but it also made for an ineffectual politics of recognition.[14]

Some evidence nevertheless provided grounds for optimism about diversity in the country. North African immigrants had recorded significant upward mobility and registered relatively high rates of intermarriage. For example, in 1990 an estimated 30 percent of men and 40 percent of women had married a spouse of a different nationality. The rate of exogamy only increased the longer migrants resided in France. Muslim integration into French society offered promise, then, the more so given most North Africans' proficiency in French.

Another reassuring indicator of integration was provided by subsequent survey results. French public opinion became more welcoming: the percentage of respondents agreeing that there were too many immigrants in France fell from 35 percent in 1988 to 25 percent in 2006. Three-quarters believed that immigration was a source of enrichment for the country, and 77 percent asserted that Muslim practices should be respected. A 2005 survey had found that about half of people of North African and Turkish origin agreed that "in France everybody can succeed whatever the color of their skin."

Immigrants themselves seemed to embrace the republican identity model even if French respondents were more guarded: only 43 percent believed in color-blind success. North African and Turkish respondents (88 percent) as well as the general population (94 percent) overwhelmingly agreed that secularism was "the only way for people with different beliefs to live together."[15] These results proved too good to be true.

Positive views of Muslim immigrants' integration into French society were shaken by a number of riots involving marginalized youth from the outer suburbs of large French cities where tall, rudimentary state-subsidized housing blocks had been built. Protest demonstrations by some Muslim organizations also became a regular occurrence. Another factor contributing to disillusion with the results of immigration was that successful integration into a receiving society tended to decline in the face of successive immigration waves. Furthermore, over time, many immigrants, and especially their offspring, began to contest the very idea of having to "melt into" French society. Their economic mobility had become blocked, and recognition of their being first-class French citizens was not always forthcoming. Most important of all, Muslims, primarily from North Africa but also from elsewhere, were of different ethnic backgrounds and were often treated in differentiated ways. For historical and cultural reasons, some were more highly respected, others more greatly distrusted or feared. Algerians are a case in point.

Harkis

Until independence in 1962, Algeria was constitutionally treated as an integral part of metropolitan France; it was not a foreign country or an overseas colony or possession. When, under General Charles de Gaulle, France signed the Évian accords granting Algeria independence after a vicious eight-year civil war, migration to the Hexagon (French mainland) spiked. Estimates of the number of those "repatriated" from Algeria ranged from 615,000 to more than one million.[16] These totals included both French people born in Algeria, the so-called pieds-noirs, and the harkis, or Muslim fighters who sided with France in the civil war. The difficult experience encountered by the latter group, once they had arrived in France, was reflected in a change of designation for them – français musulmans répatriés – a strange admixture of citizenship (French), religion (Muslim), and legal status (repatriated).

As early as 1975 harkis in France staged massive protests over their marginalized status. When François Mitterand was elected Socialist president in 1981 it was partly on the basis of a platform stressing *le droit à la difference* which promised to make France more multicultural in practice and aimed at abolishing discrimination against immigrant workers.[17] The Socialist government commissioned Henri Giordan to carry out a study of cultural democracy, and his report outlined a paradigm shift in integration policies towards immigrants.[18] "In those states where ethnic, religious, or linguistic minorities exist, those people who belong to them cannot be deprived of the right to have their own cultural life, to profess and practice their own religion, or to use their own language."[19]

For Muslim communities in France little material progress was recorded over the next decade, and another wave of demonstrations took place in 1991, this time staged primarily by descendants of *harkis* born in France. Two years later, however, the conservative party (UMP) led by Jacques Chirac, soon to be elected president, won legislative elections. Quickly, in 1993, Interior Minister Charles Pasqua lent his name to a bill which aimed to bring about zero immigration while simultaneously tightening control over the arrival, reception, and stay of foreigners in France. The law as passed targeted primarily irregular immigrants, and its impact on immigration policy may have been exaggerated. Nevertheless, it represented a policy watershed and raised the electoral profile of the *Front National*.

In this xeno-hypopsic climate it took two more decades for *harkis* to obtain "moral rehabilitation" for being abandoned by France in the aftermath of the Algerian war. In the interim the Algerian war continued to be played out in French *banlieues*. As historian Andrew Hussey has suggested, so-called anti-Muslim sentiments in France do not fuel the conflict between secular France and Islam. Rather it is that "the French Intifada" spearheaded by frustrated immigrant youth reflects a postcolonial rage: France is under attack from the dispossessed heirs to the French colonial project in North Africa.[20]

The French state made efforts to defuse this hostility. In 2012, on the fiftieth anniversary of the signing of the Évian accords, UMP President Sarkozy publicly admitted France's responsibility for having failed to protect *harkis*. By this point the community had grown to 500,000. But questions were raised about the motives and good faith of this symbolic gesture. Why had Sarkozy waited until late in his presidential term to rehabilitate this community? Was it not sparked by brazen electioneering before his reelection campaign against Socialist rival François Hollande?

Harkis have represented the vanguard of a wider set of Muslim communities. One estimate in 2013 of the size of the Muslim population in the country indicated it was as large as 6.5 million. This would make this group the largest of any Muslim community in the European Union. It accounts for about 10 percent of France's total population of 66 million. Boasting of the size of the Muslim population, a spokesperson for a controversial Muslim defense organization asked rhetorically: "Who has the right to say that France in thirty or forty years will not be a Muslim country? Who has the right in this country to deprive us of it?"[21]

Public opinion

Predictably, French public opinion reflected a backlash to such claims. In a survey carried out in 2013, 74 percent of French citizens said they viewed Islam as "intolerant" and "incompatible" with French values. In addition, 70 percent agreed that there were too many foreigners in France and 67 percent even said that they no longer felt at home in the country.[22]

To be sure, a major polling agency, the United States-based Pew Research Center, has found France to be a leader in positive attitudes towards Muslims. A 2014 seven-country survey discovered that 72 percent of French respondents had a favorable view of Muslims living in their country, significantly higher than in the United Kingdom (64 percent) and Germany (58 percent).[23] This favorable French rating occurs in the European country having the highest percentage (up to 10 percent) of Muslims in its national population. By contrast at least half of those surveyed in Italy, Greece and Poland, where Muslim minorities comprise no more than 2 percent, had a negative opinion of Muslims. An earlier survey asking Muslims in various European countries how welcome they felt also ranked France as the most hospitable.[24]

The republican model of color-blind and equal treatment appeared to exert positive influences on perceptions of difference. I suggest, therefore, that Islamophobia, when defined as hatred of Muslims, has marginal resonance in France. On the other hand Islamo-hypopsia, that is, suspicion or distrust of Muslims, more accurately captures the attitudes of those French unconvinced by the success of integration processes.

Significantly, it is France among Western European states that has always eschewed multiculturalism as a state policy of managing diversity; the United Kingdom and the Netherlands probably led the way in their advocacy of multiculturalism. The French state favors a republican approach where all citizens are treated the same way regardless of their background.

Conservative philosopher Alain Finkielkraut has expressed concern that this long-entrenched assimilationist republican model has recently been breaking down:

> Immigration used to go hand-in-hand with integration into French culture. That was the rule of the game. Many of the new arrivals no longer want to play by that rule. If the immigrants are in the majority in their neighborhoods, how can we integrate them?

> ## Box 4.1 Two solitudes?
>
> For their part, Muslims in Europe, who must confront poverty, bigotry, de facto segregation, and limited social mobility, are likely to find it difficult to embrace Europe's liberal democratic views on gender equality; sexual liberalization; and the principles of compromise, egalitarianism, and identification with the state. These are all issues that challenge the traditional views not only of Muslims but also of individuals with an Arab, Turkish, or South Asian heritage, as the vast majority of Europe's Muslims are. These cultural backgrounds have not included the Enlightenment as a central pillar, and the idea of a secular society is for the most part alien.
>
> Source: Timothy M. Savage, "Europe and Islam: Crescent Waxing, Cultures Clashing," *The Washington Quarterly*, 27:3 (summer 2004), p. 45

He concluded: "Many Muslims in Europe are re-Islamizing themselves."[25]

If we focus on turn of the twenty-first-century France then this concern is supported by evidence. A survey conducted before the 2001 terrorist attacks in the United States discovered that Muslim identification with Islam in France was stronger in 2001 than it had been in 1994 or 1989. The proportion of those declaring themselves to be "believing and practicing" Muslims rose by 25 percent between 1994 and 2001.[26]

Washington-based journalist and Islam expert Mustafa Malik explained this phenomenon: in Western European societies "resistance to liberalism was heightened by hatred for European colonialists, who represented liberal values."[27] An assertion made in 2004 encapsulating the dynamics between host and Muslim communities remains relevant today: "As intolerance toward Muslim communities grows in Europe, European Muslims are growing more self-confident but also more dissatisfied"[28] (Box 4.1).

FRANCE'S SECURITIZATION DILEMMA

In many French citizens' minds car burnings are associated with Muslim youth gangs. The point had been reached in 2010 that the official number of car burnings was no longer reported for fear that such statistics fueled negative stereotypes of Muslims. But in 2013 then Interior Minister Manuel Valls broke this short-lived convention to argue that "the French people should know the truth." He reported that 1,193 cars had been burned across France on New Year's Eve, adding that, on average, more than 40,000 cars were burned in the country every year.[29]

But France's public security problems go well beyond perceived Muslim vandalism in the country. In 2013 four suspected jihadists were arrested outside of Paris and accused of trying to join Islamist extremists in Mali which had recently developed into a haven for global jihadists. Valls argued how "We must continue the work of dismantling these networks that want to carry out acts on our territory or to smuggle individuals to carry out jihad and learn the practices of terrorism." He emphasized that "We are fighting terrorism outside of France but we are also fighting an internal enemy since there are some French people who are part of this process of radicalization." Three of the four suspected jihadists were French citizens, one of them with Franco-Algerian dual citizenship. The fourth was a Malian national.

France's chief antiterrorism judge, Marc Trévidic, underlined the domestic–international nexus of such terrorists: "We have a very large Malian community in France but also from sub-Saharan Africa as a whole. These 'black' French Muslims who had been suffering from latent racism at the hands of 'Arabs' have for the first time found their jihad." As a result, "All the ingredients exist for there to be repercussions on our soil. As France is backing those who want to intervene militarily in Timbuktu we are now the enemy."[30]

Several months later Trévidic turned to a related issue: French jihadists fighting in Syria against Bashar al-Assad's regime. As France was the first Western state to recognize Syria's rebel council as the country's legitimate interlocutor it was difficult for the Socialist government to condemn those fighting for the rebel side. On the other hand, not to act against self-described French jihadists seeking to topple the Syrian regime was risky. Cherry-picking good jihadists from among dangerous ones could blow up in France's streets.

France's security dilemma was a microcosm of a larger European predicament. The European Union's pursuit of internal security competed with its democracy promotion initiatives in two designated European "neighbourhoods" – the European Neighbourhood Policy in the east (above all, Ukraine) and the Euro-Mediterranean Partnership in the south (such as Libya).[31]

Fear of the consequences for European internal security of a spillover of conflicts occurring in Muslim-majority states across the Mediterranean was more palpable than of a ripple effect from Eastern Partnership activities. That began to change in 2014 with the escalation of armed conflict in Ukraine. In the perceptions and discourse of many of Europe's leaders, Russia even began to edge out global Islamic jihad as the most serious security threat to Europe.

Instead of the image of the Muslim suicide bomber slipping through Europe's securitization curtain, it was the opposite image of a wealthy Russian businessman abandoning Europe and relocating his money elsewhere that became regarded as an economic security threat to the European Union. Not surprisingly, the French Socialist government affirmed its determination to honor the contract signed with Russia in 2011 under Sarkozy's presidency for the construction and delivery of two Mistral-class helicopter carriers despite Russia's military interventions in Crimea and eastern Ukraine.

FRONT NATIONAL AND FEAR

In Europe *Front National* has spearheaded the path for xenophobic politics at home and abroad. In the 2014 elections to the European Parliament (EP) it emerged as the strongest French party. Cas Mudde, a specialist on populist parties, commented how "In many ways, the success of the European far right is really the success of the FN."[32]

The rise of the party known as anti-immigrant is not as straightforward as labeling it a single-issue party. For starters, immigration has not been the major concern of French voters that is sometimes made out: in a 2014 survey, conducted about the same time as the European Parliament elections were held, only 16 percent of French respondents identified immigration as an important issue facing the European Union after the economic situation, unemployment, and the state of public finances. In Italy, the Netherlands, Denmark, and the United Kingdom (in ascending order) the figure for immigration ranged from 25 to 29 percent.[33]

The *Front National* took advantage of a unique opportunity structure which had emerged in Europe that went beyond immigration fears: a conjunction of the eurozone financial crisis, highest unemployment levels in many countries in over a decade, the loss of France's triple-A credit rating, a sense of declinism across Europe brought on by the swift rise of Asia, and a reemerging cultural divide between northern and southern Europe.[34] Of course, immigration numbers, whether from third countries to Europe or from Eastern European members of the EU to Western European states, were a concern, too. Such hothouse conditions have given the FN's anti-EU and anti-immigration policies wide appeal. More factors account for its rise, then, than a politics of fear of strangers.

To be sure, Islamophobic discourse is the "brand" the *Front National* has marketed. In 2010, its leader and Member of the European Parliament (MEP), Marine Le Pen, compared Muslims taking over French streets to say prayers to the brutal Nazi wartime occupation of the country. Muslim prayers in the streets were also "occupation of territory." In 2013 the European Parliament voted to remove her legislative immunity in order to investigate her remarks.

Le Pen was critical of recommendations made in a 2013 French government report seeking to implement a "new form of secularism" that would "recognize the richness of multiple identities." The report recommended that public schools resume the practice of allowing Muslim pupils to wear headscarves in class (banned since 2004). They should be allowed to teach some courses in Arabic and African languages rather than in French. The report also recommended that the history curriculum should be revised to include broader recognition of the "Arab–Oriental dimension" to French national identity. Finally, it proposed that public authorities and the media should be prohibited from referring to people's nationality, religion, or ethnicity in public.

Le Pen attacked this program of supposedly "inclusive secularism" claiming that its implementation would amount to "a declaration of war on the French people." But even UMP opposition leader Jean-François Copé attacked the proposals as "explosive and irresponsible" because they would replace "the one and indivisible French Republic with a motley assembly of communities, ethnicities and groups of all kinds."[35] Four months later both these parties recorded strong showings across France in the 2014 municipal elections.

It is understandable that scholarly and journalistic attention has disproportionately been directed to national identity and domestic security fears emerging in European societies. Le Pen's rhetoric about domestic threats to French identity has made her a media magnet. But focusing exclusively on domestic sources of fear and neglecting or underestimating international ones is risky. Political actors, such as Le Pen, who exploit the politics of fear from below realize this. They develop discourses and programs seeking to maximize electoral support by identifying threats at home and abroad. Recent securitization literature has drawn attention to the importance of these actors' international politics because they appear to be natural outgrowths of their domestic agendas.

Anti-immigrant political parties and movements, whose influence has steadily increased across Europe, have been described in various ways as: populist, nationalist, radical right-wing, anti-immigrant, and xenophobic. They have capitalized on citizens' perceptions of a foreignization of European societies to make electoral and ideological gains. The "foreign threat within" construct has been particularly fruitful for ultranationalists.

The foreign policy programs of populist and xenophobic groups have often been lost in analysts' preferences for exposing the xenophobic politics they conduct at home. Yet the ways these groups interpret international politics so as to evoke national fears should not be underestimated: "the populist radical right's foreign political platforms play an important role in their growing appeal in Europe."[36] It may now be a truism that the "strategy of breaking political taboos allows the radical right to present itself as a fresh political force outside the established political parties and not corrupted by power."[37] But the radical right has also developed dilettante foreign policy programs that appeal to anti-establishment populist forces. In the three case studies of this book I review and analyze the key foreign policy components of xenophobic political parties beginning with those of the FN later in this chapter (Box 4.2).

> **Box 4.2 The foreign policy program of Hungary's nationalist *Jobbik* movement**
>
> *Jobbik*'s objectives are: the reincorporation into the national body of both Western and Carpathian-basin Hungarians, a resolute and independent Central and Eastern European foreign policy, an active policy towards the Balkans, closer relationships with those nations related to us by culture and descent ... the development and support of a Hungarian-to-Hungarian institutional network, and political and economic openness towards the East.
>
> *Jobbik* considers its most important task to be the reunification of a Hungarian nation unjustly torn apart during the course of the twentieth century. It is our most fundamental moral duty to represent the interests and defend the rights of Hungarian communities. We will strive, perpetually, for the collective rights of the Hungarians of the Carpathian basin, and for the realization of their territorial, economic and cultural self-determination.
>
> We will develop a partner relationship with Russia, which should bring our homeland positive economic and national-political benefits. We shall pursue cooperation with the Far-East and the South-East Asian region ... We shall also widen diplomatic relations with Arab nations, and will promote the creation of an independent Palestinian state, moreover, we shall accept a greater role in promoting the continued existence of Christian communities in the Middle East. In the case of Central Asian nations, we shall reinforce the development of political and economic relations on the basis of cultural relationships, given our ancient kinship with the peoples of that region.
>
> We will guarantee every Hungarian the right to Hungarian citizenship, and thus, to have their voices heard in matters concerning the national interest. We will review the treaties agreed with our neighboring countries, and reposition them on to more sound foundations. And with every single political instrument at our disposal we shall promote and support the efforts of Hungarians beyond the border to achieve self-determination.
>
> Source: The Movement for a Better Hungary (*Jobbik*), "Foreign Affairs Policy," http://www.jobbik.com/foreign_affairs_policy

LA POLITIQUE ARABE

Jacques Attali, special advisor to President Mitterand, once remarked that "France may be Christian, Atlantic, and European, but it is also Muslim, Mediterranean and African."[38] Several reasons account for France's special relationship with the Muslim and Mediterranean worlds. One is its geographic proximity to Arabic-speaking countries. Another is its extended period of contact with, and at times conquest of, these peoples; they date from the battle of Tours–Poitiers in AD 732 at which Franks defeated an army of the Umayyad Caliphate. Napoleon's Egyptian Campaign (1798–1801) was the precursor for a military expedition to Algeria in 1830, setting the stage for *l'Algérie française*. Algeria became France's "narrow door" to Africa. Based on at times a wrenching history, France has developed an emotional attachment to the Arab world.

Geostrategic considerations are crucial, too. One study noted that:

> France's *politique arabe* sought to counter U.S. and Soviet influence in the region, showed a preference for Arab countries in the Middle East conflict, attempted to isolate Islamist movements and was guided by strategic considerations that gave little value to the promotion of democracy.[39]

France's interest in Muslim-majority states is also amplified by the Fifth Republic president's far-reaching constitutional powers in matters of defense, foreign policy, security, and European policy. Presidents from de Gaulle to Hollande have made their personal foreign policy preferences those of France. In addition, their proximity to business leaders with economic stakes in resource-rich regions of the world can seamlessly convert foreign economic interests into the state's international politics.

France spends more on the military than any country other than the United States and Britain; its share of global military expenditures is 5 percent. Arms exports to African and Middle Eastern states – some former colonial possessions, others part of the worldwide French-speaking common-wealth known as *La francophonie*, others still dependent on France's political support or governed by elites trained in French universities – are particu-larly profitable. But another explanation for *la politique arabe* has also been advanced: the country's anti-Semitic history.

French anti-Semitism

France's pro-Arab policy cannot be decoupled from the existence of anti-Semitism throughout the twentieth century. A catalytic event was the Dreyfus affair sparked by the conviction in 1894 of Alfred Dreyfus, a Jewish officer in the French military, for treason. French society became divided over the patriotism of French Jews, and the controversy left an enduring mark on French conceptions of identity, belonging, and national security.

Anti-Semitic attitudes have not always influenced French foreign policy. France endorsed the 1924 Balfour Declaration which envisaged the creation of an independent Jewish state in the Middle East. A shameful episode fol-lowed within twenty years: the Vichy regime's political collaboration with the Third Reich in the early 1940s. The regime's official anti-Semitism led it in 1942 to agree to assist German forces in the roundup and deportation of French Jews. One of the most notorious of these roundups led to the incarceration of Jews of all ages at the *Velodrome d'Hiver* in Paris, then their transport to extermination camps in Eastern Europe. Up to 75,000 perished in Auschwitz alone.[40]

After the war Fourth Republic governments between 1948 and 1958 embraced the new Israeli state. French nuclear know-how and technology were shared with it. At home the state made efforts to improve French attitudes towards its Jewish minority. Thus, France's enthusiasm for "Franco-Israeli relations were one of the few foreign policy issues with a strong domestic resonance – both because of their implications for domestic attitudes to French Jews, and because of the existence of relatively well organized lobbies."[41]

At this time French state and society were going in different directions in their approaches to Jews and Muslims in their midst. It has been argued that, for a time, Jews migrating to France found themselves in a more privileged position than their Muslim cohorts. According to historian Maud Mandel, both groups were framed by their religion regardless of whether they wished it. Master narratives could construct and maintain the foreignness of specific groups or they could undermine it. For Mandel "the very terms 'Jew' and 'Muslim' hide as much as they reveal, because they cluster various national and ethnic origins under broad religious categories that imply homogeneity and communal identifications in place of the profound heterogeneity that characterizes each population."[42]

Mandel described the different roles that the two groups were expected to play in France's colonial project in North Africa. When, in 1954, armed rebellion broke out against French rule in Algeria, Algerian Muslims were turned into "the central and even unique symbol of 'the enemy within.'"[43] Simultaneously, France recognized the French citizenship of Jewish Algerians, thereby enfolding them into the wider European family. In the decades that followed, Jews arriving in France joined a rooted French Jewish community. By the time Algeria obtained independence in 1962, France had eliminated legal "distinctions between Jews and other 'Europeans' thereby juridically sealing the 'Frenchness' of Algeria's Jewish population."[44] A "Jewish Story" was spun that differed markedly from a "Muslim Story."

Relations between the two Algerian communities which had migrated to France after Algeria's independence were shaped by lasting images of each other: "In Jewish memories, Muslims seem to embody the negative representation of the 'other,' while the hostility of the Europeans has been minimized." Not so for Muslims, "presented as an existential threat to the Western world."[45] Thus "the inequities built into the colonial structure and transferred to the metropole created the context in which Muslim–Jewish relations would evolve in France." Some Jewish leaders in the metropole emphasized "the fusion of Jewishness and Frenchness in contradistinction to Muslim foreignness."[46]

In her study Annie Kriegel compared the reconstructed identities of the two groups. Jews constituted a voluntary, religiously based community while Muslims comprised a minority group.[47] The latter were permanently framed as a minority of foreigners and aroused distrust and fear. Returning to Mandel's analysis, these "socially constructed categories had legal, adminis-trative, and cultural implications for those categorized as 'Muslims' whether they embraced the label or not."[48] But two Middle East wars in 1967 and 1973 affected the status of Jews and Muslims in France.

The Franco-Israeli bond came to an end with the Six Day War of 1967. Israel's military routed Arab states' armies and initiated an occupation of Arab lands only some of which were ceded back in subsequent decades. President de Gaulle criticized Israel's actions and imposed an arms embargo on it. Some Arab leaders interpreted the move as a decisive tilt towards a pro-Arab politics. At a minimum it "provided French diplomats with both political capital and commercial leverage within the Arab world."[49]

Was the Six Day War just a pretext for France shifting its support to Muslim-majority states? Was the anti-Israeli foreign policy shift shaped by a domestic factor – anti-Semitism among a part of the political elite in Paris?[50] Or were the Muslim world's resources becoming more important to France? The 1973 Arab–Israeli war dealt Israel a limited diplomatic defeat. Shortly after it had ended with Israeli Defense Forces in control of the Sinai Peninsula, the Organization of Arab Petroleum Exporting Countries (OAPEC) declared an embargo on the export of oil to the West. Within a year the price of a barrel had quadrupled from $3 to $12. The first signs of European *dhimmitude*, or subservience to Islam, and of a Eurabia where Arab interests began to prevail on the European continent emerged. Was an accompanying role reversal occurring in France and elsewhere where Muslim communities became the privileged and Jewish ones at risk?[51]

Une puissance musulmane

The framing of France as *une puissance musulmane* became a cornerstone of the foreign policies of Fifth Republic presidents until Sarkozy's election in 2007.[52] To be sure, friendly policies towards Islamic political leaders were not without problems. The French government had assisted Ayatollah Khomeini when he lived in Paris as an exile by extending his visa; then it initially backed his takeover of power in Teheran in 1979. The timeless principle explaining this support was again that one's enemy's enemy (Iran as the enemy of the United States) is one's (France's) friend.[53]

The way that the Iranian revolution subsequently played out made French leaders reconsider their position. Support for a theocratic republic in Iran, and even secular ones in the Arab world, became more circumspect. Sympathy for Saddam's secular Iraqi state vanished after Iraq invaded Kuwait in 1991, and President Mitterand joined the United States-led coalition driving the Iraqi military out of the Gulf state in 1993. A contributing factor at home may also have contributed to increased circumspection: "The creeping Islamicization of France's Muslim population and the perpetration of Islamist terrorist attacks on French soil served to turn French policy further against political Islam."[54]

Yet this shift did not mark a definitive turning point in French foreign policy. Jean-Pierre Chevènement, defense minister of Mitterand's Socialist government in the late 1980s, had been the chief strategist behind an approach to support secular governments in Muslim states. As an analyst summarized,

> One of Chevènement's longstanding central arguments has been for the need for French foreign policy to combat religious revivalism in the Maghreb and Middle East – not as an end in itself, but as a bulwark against the influence of Islamist groups within France's own population, influence which continued to inform French policy towards Iraq in 2002–03.[55]

Again we observe the interplay of international and domestic considerations in the making of policy.

In 1996 President Chirac became the first world leader to address the Palestinian Legislative Council in Ramallah. In 2003 he was outspoken in his criticism of the US invasion of Iraq and was backed by major French multinational corporations, the higher echelons of the civil service, and the vast majority of French citizens. France and Russia had vetoed a United Nations Security Council resolution which would have authorized United States military intervention. Chirac's foreign minister, Dominique de Villepin, made an impassioned speech against going to war: "No one can assert today that the path of war will be shorter than that of the inspections" (referring to the unfinished mission of United Nations weapons inspector Hans Blix).[56] But "many American commentators suggested that France's antiwar position was dictated by the country's five million Muslims, or at least that this population significantly limited the options available to President Jacques Chirac."[57]

Admittedly what happened in the Middle East or North Africa was a function of regional balances of power, security threats, and the alignment of global forces. But how France reacted to them had a domestic dimension: anticipation of what might happen on the "Muslim street" in France.

The French president was nicknamed *Chirac d'Arabie* for his attention to Arab state interests. While the Middle East held vital energy interests for

France, across the Mediterranean in the 1990s, the Maghreb became the primary destination for French assistance, investment, and cooperation on military and counterterrorism operations. Given its colonial past and how many migrants it had been sending to France, Algeria had particular importance for Chirac. The Algerian civil war which had broken out between Islamists and military-backed government forces in 1992 and lasted until 2002 had a destabilizing effect on the region and indirectly on France's role in it.

Shortly after the fighting ended, the French president visited his counterpart, Abdelaziz Bouteflika, in 2003. They signed the Algiers Declaration creating a privileged partnership – partenariat d'exception – between the two countries in political, economic, cultural, and humanitarian (which included migration policy) cooperation. Subsequently, Sarkozy renewed the cooperation agreement, renamed by technocrats as Document Cadre du Partenariat (DCP) for 2007–12. Hollande was to do the same (DCP 2013–17) during his visit to Algiers in 2012. Chirac also signed DCP framework agreements with Morocco and Tunisia for 2006–10 but these were not extended.

Algeria has remained France's largest trading partner in Africa, with growth increasing by more than 10 percent between 2010 and 2012. France also remained Morocco's and Tunisia's largest trading partner. The long-established development agency Agence Française de Développement has been the pivotal funnel for economic assistance to Maghreb countries as well as to sub-Saharan Africa.

President Chirac's pro-Arab policies had its critics: "Chiraquien diplomacy brought neither France nor any other country anything since it only encouraged extremist, adventurist tendencies of the worst type, such as in Saddam Hussein, Muammar Quadafi, and Khomeini."[58] Significantly, then, while Chirac was still president, the 2007 Rapport Avicenne, written by French diplomats, proposed a stronger engagement with moderate Islamic actors.[59]

The 2005 riots that rocked several French cities demonstrated how no domestic payoff was guaranteed by conducting friendly bilateral relations with Muslim-majority states. It was said that the Tablighi (a Sunni missionary movement) and the Muslim Brotherhood were recruiting young French Muslims to their cause. Philippe de Villiers, a conservative politician, warned of the "Islamicization" of French minds, speech, and territory.[60]

Was Islamicization of French society correlated with la politique arabe, that is, did they occur simultaneously with each other? Pro-Arab foreign policy predated the arrival of large numbers of Muslims to France. Moreover, French Muslims represent diverse ethnic, linguistic, and political communities. In elections, those who vote – only about three in five are voting citizens – do not vote as a bloc. As a whole "The political impact of the Muslim population is very minimal on foreign policy or the fight against terrorism."[61] Among the reasons for this are their greater interest in issues concerned with employment, the economy, education, and discrimination.

From the perspective of Muslim residents, foreign policy is of secondary concern. As early as 2002 a study of self-identified Muslims in France found foreign policy issues to be at the very bottom in importance of a list of sixteen issues. For them the role of France in the world ranked twelfth in importance (compared to ninth for self-identified Roman Catholics), globalization thirteenth (for Catholics, sixteenth), and European integration sixteenth (for Catholics, fifteenth). Security, employment, social inequality, and pensions were ranked at the top of each group's lists in the same rank order.[62]

The single most important international issue for French Muslims has been the Palestinian cause which has overshadowed other matters such as the Iraq and Syrian wars. "French Muslims have never mobilized on behalf of Chechnya, Kashmir, or even Bosnia as they have for Palestine."[63] Tellingly, an ethnic voting bloc in France running for the 2004 European Parliament was called "Euro-Palestine."[64]

In 2014 French Muslim sensitivity to the Palestinian cause led to demonstrations against Israel's military intervention in the Gaza Strip. Interior Minister Bernard Cazeneuve had to order a ban on protests in Paris, the Sarcelles suburb, and Nice claiming the security risk was too great in these areas. President Hollande declared he would not allow violence in the Middle East to spill over to France.[65] Some Muslim and radical groups condemned the ban as Islamophobic.

On the big issues, French Muslims and the French population at large have usually been in agreement. More than 70 percent of both groups said that they worried about Islamism and that they believed there is no "conflict between being a devout Muslim and living in a modern society." The two populations also expressed mutual respect: not long after the 2001 terrorist attacks in the United States, close to two-thirds of all French people thought favorably of Muslims – the highest proportion of any of the Western countries polled. Reciprocally, more Muslims had favorable views of Christians and Jews (91 percent and 71 percent respectively) in France than anywhere else.[66]

Adopting a counterfactual approach, it still would appear that the Muslim fact in France has had limited direct impact on foreign policy: "The historical record of French policy in the Arab world since Charles de Gaulle suggests that France's position on international affairs would not look much different even if there were no Muslim minority in France."[67] We can endorse the cautious conclusion of two researchers that "While there is no evidence of the Muslim minority's direct influence on French foreign policy, the presence of five million Muslims does have an indirect impact on diplomacy with respect to the Middle East. But it seems mostly to confirm France's preexisting policies toward this region."[68] But a closer look at the linkage under the Sarkozy and Hollande presidencies may raise questions whether it remains of limited significance.

SARKOZY: *L'HOMME DE RUPTURE OU NON-RUPTURE?*

As presidential candidate in 2007, Sarkozy cast himself as *l'homme de rupture* – the leader who would break with past French policies. His electoral campaign borrowed anti-Muslim themes from the *Front National*, such as cracking down on those involved in urban violence and deporting more illegal immigrants. In terms of style, if not necessarily substance, he delivered on his promise to break with the past.

International relations expert Pascal Boniface termed Sarkozy's diplomatic stratagems over his one presidential term *une non-rupture sarkozyste*. It began with an Atlanticist world view and ended with air strikes on Libya so it represented a scattergun approach rather than a clean break.[69] In turn, Jean-François Bayart, another critic, condemned Sarkozy's policies as anti-intellectual and anti-societal for their simplistic formula of attacking poor people rather than poverty both at home and abroad.[70]

An influential book on foreign policy published in the year Sarkozy became president was by former UMP Prime Minister Edouard Balladur. Offering a blueprint to Sarkozy, it outlined how France was, like Israel, located on an axis of the Western world facing the same threats: Islam, Russia, China.[71] For Balladur, France's *politique arabe* had been a sellout of Western ideals. To meet these external threats, the French state had to rein in the influence of large corporations. It had also to shake up a culture in which "Arabs have been accustomed to the cajolery of the French state, and the expected privilege that goes with it."[72]

This blueprint shared features with the *Front National*'s securitization narrative. One analyst summarized the FN view: "Muslim fundamentalism in North Africa and the Middle East is seen as a new strategic threat – missile launchers along the southern Mediterranean coast could reach France, and proto-nuclear power Iran and illegal arms trading from the ex-Soviet Republics could supply weaponry to these countries."[73]

Both Sarkozy's UMP and the FN had grounds for concern about Mediterranean security. Threats of piracy, arms smuggling, and terrorist movements between North Africa and France had grown. In 1996 the Salafist Group for Preaching and Combat (GSPC) broke away from the Armed Islamic Group (GIA) to concentrate on terrorism against security forces and foreign interests in Algeria as well as in Europe. In 2007 GSPC merged with al-Qaeda to pursue a shared goal: "Reaching Europe by setting up an organization in a nearby region with close ties to the continent, especially through the North African migrant community travelling back and forth across the Mediterranean."[74]

The most influential advisory group in the first years of the Sarkozy presidency was made up of pro-American intellectuals, journalists, and business leaders drawn from the ranks of the center-right UMP. Called *occidentalo-atlantiste*, its influence on the new president was profound. The "White Book on Defense and National Security" published in Sarkozy's first year as president used the word "Occident" (or West) eighteen times.

Occidentalism was reflected in two key foreign policy changes under Sarkozy. The first was his 2009 decision to rejoin the military structures of the North Atlantic Treaty Organization. This appeared more a symbolic than substantive change: France had already been conducting military operations from Kosovo to Afghanistan as part of NATO.[75] Rejoining NATO's military structure and fighting a war in Afghanistan were policies that could drive a wedge between France's Muslim minority and its mainstream. Sociologist Emmanuel Todd was critical of these moves and attributed them directly to Islamophobia. The French president was joining the United States on a "mission of conquest" against Islam. "France was positioning [itself] in an ideological construction against the Muslim world. This posture is also very much of a piece with Sarkozy's interior politics . . . The search for scapegoats, the emergence of an Islamophobic ideology hostile to immigrant children."[76]

The second dimension to Occidentalism entailed relations with the Muslim world. Here Sarkozy was determined to reverse the policies of his Fifth Republic predecessors. One writer noted how "For the first time, an openly pro-Israeli Presidential candidate made it to the Élysée . . . making a mockery of old conjectures about the communitarian electoral breakdown in France: 6 million Muslims versus 600,000 Jews!"[77]

President Sarkozy carried out other major foreign policy changes. In a speech to French troops fighting in Afghanistan in late 2007, he described the combat as the front line of a global war on terror waged by the Occident. Policy on Iran shifted, too. Chirac had made the cynical observation that, if Iran had one or two atomic bombs aimed at Israel, it would not be dangerous because Teheran would be destroyed in minutes.[78] By contrast, Sarkozy made clear that an Iran armed with nuclear weapons was simply unacceptable; tougher sanctions should be imposed in order to avoid a catastrophe defined as either an Iranian nuclear bomb or the bombing of Iran. When Israel launched an air attack against a target in Syria in 2007, the French government remained silent. When in 2008 the CIA produced documents suggesting it had been a nuclear site, France's official response echoed that of the United States: Syria should reveal all its nuclear activities, past and present.

Perhaps Sarkozy's most audacious move was to strengthen bilateral relations with Israel. One of his aides met with leaders of *Le Conseil représentatif des institutions juives de France* (CRIF) in 2007 and announced that a Franco-Israeli alliance would be "at the heart of the Mediterranean Union." Sarkozy, whose grandfather was Jewish, visited Israel in 2008 and expressed his sympathy for the suffering of Israelis without referring to Palestinians or the occupation of Arab lands. Israel and France were in the same democratic camp, he emphasized. He even "forgot" to read the phrase in his speech recommending a return to Israel's pre-1967 borders.

Sarkozy also supported Israel's bid for closer relations with the European Union, including having an annual meeting with the EU Council of Ministers as great powers like the United States, Russia, and China enjoy. Arab states threatened to boycott the next Mediterranean Union summit in retaliation. Shortly afterwards, an EU meeting diplomatically turned down the idea of holding EU–Israel annual meetings.[79]

While these realignments represented a break with some aspects of past policy, Sarkozy did not carry out a complete volte-face of France's international politics. The issue of controlling migration to Europe by transit countries remained pressing. Libyan leader Gaddafi was particularly assertive and candid about this subject and had demanded a large financial "reimbursement" in return for helping Europe avoid becoming what he called "Black Europe." At the end of 2007, Sarkozy played host to Gaddafi in Paris. The visit resulted in the sale of twenty French-made Airbus jets to Libya and large contracts for other French firms, such as Areva, Vinci, Veolia Environnement, and Gaz de France. An additional agreement cleared the way for nuclear cooperation in the civilian area; one commentator condemned such "nuclear diplomacy" as mercenary.[80] Rama Yade, a Senegalese Muslim whom the president had appointed Minister of Human Rights, criticized Gaddafi's visit: France was being used as "a doormat for wiping off the blood of his victims."[81]

A key international success for Sarkozy came in 2008 when he played host to the founding meeting of the Mediterranean Union. Leaders from Middle Eastern and North African countries, many at odds with one another, arrived in Paris to sign the agreement. Israel became a member alongside many Muslim-majority states which refused to recognize Israel's existence. All EU member states were also made part of "Club Med". Among invited guests was Syrian President al-Assad which drew criticism from the United States and Israel. Sarkozy's embrace of such controversial leaders appeared to be a compensatory mechanism for harsher policies he was adopting at home towards Muslim communities.

In December 2010 public protests broke out in Sidi Bouzid, Tunisia, against the rule of longtime strongman Zine el-Abidine Ben Ali. They marked the opening salvo of anti-government movements that spread beyond North Africa to as far away as Egypt and Yemen. But rumblings of dissent in Tunisia had been detectable for many years. A *WikiLeaks*-released 2005 US embassy cable had noted how "human rights policy on Tunisia would remain unchanged as long as Chirac remained President . . . the French leader's ties with Ben Ali were too long-standing for the French president to adopt a new approach." The American embassy analyst commented: "We view this controversy as indicative of the degree to which President Chirac's 'stability first' and tradition of cultivating close relations with aging Arab world dictators is increasingly out of step with current realities."[82]

Predictably, President Sarkozy was slow to throw France's support behind Tunisia's dissidents (discussed in the next section). As the opposition movement grew, he chose this period to express criticism of European multiculturalism, having received cues from Chancellor Merkel and Prime Minister Cameron. France may not have adopted the multicultural model of managing diversity (of course, multiculturalism in France had long been a social reality) so Sarkozy's remarks seemed particularly poorly timed and lacking in sympathy for Muslim communities. His return to the formula that there could be an Islam *in* France but not an Islam *of* France deepened suspicion of a disjuncture in his approach to Muslim states abroad and Muslim groups at home.

In sum, President Sarkozy, who came in for increasing criticism for his Glampolitics style, broke with many aspects of Fifth Republic foreign policy. But he did not neglect the importance of continuity as well. He did not alter France's close economic relations with oil-exporting Gulf states. The creation of Club Med was effectively an extension of existing French policy: "the Maghreb policy means essentially, for France, the management of immigration, the *francophonie* policy, the tolerance of human rights violations, and the defense of French economic interests."[83] Indeed, it is argued that Club Med came at the expense of the European Union's Euro-Mediterranean Partnership program and it had not been coordinated well within the Franco-German cooperation framework.[84]

Despite opportunistic discursive borrowings from the *Front National*, Sarkozy still embraced cultural Islam. In 2008 he laid the cornerstone for an Islamic arts addition to the Louvre, financed largely by Saudi Arabia. Departing from his election-time motifs he announced that "Islam represents progress, science, finesse, modernity."[85]

There are caveats to what may seem a linear shift by Sarkozy away from pro-Arab policies that can be linked to the pressure of public opinion. Before Sarkozy was elected, it may have been that both a phobia – anti-Israeli views – and *philia* – pro-Arabism – were embraced by swathes of the French political elite. But French society did not necessarily share these sentiments. One writer claimed that

> In contrast to the foreign policy establishment and its determination to act and speak as though the national interest demanded siding with the Muslim Middle

East in all its issues and prejudices, public opinion in France has been in the main supportive of Israel and Jews generally, while wary of a *France musulmane*.[86]

If that was the case, then Sarkozy's foreign policy tilt may have represented realignment with citizens' longstanding political orientations: Islamo-hypopsia on the one hand, empathy for assimilated French Jews and a Westernized Israel in the Middle East on the other. If this was indeed the case, then citizens' hypopsia of Muslims covaried with the foreign policy tilt away from the Muslim world. For reasons given above, French Muslims' influence on foreign policy was circumscribed but not that of *français-français* – mainstream French.

HOLLANDE: THE MAGHREB, SAHEL, AND BEYOND

François Hollande's presidency had to deal with the continued electoral rise of the *Front National*. Le Pen's nested game linking domestic and external security threats and fears appeared credible to an expanding electoral constituency. Following its strong national showing in the 2012 legislative elections and even better results in the 2014 municipal and European Parliament elections, the FN had developed greater leverage to influence the Socialist government and Socialist president than the UMP government and President Sarkozy before them. Did the Hollande presidency mimic the two-level games the FN played in order to undermine its support base?

Like many Western states, France's reaction to popular uprisings against authoritarian leaders in the Arab world in early 2011 was cautious. Sarkozy had backed the authoritarian Tunisian regime headed by Ben Ali longer than seemed decent. Several months before the popular uprising against his rule, Foreign Minister Michèle Alliot-Marie had borrowed Ben Ali's private jet to holiday in Tunisia. She approved the sale of tear gas to Tunisian police and offered assistance in crowd-control techniques to Ben Ali days before he was forced to flee the country. The French foreign minister thereby incurred the wrath of Tunisians living on both sides of the Mediterranean. French foreign policy became susceptible to the criticism that it was of a piece with Sarkozy's anti-Muslim policies at home.

A more nuanced foreign policy approach was taken towards massive demonstrations in Cairo's Tahrir Square. Admittedly, a scandal similar to the Tunisian one erupted when it became public that Prime Minister François Fillon had made use of Egyptian President Hosni Mubarak's plane during his all-expenses-paid holiday in the country. But this time Sarkozy worked closely with other EU leaders to present a coordinated response to the Egyptian revolution that overthrew Mubarak. As for the Libyan revolt (outlined in Chapter 2) and President Qaddafi's defiant attitude towards the

West, Sarkozy drew closer to the Western coalition and in 2011 took the lead in launching air strikes on parts of the country.

Hollande's presidency broke with the mutually reinforcing dynamic of growing anti-Muslim sentiment at home and more wary relations with Muslim-majority countries abroad.[87] He effectuated greater policy convergence rather than compensatory divergence in the two arenas. Could it be, however, that Hollande's policy convergence was based on an FN template?

The FN's eleven-point foreign policy program documented all that was wrong with French foreign policy. It identified France's role as *une puissance souveraine, une puissance d'équilibre, and une puissance mondiale* – a sovereign global power promoting a strategic balance. For the FN, successive conservative and Socialist governments had produced the reverse: France backed away from *la grande politique mondiale* to focus on Europe and alliance with the United States. It abandoned a strategy of equilibrium as well as its own sovereignty by merging into a European empire deprived of a real identity.[88]

For the *Front National*, opportunities in Africa had been left to emerging powers such as the BRICS countries (Brazil, Russia, India, China, and South Africa) to exploit. The FN program therefore called for a break with the *Françafrique* approach – a policy of maximum contact and advantage which had been initiated by President de Gaulle half a century earlier. This policy had become abused and corrupted. The FN asserted that France should demonstrate respect for African states' sovereignty while simultaneously supporting French private investment there. In return, the FN program insisted, African countries had to reverse migratory flows to Europe.

Related to this was the need to restore *la politique arabe*. The war in Iraq and the Arab revolutions had weakened France's footprint in the region. The FN called for a French policy of equilibrium between Palestine and Israel that would enhance French authority.

For a time, Hollande's presidency resisted FN programmatic influence. Many French Muslims split from the mainstream by opposing the war in Afghanistan; they had been a factor helping Hollande win the 2012 election. As a result, early in his term he pulled French troops out of combat operations in Afghanistan, in this way removing one grievance of French Muslims. His calculation may also have been that the appearance of harmonious relations and congruent views between majority and Muslim populations in France would project a positive French image abroad and elicit the backing of much of the Muslim world.

Hollande's Foreign Minister, Laurent Fabius, offered a defense of the positive role played by religion, including Islam: "the religious fact is a growing force in international life. In these conditions, no foreign policy can dispense with expertise on religions."[89] Fabius highlighted how "international terrorist groups, notably those linked to Al Qaida, present themselves as inheritors of past religious wars. They attempt to insert themselves into local conflicts and radicalize them." But he underlined France's unique experience in dealing with religious questions. Already in 1920, the Quai d'Orsay (Foreign Ministry) had created an office for diplomatic relations with the Holy See. Subsequently, it was broadened to maintain regular contacts with all major religions and confessional leaders in France as well as abroad.

The 2011 revolutions in the Arab world revived the question of France's relations with political Islam. The foreign minister was optimistic: "The principle of neutral *laïcité* furnishes us with a compass that allows us to follow an approach simultaneously pragmatic and robust." He cited the Roman poet Lucretius: *Tantum religio potuit suadere malorum* – "To such heights of evil are men driven by religion." But Fabius singled out France's strength in resolving this dilemma: religion can be a force for dialogue and peace and "in this domain France possesses a precious experience."[90]

As Socialist candidate Hollande had stressed traditional Socialist foreign policy principles. He promised:

> I shall develop France's relations with the countries of the south bank of the Mediterranean on the basis of an economic, democratic, and cultural project. I shall break with *Françafrique* policy by proposing relations based on equality, trust, and solidarity. I shall relaunch *la Francophonie*.[91]

There was little new in Hollande's assertion: many French leaders had previously announced the death of *Françafrique* – the corrupt practices with which France has maintained its influence in Africa since decolonization. In turn, *l'Organisation internationale de la francophonie* (OIF), founded under a different name in 1970, never approached the status of the British Commonwealth in forming a solid international governmental organization with regular summits.

If France's image in Muslim-majority countries reflected increasing congruence in constructive domestic and international policies towards Muslims, why did Hollande put this encouraging development at risk with military action in Mali?

Military intervention in Mali

In explaining French intervention against radical Islamists in Mali in January 2013, Foreign Minister Fabius stressed: "We must stop the rebels' offensive, otherwise the whole of Mali will fall into their hands creating a threat for Africa and even for Europe." Like Sarkozy's use of air strikes against the Libyan regime in 2011, which were backed by the United States and NATO, President Hollande had the support of the United Nations, Britain, and the

United States for dispatching 750 French troops which were to increase to 2,500.

Similar to many leaders justifying military action abroad, Hollande claimed that in Mali "France has no interest other than the goal of fighting terrorism." The French national Muslim organization, *Conseil français du culte musulman*, praised the language he employed to explain the invasion. Terrorism and not Islamism was the *casus belli*. Mafia groups and bandits, not so-called Muslim groups, were the terrorists. Euro-Islam philosopher Tariq Ramadan noted that "It is in the north of Mali where France sees the reflec-tion, finally, of a strong and committed President."[92] Otherwise disillusioned with Hollande's error-prone presidency, French public opinion also endorsed his intervention in the Sahel state. A political consensus spanning the UMP and FN backed the military action. Only left-wing parties opposed Hollande's decision.[93]

To be sure, FN support was circumspect. Le Pen noted that the "legiti-mate" action only drew attention to how France had "paved the way" for the resurgence of Islamist groups in the first place following its 2011 air strikes against Qaddafi's forces which the FN opposed. She contended that French anti-Islamist military action in Mali and elsewhere in Africa (including in the non-Muslim-majority state of Central African Republic) had mobilized jihadi groups to retaliate against France.

Indeed, just days after the Mali invasion al Qaeda-allied Islamist radicals overran the Tigantourine gas plant in Algeria taking over eight hundred European and American employees as hostages. In an ill-conceived rescue attempt by Algerian forces, forty foreign hostages were killed. In Somalia the al-Shabab militia executed a French citizen it had been holding for more than three years. In Mali itself a jihadi leader warned that by attack-ing Islamist forces in Africa "France has opened the gates of hell for all the French. She has fallen into a trap which is much more dangerous than Iraq, Afghanistan or Somalia."[94]

Hollande's decision to intervene was not taken suddenly. An important philosophic influence on him was exerted by former Socialist Party member and Sarkozy's foreign minister between 2007 and 2010, Bernard Kouchner. Founder of *Médecins Sans Frontières*, an international non-governmental humanitarian organization delivering medical assistance to groups in con-flict zones, Kouchner had developed the idea of the "right to intervene" which, in 2001, was transformed into the principle of "Responsibility to Protect" (R2P). It was ratified by the United Nations in 2005. This concept emphasizes states' responsibility to protect their populations and, where they cannot, the actions that the international community can take on their behalf. R2P set out the conditions for a resolute response to crises including coercive military intervention when approved by the Security Council under

Chapter VII of the United Nations Charter. It was an appeal to this international principle that gave the French president the legal basis on which to intervene in Mali.

Hollande had made diplomatic efforts to persuade West African states and the United Nations to do so. In 2012 French officials had worked out a plan for a UN-backed African force to restore the Malian government's control over its own territory. When Islamists, who had already seized control of the north of the country, threatened to launch an offensive on the south, Hollande finally acted despite American officials' skepticism. In the opinion of some analysts he won a quick and brilliant victory.[95]

One observed how

> The Mali crisis was of the highest concern to France because it stood on the intersection of two problematics: the terrorist theme which had become a priority of security structures, and the African theme. This region of the world remains one of the few if not the only one where France's expertise is more significant than that of the United States.[96]

International relations theorist Immanuel Wallerstein was struck by Hollande's unexpected activism (Box 4.3). "What happened to explain this turnaround?" after France refused to take part in the war against Iraq in 2003. One factor was the decline of American effective power in the international arena. That was not all, however. For Wallerstein the new foreign policy was affected by domestic considerations:

Box 4.3 Jihadist fears: France's expanding presence on the international stage

In the last few years, France has asserted itself on the international scene in a very active way – first under President Nicolas Sarkozy and then even more under President François Hollande. It led the way among Western powers to intervene in Libya in order to oust Muammar Gaddafi. It has pushed the hardest line of all Western powers on Syria's Bashar al-Assad. It has intervened unilaterally in Mali to stop the downward sweep of Islamic armed movements. Hollande was received virtually as a hero when he went recently to Israel, because of his hard line on negotiations with Syria and Iran. And now France has sent troops to try to restore order in the Central African Republic.

Source: Immanuel Wallerstein, "France's Aggressive Foreign Policy: What is behind François Hollande's assertiveness on the world stage," *Al Jazeera America*, 2 December 2013, http://america.aljazeera.com/opinions/2013/12/france-foreign-policymilitaryintervention.html

---

There are, of course, some internal factors that contributed to these develop-ments. Because of its colonial history, France today has a large number of Muslim residents and citizens who are largely an economic underclass. Many of the younger Muslims have become increasingly militant, and some of them have been attracted to the more radical versions of Islamist politics. While this shift has occurred throughout much of Europe, it seems particularly strong in France. It has therefore evoked a political reaction not only from extreme-right xenophobic groups like the National Front party but also from people holding unyielding ver-sions of secularism (laicité) on the political left. Today the most popular Socialist minister seems to be Interior Minister Manuel Valls, whose major activity is taking extra-strong measures against illegal migrants, mostly Muslim migrants, to France.[97]

This was a one-sided view of Valls who, in 2014, became prime minister. A website dedicated to information about Islam favorably cited his tour of French mosques in 2013 during Ramadan and his reassuring comment that "France will always protect the Muslims of France."[98] But Valls had acknowledged "We are facing an exterior enemy and an interior enemy."[99] Immediately after the Mali invasion, as interior minister he ordered hundreds of armed soldiers to patrol Metros, train stations, airports and tourist sites across France. For a time the country had moved to the top of the list of ter-rorist targets in Europe. But the risks in carrying out the intervention had to be compared to the benefits of doing so.

Reinvigorating Françafrique

Despite Hollande's pledge to end Françafrique policy, the country could not abandon its enormous energy and mining interests in the Sahel region, a belt south of the Sahara extending from Mauritania and Senegal on the Atlantic Ocean through Mali, Algeria, Niger, and Chad to Eritrea on the Red Sea. The region, which some local Muslim groups call Sahelistan, represents an "El Dorado" for exploration of oil and gas resources.[100] French (Total), Italian (ENI), and Algerian (Sipex) corporations already have large energy stakes here.

In explaining the factors lending widespread support for military action in Mali, hypopsia towards people from the Sahel who reside in France should not be overlooked. In 2010, sociologist Hugues Lagrange had provoked a national debate with the publication of his book Le déni des cultures ("The denial of cultures").[101] He argued that cultures did matter in explaining differ-ences in rates of delinquency (broadly defined as "encounters with the law") in France. Culture and, by extension, ethno-religious and racial attributes helped explain why blacks, especially those of Sahel background, were over-represented in delinquency statistics. Lagrange believed that this propensity to crime was the result of the pervasiveness of polygamy, the subordination of women (above all in their role as mothers), and the authoritarianism of fathers permeating Sahel culture.

While unlikely to be a decisive factor, a nuanced French fear about Muslims originating in this obscure part of Africa may have served as an opportune cultural environment for launching an armed intervention – which proved to be a popular move by an otherwise unpopular president. France became the "Gendarme-in-chief of the Sahel" and, with the United States, deployed forces across the extended region in their war on jihadism.[102]

For his military interventions in the Sahel, as well as in the Central African Republic in 2013, Socialist President Hollande became characterized as a "strident neocon" and "decisive war leader." His willingness to send French soldiers to *Françafrique* was juxtaposed with his "shaky" performance at home; for example, in a highly publicized deportation case, he recommended that a young Roma schoolgirl should remain in France but her family sent back to Kosovo.[103] In Mali had Hollande stumbled into success?

CONCLUSIONS

The war on terror initiated in 2001 has produced a recognized blowback effect leading to a strengthening of the very groups that the West wishes to destroy. Repeated military interventions in Muslim-majority states have created what has been called "an interstate highway of international insurgency" running from Pakistan through Iraq and Somalia into the Sahel. Iraqi fighters have organized units in Afghanistan while Maghrebi and Sahel groups have honed combat skills in Iraq. Along this highway travel combatants, ideas, tactics, and arms used by those determined to fight the "new Crusaders."[104]

Radical Muslim groups do not distinguish between Islamophobic and Islamo-hypopsic policies. For them France and other Western states show a hatred for Islam in both their domestic and international behavior. But, from an empirically based analytic perspective, there is little evidence of a chronic and profound French Islamophobia; a low-intensity Islamo-hypopsia is suggested from public opinion surveys. Even less plausible is that FN-framed hatred of Muslims has hijacked French foreign policy. Most unlikely of all is that Muslim radicals have commandeered the country as Eurabia advocates suggest.

The fluctuating relationship between the agenda of the agents of fear and the type of foreign policy a country gets points to the importance of exploring the domestic–international policy connection. Therefore "domestic factors deserve a special attention in the study of world politics, as they influence national foreign-policy making." They have an "impact on whether the incentives, policies, and values promoted by the 'West' are acceptable."

Moreover "domestic factors related to political identity may be decisive" to a country's normative empowerment in world politics.[105]

In the case of France, harmonious relations between majority and Muslim populations at home can be more meaningful to French influence abroad than its many forms of diplomacy. If France is to have a demonstration effect on African countries in the Maghreb and Sahel, it needs to show that the republican model indeed treats all groups fairly.

French presidents have not acted in a vacuum. Each faced unique circumstances and, to a degree, made distinctive foreign policy choices. But they also took cues from a national action script. These could have idealistic motifs, such as the Third Republic-derived *mission civilisatrice*. Just as probably, they could have self-serving, utility-maximizing qualities, such as *Françafrique* politics.

The games French leaders played in two arenas have produced variable payoffs. When France needed cheap labor to fuel economic growth, as in the 1960s and 1970s, immigration policy was liberal. Economic actors were the major beneficiaries of such policy. By Sarkozy's presidency and even before, France had an overabundance of cheap unskilled labor. So Sarkozy adopted the restrictive policy of *immigration choisie*. Observing the game in just one arena offers only a partial assessment of the optimality of the choices made.

Both *la politique arabe* and Sarkozy's Occidentalist turn agreed on the principle of the French state's support for public and private investment abroad. Even Hollande's foreign policy of increased French engagement in the Sahel involved rent-seeking. For both presidents a suboptimal outcome in the domestic game was choking off emigration, typically by providing incentives to sending societies to circumscribe it. The suboptimal outcome at home – fears of a continued influx of immigrants though smaller in number and more selective in nature – is more than balanced by aggressive economic activity by the French state and corporations globally.

Significantly this nested game is consistent with the objectives of the *Front National*. It is not necessarily benign for many Muslims whether they reside in France or in the target countries for French direct foreign investment. Radical Islamist groups exploit fears of neocolonial resurgence in African states in the way that the FN rides fears of foreigners in France to electoral success.

The shift under President Sarkozy from *la politique arabe* to more balanced foreign policy may be the strongest case we have of FN-influenced Islamophobic ideas influencing foreign policy. Even here caveats are in order. Sarkozy's closer relations with Mediterranean littoral countries may have signaled how Club Med was to be an antidote to Islamo-hypopsia at home: it reached out to Maghreb countries almost as recompense for the poor treatment many of their nationals and their descendants were receiving in France.

With his bold military interventions in North and sub-Saharan Africa as well as support for anti-Assad rebels in Syria and anti-"Islamic State" Kurdish forces in Iraq, President Hollande staked out a strong claim to be *l'homme de rupture*. He acted on the conviction that French perceptions of a Muslim threat at home and abroad had to be aggressively countered. But little evidence suggested that he was under pressure from French public opinion to do so. Only indirectly, through witnessing how FN electoral success in 2014 was founded on expressed hostility towards Muslims, was Hollande's foreign policy a product of a populist Islamo-hypopsia.

Domestic fears of an immigrant minority do not always translate into foreign policy hostility towards their country of origin. On occasions, however, they set parameters as to what kind of bilateral relations can exist. The case of France demonstrates how the time-honored font of international politics is the national interest, not caprices of animosity by elites or citizens. But this does not undermine the maxim of *la politique du dehors avec les raisons du dedans*. Nor does it contradict Thucydides' Theorem based on the statement: "the Athenians becoming great and furnishing fear to the Spartans drove them to war."[106]

This statement may encapsulate the perspective of radical Islamist groups abroad which inspire fear in French society with each armed feat they record. They drive France to war. This is coupled with unease stirred by the longer-term threat to the country's cohesion and identity posed by many "foreigners." To this extent the social fabric of fear does condition the making of foreign policy. Currently unforeseeable longer-term foreign policy changes together with increased securitization domestically may be the products of the Islamist terrorist attacks in Paris in January 2015.

Notes

1. Jocelyn Evans, "'La politique du dehors avec les raisons du dedans:' foreign and defense policy of the French *Front National*," in Philippe Burrin and Christina Schori-Liang (eds), *European Right-Wing Populism and Foreign Policy* (Aldershot: Ashgate, 2007).
2. Georg Simmel, *Conflict* and *the Web of Group Affiliations* (New York: Free Press, 1955 [1908]), pp. 98–9.
3. The de Vieuzac report is cited by Michel de Certeau, Dominique Julia, and Jacques Revel, *Une politique de la langue: La Révolution Française et les patois* (Paris: Gallimard, 1975), p. 295. Also by Leigh Oakes, *Language and National Identity: Comparing France and Sweden* (Amsterdam: John Benjamins Publishing Company, 2001), p. 60.
4. Stéphanie Giry, "An Integrated France," *Prospect*, 131 (February 2007).
5. Sally Marthaler, "Nicolas Sarkozy and the politics of French immigration policy," *Journal of European Public Policy*, 15:3 (April 2008), p. 382.
6. João Carvalho, "President Sarkozy and broken promises: the development of French immigration and integration policies," Academia website, http://www.academia.

edu/5409393/President_Sarkozy_and_broken_promises_the_development_of_
French_immigration_and_integration_policies

7. "Nicolas Sarkozy dénonce l'échec du multi-culturalisme," *Les4verites Hebdo*, 15
February 2011, http://www.les4verites.com/societe/nicolas-sarkozy-denonce-lechec-
du-multi-culturalisme

8. Florent Villard and Pascal-Yan Sayegh, "Redefining a (Mono)cultural Nation:
Political Discourse against Multiculturalism in Contemporary France," in Raymond
Taras (ed.), *The Challenge of Multiculturalism: Managing Diversity in Europe*
(Edinburgh: Edinburgh University Press, 2012), p. 250.

9. Gilles Kepel, *Passion française. Les voix des cités* (Paris: Collection Témoins,
Gallimard, 2014). See also his earlier *Passion arabe: Journal, 2011–2013* (Paris:
Gallimard, 2013).

10. Coincidentally, in Quebec a similar process led to the same result. A secular charter
of values was tabled in May 2013 by nationalist Prime Minister Pauline Marois's
government. It was opened up to public hearings about state secularism and religious neutrality which proved polarizing, as Marois had calculated. She called an
early election hoping French Quebecers would give her minority government a
stronger mandate. Instead, in April 2014, her party was soundly defeated showing
how, as in France, identity debates can be volatile and have unanticipated consequences.

11. Claude Guéant, "Les résultats de la politique migratoire," January 2012, http://www.
interieur.gouv.fr/Archives/Archives-Claude-Gueant-2011-2012/Les-interventions-
du-Ministre/10.01.2012-Les-resultats-de-la-politique-migratoire. For detailed immigration data see Rapport du Gouvernement au Parlement, *Les étrangers en France:
année 2012*. Dixième rapport établi en application de l'article L.111-10 du Code de
l'entrée et du séjour des étrangers et du droit d'asile (2013).

12. "France's Ruling Party Proposes 26-point Secularism Platform," *Islam Today*, 6 April
2011, http://en.islamtoday.net/artshow-229-4017.htm

13. "President Nicolas Sarkozy calls for a fight against anti-Semitism and Islamophobia
in France," *Euro-Islam.info*, 3 March 2009, http://www.euro-islam.info/2009/03/03/
President-nicolas-sarkozy-calls-for-a-fight-against-anti-semitism-and-islamophobia-
in-france/

14. William Safran, "Islamization in Western Europe: Political Consequences and
Historical Parallels," *Annals of the American Academy of Political and Social Science*,
485 (May 1986), p. 101.

15. 2005 RAPFI survey, conducted by CEVIPOF and reported by Ariane Chebel
d'Appolonia, "Race, Racism and Anti-Discrimination in France," in Sylvain
Brouard, Andrew M. Appleton, and Amy G. Mazur (eds), *The French Fifth Republic
at Fifty* (Basingstoke: Palgrave, 2009), pp. 275–6.

16. Daniel Lefeuvre, "Les Colons," in Jean-Pierre Rioux (ed.), *Dictionnaire de la France
Coloniale* (Paris: Flammarion, 2007), p. 571.

17. Oakes, *Language*, p. 98.

18. Timo Behr, *France, Germany and Europe's Middle East Dilemma: The Impact of
National Foreign Policy Traditions on Europe's Middle East Policy* (Ann Arbor, MI:
ProQuest, 2009), p. 97.

19. Henri Giordan, *Démocratie culturelle et droit à la difference* (Paris: La documentation
française, 1982), p. 16.

20. Andrew Hussey, *The French Intifada: The Long War between France and its Arabs* (London: Granta, 2014).

21. Marwan Muhammed, spokesman, Collective Against Islamophobia in France (CCIF), Paris. Quoted by Soeren Kern, "The Islamization of France in 2013," Gatestone Institute website, 6 January 2014, http://www.gatestoneinstitute. org/4120/islamization-france#

22. Ipsos survey, *Le Monde* (24 January 2013). For earlier attitudinal survey results on Muslims in France see my *Xenophobia and Islamophobia in Europe* (Edinburgh: Edinburgh University Press, 2012), Chapters 4–5.

23. "Spring 2014 Global Attitudes Survey," Pew Research Center website, May 2014, Q37c, http://www.pewglobal.org/2014/05/12/chapter-4-views-of-roma-muslims-jews/

24. Congressional Research Service, *Muslims in Europe: Integration in Selected Countries* (Washington, DC: CRS, 2005).

25. "Alain Finkielkraut Interview," *Der Spiegel* (6 December 2013), to discuss his latest book *L'identitée malheureuse* (Paris: Stock, 2013).

26. Open Society Institute, *EU Accession Monitoring Program*, 2002, p. 76.

27. Mustafa Malik, "Islam's Missing Link to the West," *Middle East Policy*, 10:1 (spring 2003), p. 126.

28. Timothy M. Savage, "Europe and Islam: Crescent Waxing, Cultures Clashing," *The Washington Quarterly*, 27:3 (summer 2004), p. 45.

29. David Jolly, "France's less joyous New Year's tradition," *New York Times*, 2 January 2013, http://www.nytimes.com/2013/01/03/world/europe/frances-less-joyous-new-years-tradition.html?_r=0 For similar figures reported at the beginning of 2014 see "France's odd New Year tradition: Counting torched cars," *France24*, 6 January 2014, http://www.france24.com/en/20140102-france-car-burning-new-year-tradition-urban-violence-media/

30. "Marc Trévidic: La France, ennemi bien identifié," *Le Journal du Dimanche*, 5 January 2013, http://www.lejdd.fr/Societe/Justice/Actualite/Le-juge-antiterroriste-Marc-Trevidic-La-France-ennemi-bien-identifie-584526

31. See Giselle Bosse, "From 'Villains' to the New Guardians of Security in Europe? Paradigm Shifts in EU Foreign Policy towards Libya and Belarus," *Perspectives on European Politics and Society*, 12:4 (2011), pp. 440–61.

32. Cas Mudde, "The far right in the 2014 European elections: Of earthquakes, cartels and designer fascists," *Washington Post*, 30 May 2014.

33. "Public Opinion in the European Union," *Standard Eurobarometer 81: Spring 2014* (July 2014), p. 13, http://ec.europa.eu/public_opinion/archives/eb/eb81/eb81_first_en.pdf. France also did not place high along a set of anti-immigration indicators measured in a twenty-three-country global survey conducted by Ipsos in 2011. See "Nearly Half of World Citizens Believe Immigration Has Had a Negative Impact on their Country," *Ipsos*, 4 August 2011, http://www.ipsos-na.com/news-polls/pressrelease.aspx?id=5298

34. "Face à la crise, les Français passent du ras-le-bol à la révolte," *Le nouvel observateur*, 1 February 2012, http://tempsreel.nouvelobs.com/politique/20111101.OBS3596/face-a-la-crise-les-francais-passent-du-ras-le-bol-a-la-revolte.html

35. Soeren Kern, "The Looming Battle over Muslim Integration," Gatestone Institute website, 31 December 2013, http://www.gatestoneinstitute.org/4113/france-muslim-integration#

36. Christina Schori Liang, "Europe for the Europeans: The Foreign and Security Policy of the Populist Radical Right," in Liang, *Europe for the Europeans*, p. 2.
37. Ibid., p. 6.
38. Jacques Attali, "A Continental Architecture," in Peter Gowan and Perry Anderson (eds), *The Question of Europe* (London: Verso, 1997), p. 355.
39. Timo Behr, "Enduring Differences? France, Germany and Europe's Middle East Dilemma," *Journal of European Integration*, 30:1 (March 2008), p. 83.
40. "The Holocaust in France: The Deportation of the Jews from France," *Yad Vashem* website, http://www.yadvashem.org/yv/en/holocaust/france/deportations.asp
41. David Styan, *France and Iraq: Oil, Arms and French Policy Making in the Middle East* (London: I.B. Tauris, 2006), p. 34.
42. Maud S. Mandel, *Muslims and Jews in France* (Princeton, NJ: Princeton University Press, 2014), p. 2.
43. Ibid., p. 4.
44. Ibid., p. 35.
45. Ibid., pp. 58, 65.
46. Ibid., pp. 79, 126.
47. Annie Kriegel, "Juifs et Musulmans," *L'Arche* (November 1987), pp. 28–30.
48. Mandel, *Muslims and Jews*, pp. 8–9.
49. Styan, *France and Iraq*, pp. 46, 50.
50. See David Pryce-Jones, *Betrayal: France, the Arabs, and the Jews* (New York: Encounter Books, 2006).
51. This argument was made by Bat Ye'or (Gisèle Littman) in *Eurabia: The Europe–Arab Axis* (Madison, NJ: Fairleigh Dickinson University Press, 2009). I have presented the argument and its critique in my *Xenophobia and Islamophobia in Europe*, pp. 198–200.
52. Frédéric Charillon, "La politique étrangère de la France: l'heure des choix," *Politique étrangère*, 1 (spring 2007), pp. 139–50.
53. Pryce-Jones, *Betrayal*, p. 128.
54. Behr, "Enduring Differences?" p. 85.
55. Styan, *France and Iraq*, p. 199. See Jean-Pierre Chevènement, *Le vert et le noir: intégrisme, pétrole, dollar* (Paris: B. Grasset, 1995).
56. Quoted by Patrick Tyler, "If, and When: War's Timing," *New York Times*, 15 February 2003, http://www.nytimes.com/2003/02/15/world/threats-and-responses-news-analysis-if-and-when-war-s-timing.html
57. Jonathan Laurence and Justin Vaisse, *Integrating Islam: Political and Religious Challenges in Contemporary France* (Washington, DC: Brookings Institute, 2008), p. 204.
58. Amir Taheri, "La politique arabe de Chirac: un échec cuisant," *CourrierInternational.com* 848 (1 February 2007).
59. Rapport Avicenne, "Maghreb–Moyen-Orient: Contribution pour une politique volontariste de la France" (Paris: Ifri, 2007).
60. Pryce-Jones, *Betrayal*, p. 5.
61. Laurence and Vaisse, *Integrating Islam*, p. 204.
62. Ibid.
63. Ibid., p. 219.
64. Ibid., p. 208.

65. "Anti-Israel protesters rally across France, defying ban imposed after synagogue clash," *Haaretz*, 19 July 2014, http://www.haaretz.com/news/diplomacy-defense/1.606036
66. Pew Global Attitudes Project, "Unfavorable Views of Jews and Muslims on the Increase in Europe," 17 September 2008, http://pewglobal.org/reports/pdf/262.pdf
67. Laurence and Vaisse, *Integrating Islam*, p. 219.
68. Ibid., p. 221.
69. Pascal Boniface, *Le monde selon Sarkozy* (Paris: Jean-Claude Gawsewitch, 2012).
70. Jean-François Bayart, "Quelle politique africaine pour la France?" *Le blog de Jean-François Bayart*, 25 October 2010, http://blogs.mediapart.fr/blog/jean-francois-bayart/251010/quelle-politique-africaine-pour-la-france
71. Edouard Balladur, *Pour une Union occidentale entre l'Europe et les Etats-Unis* (Paris: Fayard, 2007).
72. Pryce-Jones, *Betrayal*, p. 151.
73. Evans, "'La politique du dehors,'" p. 135.
74. Ammer Jaffal, "Uniting Radical Forces: The Evolution of al-Qaeda in the Maghreb," *Arab Insight*, 2:6 (winter 2009), p. 69.
75. Philippe Moreau-Defarges, "La politique étrangère de Nicolas Sarkozy un an après: insaisissable rupture," *l'Essentiel des relations internationales* (Juin–Juillet 2008), pp. 68–71.
76. From Emmanuel Todd interview in *Marianne2.fr*, 3 April 2008. For an English summary, see Alex Lantier, "France moves towards reintegration into NATO," *Global Research*, 19 March 2009, http://www.globalresearch.ca/index.php?context=va&aid=12801
77. Frédéric Encel, "France-Israël: Passé et présent d'une relation spéciale," *l'Essentiel des relations internationales*, (Juin–Juillet 2008), p. 79.
78. See "Chirac et l'Iran. Quand la presse s'emballe," blog *Nouvelles d'Orient*, at Le *Monde diplomatique*, 2 février 2007.
79. Alain Gresh, "OTAN, Proche-Orient, Afrique . . . Enquête sur le virage de la diplomatie française," *Le Monde Diplomatique* (Juillet 2008), pp. 1, 8–9, http://www.monde-diplomatique.fr/2008/07/GRESH/16104
80. Ibid.
81. Doug Sanders, "Five women and 365 days," *Globe and Mail*, 9 May 2008.
82. United States embassy in Paris, "Assault of French Journalist in Tunisia Prompts Media Outcry, Domestic Criticism of GOF Human Rights Policy," cable 03 PARIS 8954, 16 November 2005, http://www.theguardian.com/world/us-embassy-cables-documents/45270
83. Jean-François Daguzan, "France and the Maghreb: The End of the Special Relationship?" in Yahia H. Zoubir and Haizam Amirah-Fernández, *North Africa: Politics, Region, and the Limits of Transformation* (London: Routledge, 2008), p. 335.
84. Aleksandra Kling, *Stosunki Francji z krajami Maghrebu: przeszłość kolonialna a współczesność* (Warsaw: AWR Skarpa, 2013), p. 131.
85. Cited in Ivan Rioufol, "'La France veut la paix' (mais à quelle prix?)," *Le Figaro*, 18 July 2008.
86. Pryce-Jones, *Betrayal*, pp. 132–3.
87. This section was first presented as a paper titled "Xenophobic actors in nested

games," Annual Conference of the International Studies Association, April 2013, San Francisco.

88. "Notre politique étrangère, la politique du Grand large! Retrouver notre influence, être un facteur de paix," *Front National* website http://www.frontnational.com/le-projet-de-marine-le-pen/politique-etrangere/notre-politique-etrangere/

89. "Intervention de Laurent Fabius au colloque 'Religion et politique étrangère,'" Clôture du colloque "Religions et politique étrangère," Sciences Po (CERI), 6 November 2013, http://www.diplomatie.gouv.fr/fr/les-ministres-818/laurent-fabius/discours-21591/article/intervention-de-laurent-fabius-au-109024#

90. "Intervention de Laurent Fabius."

91. "Interview de François Hollande du 27 mars 2012 dans *Afrik.com*," http://www.afrik.com/article25144.html

92. Tariq Ramadan, "Le Mali, la France et les Extrémistes," 17 janvier 2013, http://www.tariqramadan.com/spip.php?article12693&lang=fr

93. Alain Gresh, "Mali, Afghanistan, les leçons oubliées," *Le monde diplomatique*, 14 janvier 2013, http://blog.mondediplo.net/2013-01-14-Mali-Afghanistan-les-lecons-oubliees

94. Mike Pflanz, "Islamist fighters in Mali seize control of southern town in daring counter offensive," *The Telegraph*, 14 January 2013, http://www.telegraph.co.uk/news/worldnews/africaandindianocean/mali/9801329/Islamist-fighters-in-Mali-seize-control-of-southern-town-in-daring-counter-offensive.html

95. Richard Gowan, "Diplomatic Fallout: For France's Hollande, African Interventions a Strategic Failure," *World Politics Review* (9 December 2013), http://www.worldpoliticsreview.com/articles/13430/diplomatic-fallout-for-france-s-hollande-african-interventions-a-strategic-failure. See also Michel Goya, "La guerre de trois mois: l'intervention française au Mali en perspectives," *Politique étrangère*, 78:2 (summer 2013), pp. 157–68.

96. Hélène Quénot-Suarez, Aurore Loste, "L'Afrique en questions n°13, 'Hollande l'Africain?' La politique africaine de la France à la croisée des chemins – Interview de Yves Gounin," *Actuelle de l'Ifri*, September 2012 (18 October 2012), http://www.ifri.org/?page=detail-contribution&id=7360

97. Immanuel Wallerstein, "France's Aggressive Foreign Policy: What is behind François Hollande's assertiveness on the world stage," *Al Jazeera America*, 2 December 2013, http://america.aljazeera.com/opinions/2013/12/france-foreign-policymilitaryintervention.html

98. "'France will always protect its Muslim communities,' declares Minister," *Euro-Islam.info*, 23 August 2013, http://www.euro-islam.info/2013/08/23/france-will-always-protect-muslim-communities-declares-minister/

99. "France girds for new threats after Mali operation," *Washington Times*, 15 January 2013, http://www.washingtontimes.com/news/2013/jan/15/france-girds-new-threats-after-mali-operation/

100. Samuel Laurent, *Sahelistan* (Paris: Seuil, 2013). His focus is primarily on Islam in Libya.

101. Hugues Lagrange, *Le déni des cultures* (Paris: Seuil, 2010).

102. "La France gendarme en chef du Sahel," *Le monde diplomatique*, 6 February 2014, http://blog.mondediplo.net/2014-02-06-La-France-gendarme-en-chef-du-Sahel

103. "Strident neocon, lame socialist," *The Economist*, 30 November 2013, http://www.economist.com/news/europe/21590919-gap-widening-between-french-Presidents-decisiveness-abroad-and-dithering-home-strident
104. Philippe Rekacewicz, "Autoroute de l'"Internationale insurgée'", *Le monde diplomatique* (November 2007).
105. Raffaella A. Del Sarto, *Contested State Identities and Regional Security in the Euro-Mediterranean Area* (Basingstoke: Palgrave, 2006), p. 233.
106. Thucydides, *History of the Peloponnesian War*, Book I, Chapter 23, p. 6.

CHAPTER FIVE

Poland's fixation with Russia: fear or reason?

CIVILIZATIONAL FEARS?

As in the case of relations between many neighbors – England and Ireland, Greece and Turkey, even Denmark and Sweden – attitudes of Poles and Russians towards each other are shaped by a thousand years of tumultuous history. Over centuries mutual vindications, irredentist claims, cultural chasms, incompatible value systems, religious and philosophic conflicts, and other historical grievances have created reciprocal suspicion, distrust, dislike, and, at times, hatred.

Fyodor Dostoyevsky claimed that "A Pole from Old Poland instinctively and blindly hates Russians and Russia . . . Old Poland will never exist because it cannot coexist with Russia."[1] But Russian émigré poet and Polish citizen Natalya Gorbanevskaya, who died in 2013, was convinced that Poles and Russians are essentially similar. She observed that "It would be good if Poles understood that Russians also have the right to love their fatherland."[2] Before examining Poland's legitimate concern with Russia and the threats it may pose, let me step back and review the more sweeping civilizational context within which the two countries have confronted each other.

The clash-of-civilizations thesis advanced by Huntington explained the cleavage between Russia-led Eastern Orthodoxy and Western Christianity.[3] Dostoyevsky had already recognized such a civilizational divide in his interpretation of the 1863 Polish revolt against tsarist Russia. In his private notebook he wrote: "The Polish war is the war of two Christianities, this is the beginning of the future war of Russian Orthodox Christianity with Roman Catholicism, in other words, of Russian genius and European civilization."[4]

Dostoyevsky's thinking may have been more precocious but Huntington's was more sublime. The American political scientist recognized that one country straddled Orthodox and Western civilizations – Russia and Poland – and he therefore described Ukraine as a "cleft country" containing large

114

Orthodox and Catholic communities identifying with different civilizations. For Huntington, Ukraine was not a "torn country" in which people generally "agree on who they are but disagree on which civilization is properly their civilization."[5]

Later in this chapter I examine how Russia's involvement in Ukraine and annexation of Crimea after the overthrow of the Yanukovych regime in 2014 have made it difficult to speak of an unfounded russophobia whether in Poland, western Ukraine, or Lithuania.

Historian Andrzej Nowak endorses Huntington's thesis. It represents "not just some speculative thinking removed from reality but is easily discernable as reflecting the most current reality." Nowak cited the example of NATO (Western) bombardment of Serb (Eastern Orthodox) military positions in Bosnia in 1999. It "reanimated the antagonism between the West and a [pro-Serb] Russia which was no longer a communist but a civilizational other."[6]

Do Russians agree that their country constitutes a distinct Orthodox civilization? Political scientist Andrei Tsygankov, author of an important study of russophobia in the United States, believes that President Vladimir Putin's idea of Russia as "state–civilization" offers guidance. The concept holds that ethnic Russians form the core of this state–civilization but that it cannot be equated with a "Russian 'national', mono-ethnic state." For Putin this would contradict Russia's thousand-year history of multinationalism. This state–civilization undergirds "Moscow's new civilizational discourse" and shapes the country's foreign policy.[7]

In the case of Poland and Russia, the existence of contrasting religious institutions and traditions support the idea of separate civilizations. One Turkish academic study focused on the comparative roles played by the Polish Roman Catholic Church and Russian Orthodox Church in shaping

> church–state relations, public space, civil society and democratization in two post-communist countries. In these two countries, Catholicism and Orthodox Christianity, despite interruptions during communist rule, play a determining role in church–state relations, political patterns, national identity and the social sphere.[8]

The proposition is that religious institutions have carved out separate civilizations.

Another way to gauge whether the distinction between Orthodox and Western Christianity remains salient is to consider public perceptions. Is there such a prejudice as Orthodoxophobia in Catholic Poland, for example? Polish surveys consistently show that largely Orthodox nations – Romanians, Russians, Serbs, Ukrainians, Belarusians – are not much liked.[9] Paradoxically, official census figures reveal that these targets only have small communities in Poland: Belarusians (50,000), Ukrainians (30,000), Russians (6,000).

To be sure, the numbers of Russian speakers in the country have increased significantly after the 1991 collapse of the Soviet Union. These include some of the 20,000 students from Ukraine who reside in Poland. This influx has not caused any backlash against Russian speakers whether measured by popular attitudes, public discourse, or discriminatory acts. So if there is hypopsia of Eastern Orthodoxy it is directed outwardly, towards neighboring states where this religious identity is anchored.

Poland is an ethnically and religiously homogeneous society: over 90 percent of inhabitants are ethnically Polish and nominally Roman Catholic, though the numbers of churchgoers and believers have been declining. If fears of foreigners, particularly defined in religious terms, figure in national politics, they are directed primarily at foreign countries, therefore, not at minorities in the country. To be sure, anti-Semitism persists even in the absence of a sizeable Jewish community. For example, a 2013 national study by the Center for Research on Prejudice at Warsaw University discovered that 63 percent of Polish respondents believe in a Jewish conspiracy.[10]

Analogously, distrust and dislike of Russians is not a manifestation of hostility to the few thousand who live in Poland. It has everything to do with the long history of relations between the two nations. Sociological research into how social inequality may generate discrimination and intolerance towards vulnerable groups which serve as scapegoats is of importance, though it has not produced conclusive evidence that inequalities cause prejudices.[11] Even less likely is that social disadvantage rouses antipathy to another country, especially when that country is less economically developed, as in the case of Russia. In Poland, therefore, a fear of Russia is not a trait of a specific socio-economic group but a characteristic of all social strata. If any group is to be singled out for particularly negative views of Russia it is farmers who are hardest hit by Russia's embargos on Polish food products.

Polish national identity has, then, been shaped by negative images of Russia which have been worsened by recent history. If Poland underwent self-redefinition after the Communist takeover in 1945 and its insertion into the Soviet bloc, then, after the 1989 democratic transition, a "fundamental reorientation of its place in the world" occurred. Changes in Polish national identity were caused by integrating into European structures such as the European Union in 2004. These moves led to a "new definition of Polish civilization" and a stress on its European credentials.[12]

Other countries' perceptions about Poland's Europeanness are not as Pollyanna-ish. In mapping European cultures, philosopher Étienne Balibar imagined a set of concentric circles leading from the "true" Europe (the advanced Western states) to an "outer" one still *wishing* to be Europeanized (the Eastern part).[13] As discussed below, some Western European leaders have been skeptical about Poland's status in Europe, particularly following its accession to the European Union.

In turn, some Polish leaders are convinced that outer Europe, indeed non-Europe, starts at Russia's western borders and stretches eastward. Those who do not acknowledge a civilizational divide believe that a *political* wall – not a *cultural* gulf – separates Europe and non-Europe, Poland and Russia. Thus, Polish politicians and public intellectuals may stress that Western Slavic Poland shares liberal political values with Eastern Slavic Ukraine, thereby transcending their cultural and religious divide.

From the Russian perspective, this Polish imaginary is an effort to legiti-mate the establishment of a ring of hostile states around Russia. Western politics and its institutions – the European Union, the North Atlantic Treaty Organization, the Eastern Partnership – produce a divide, not civilizations. As far as the Kremlin is concerned, the (re)construction of Polish national identity as exclusively European is of a piece with the European Union's geopolitical mapping. From Moscow's perspective the unstated assumption of the European Union is that any country is eligible for membership – except Russia.

RUSSO-HYPOPSIA

Writing in the interwar period, celebrated novelist Witold Gombrowicz claimed that "Poland is a transitional country between west and east where both these worlds mutually weaken."[14] Poland's importance lies in supplying Western Europe with ideas, impressions, and information about Russia. The image of the "Eastern demon" spread by Poles, which stresses "Russian lies, enslavement, lawlessness, and aesthetic ugliness in order to underscore our love of truth, freedom, and beauty, has always been lightly treated by the West." Referring to right-wing conspiracy theories circulating today that, in 2010, Russians brought down the airplane carrying the Polish president and the Polish political and military elite, the author added: "With Smolensk [site of the air crash] it will be the same."[15]

A national role conception impressed upon Poles is, as noted in Chapter 2, of an *antemurale christianitatis* – Christianity's rampart on the eastern border. Poland also serves as the West's listening post in the east. These have fur-nished reasons for Russian leaders over the ages to harbor hypopsic attitudes towards Poland.

If Poles are on their guard in dealings with Russia, it is by virtue of Russia being a major neighboring power. Allegations of disloyalty, as in France of Muslims as external foe and internal fifth column, are difficult to sustain in the case of Russians living in Poland. Does it matter if xenophobia targets an external actor rather than a national minority?[16] Is there a difference between

117

distrusting or disliking a neighboring nation as opposed to a faraway one – in the impact this has on foreign policy? Intuitively, it seems that antipathy or hypopsia towards a great power such as Russia will carry more weight in the formulation of foreign policy. Phobia of an external actor rather than of an internal "stranger" may be harder to undo; countries rarely disappear but a stranger may stay and actually come to belong. Distrust of an internal minority can wane as majority and minority groups negotiate accommodation of each other. One example: previous hypopsia of Ukrainians in Poland has been replaced by post-1989 government policy of championing the cause of Ukraine. At the grassroots level, too, a marked shift to more favorable attitudes towards Ukrainians has occurred.

In an electoral democracy, targeting a historically antipathetic foreign nation or a disliked national minority can have payoffs. This is truer when the target of distrust adopts inimical politics that play into the hands of a suspicious neighboring nation or a minority group. Russia's politics, ranging from energy security to expanding definitions of a collective "us" to land grabs, present challenges to other states. For Tsygankov, russophobia originates in a number of presumptions. Russia has ruthlessly pursued expansionist and imperialist agendas. It has a unique culture dooming it to eternal backwardness. It is a captive of its anti- and un-Western historical experiences. It is dominated by an ingrained authoritarianism which cannot be dismantled.[17] These criticisms may be based on history but, when the Russian state today makes territorial claims on other countries, it becomes current events.

Presumptions about Russia's inescapable backwardness exaggerate the role of historical determinism. But fears of a foreign threat may perform positive functions in the fearful society. Social scientist Tomasz Zarycki has identified five uses which a negative image of Russia has in Poland. The first is "rescaling" Poland's own shortcomings:

> Most Polish weaknesses, including backwardness, poverty, corruption, the general frailty of civil society and so on are supposed to appear as almost insignificant, or at least not unusual in the European context, compared to the gigantic scale of Russia's social, economic, and political backwardness.[18]

Thus, any Polish inferiority complex stemming from lying on the periphery of Europe is balanced by the image of Russia as even more peripheral.

Related to this is the second use: Russia is stereotyped as Asian, Poland as European. An Orientalizing frame defines Polish attitudes to the east. Zarycki contends that the part of Poland under Russian partition in the nineteenth century is usually depicted as less advanced economically than the areas that fell under Austrian or Prussian rule. In fact, this Congress Poland was the most industrial and vibrant of occupied Polish lands. Through such biased

118

and inaccurate historicism, Poland's European credentials are strengthened by highlighting Russia's supposed lack of them.

The third use of a negative image of Russia is to frame the country as a constant threat while, as a corollary, underscoring Poland's unifying endeavors. Historian Nowak summarized the history of Polish–Russian relations after the collapse of the Soviet bloc this way:

> ... after sixteen wars two of which were wars of aggression by the Polish–Lithuanian Commonwealth and the other fourteen which represented a series of Russian expansionist movements; after 250 years of Russian domination in Poland that provoked six Polish uprisings (Poland ruled Russia for only two years and was driven out by Russia's one and only uprising), Poland appears now to be free.[19]

A social psychologist concluded that "A realistic analysis of history leads to the conclusion that a sense of danger among Poles is justified."[20] It is no surprise that, even in the first years following the democratic transition, Poles still singled out Russians as their least liked national group.[21]

Fourthly, negative stereotypes of Russia evoke the motif of Polish suffering caused by Russian oppression. An extended history of being persecuted by Russia is critical to justifying Poland's claim of holding the moral high ground in relations with East and West. Poland's miseries at the hands of Soviet Russia, for which the West was partly responsible by ceding the country to Joseph Stalin at Yalta and Potsdam, are used to suggest a debt that the West owes Poland.[22] For Zarycki, Poland's own aggressive acts against eastern and southern neighbors, primarily in the interwar period, are lost in its victimhood.

Finally, the use of negative images of Russia contributes to casting Russia as an inscrutable country and Poland as a resourceful one. Poles realize they must work hard to overcome a reputation for being biased against Russia:

> Most Poles, at least those interested in foreign affairs, realize that they are often thought to have an anti-Russian bias and their accounts are dismissed as russophobic. Hence, worries about credibility are a permanent element of Polish discourse on Russia. One symptom is attempts to obtain from Western personages recognition of the legitimacy and objectivity of Polish perceptions.[23]

I propose a sixth domestic reason for the advantages to Poland of disseminating negative images of Russia. It constructs a political cleavage that carries issue valence in the Polish party system. Applying the distinction used in this book, at election time parties choose between promoting russophobic or russo-hypopsic campaign programs. Competing parties cultivate electoral constituencies which are either more traditional and nationalist or more pragmatic and European. Russophobic discourse can express a form of cultural racism appealing to nationalist extremists and primordialists.

Russo-hypopsis, on the other hand, can be marketed as a manifestation of rational politics, of threat perceptions rooted in realities. Choosing one over the other provides a party with a different strategy to win votes.

Fearsome bear as metaphor for Russia

It is hard to be indifferent to Russia – and impossible for countries geographically adjacent to it. An advisor to President Putin identified nearby countries as comprising the vanguard of russophobia in Europe: Sweden, Poland, the Baltic countries and recently Finland, too. The Kremlin official claimed that, even though Finland gains economically from its trade with Russia, Sweden and the Baltic countries pushed Finnish leaders to bandwagon against Russia.[24]

Being labeled russophobic is a stigma but not of the order of being called anti-Semitic, racist, or Islamophobic. In Poland it can elicit a scornful reaction. Two analysts of Polish international relations argued that "Warsaw should not be afraid of the charge of russophobia, that not having the best relations with Russia will worsen its ranking in the West." More important is the opportunity to "increase in the West, particularly in Germany, awareness of the character of the Putin regime."[25] The supposed payoff for the European Union is therefore a more hard-nosed and realistic policy on Russia transcending economic ties.

Not all Poles agree that Poland serves the West as a reliable narrator on Russia. The eminent historian of Russian and Polish nationalism, Andrzej Walicki, condemned the tendency in Poland, past and present, to demonize and exclude Russia from the family of European nations. Instead, he exhorted Poland's elites to help bring about the Westernization of its eastern neighbor rather than to marginalize it.[26]

No better symbol of the fear of Russia is available than the caricature of the country as an enormous, frightening bear. First drawn in the West in the eighteenth century, the symbol of the bear connotes aggression, barbarism, cruelty, laziness, threat, and behemoth. In their seminal book on semiotics, Andrzej de Lazari, Oleg Riabow, and Magdalena Żakowska describe how the image of Russia as bear has been used to mark the limits of the civilized world: "The predatory bear more convincingly makes the case for expanding NATO to the average person in the West than the most elaborate political treatise."[27] Though he did not explicitly conjure up the image of the predacious bear, Ukrainian president, Petro Poroshenko, referring to the conflict with Russia in Donbass, told a joint session of the United States Congress in 2014 that "If they [the Russians] are not stopped now, they will cross European borders and they will absolutely spread throughout the world. The choice is simple: it is between civilization and barbarism."

"In the beginning was fear," wrote Poland's greatest specialist on bears.[28] Lamentations 3: 10 uses the metaphor "He is unto me as a bear lying in wait." Proverbs 28: 15 relates how "Like a roaring lion and a rushing bear is a wicked ruler over a poor people." Philosopher Gottfried Wilhelm Leibniz called Russians little more than "baptized bears."[29] One of the most russophobic books of all time, Gustave Doré's album published in 1854, has as its first drawing the birth of the first Russian, sired by a polar bear and out of a sea lion.[30]

While most of the world has clutched the image of Russia as a bear, Poland's approach is instructive. In 1832, a Polish cartoonist drew a bear dressed in Russian military uniform as the symbol of oppressor of Poland and crusher of the November 1830 anti-tsarist uprising. Poles exiled to Siberia were pictured as forced to hunt for ferocious polar bears. Parisian circles of exiled Poles after 1830 made frequent recourse to the symbol of the bear as Russia. These Poles were the ones who exerted great influence on shaping European understanding of Russia of that time.

Political caricatures have always shown special skills in portraying the enemy of the day. They hold up a mirror to national stereotypes and biases. But semioticians have also identified benign and endearing associations of the bear with Russia, not russophobia. The 2014 Sochi Olympics furnishes an illustration.

Western media coverage of the buildup to the Olympics was generally negative and focused on problems facing the Games;[31] the same applied to coverage of the run-up to the World Cup in Brazil a few months later. A Canadian newspaper invoked the imagery of a growling Russian bear for a different purpose. The headline (prescient as later results were to show) was a parody of the bear threat: "Russian bear getting its figure skating growl back."[32] Indeed, the bear was the *mascotte à clef* of the Games charged with blowing out the Olympic flame at their closure. One American media source was even moved to write: "Fittingly, the bear cried a single bear tear down his left bear cheek. We'll miss you too, big fella."[33] Within weeks Russia had annexed Crimea and the Sochi charm had vanished.

In Russia itself the sign of the bear is now widely used in marketing. Prime Minister Dmitry Medvedev is inevitably associated with a bear given that is what his last name means. President Putin has, by contrast, been associated with a lion and, by Proverbs's association, with wicked rule.[34]

Whether endearing or fearsome, the symbol of the bear has endured. "The Russian bear apparently remains the last animal from the rich bestiary of European states of just 70 years ago. It is difficult today to find the British lion or the brave French cockerel; at most one can talk about the sluggish bull of the European Union." Europeans in other countries may therefore grudgingly harbor "a hidden nostalgia for the times when other European states also could show their claws."[35]

Instrumentalizing history

About a century ago, in 1919–21, newly independent Poland and newly Bolshevik Russia fought a war called by some Western historians the Forgotten War – an ironic term given its importance to the independence of the Baltic states, the status of Belorussia and Ukraine, the ethnic composition of Poland, and interwar state boundaries in the region. The result on the battlefield swung wildly – from the eastward advance of the Polish army beyond Minsk and an offensive on Kiev, then subsequently the advance of Russian forces to the Vistula river and Warsaw itself

Both Soviet leader Vladimir Lenin and Polish strongman Józef Piłsudski shared similar objectives. For Lenin it was the establishment of an enlarged socialist federal state larger than the Russian empire of the tsars. For Piłsudski the goal was to consolidate an independent multinational Polish state approaching the size of the Polish–Lithuanian Commonwealth of the sixteenth to eighteenth centuries. It would certainly not be socialist; Piłsudski admitted that he got off the red streetcar of socialism at a stop called independence.

The war was inconclusive. Both countries had to settle for shared occupation of today's Ukrainian and Belarusian territories. But, from this battle, Piłsudski concluded that "mutual hostility became our distinct attribute, our organic trait."[36] For Poles the historical memory of that war centers on Piłsudski and the "Miracle on the Vistula" in 1920 in which his forces repelled the Russian advance on Warsaw. It evokes a sense of kinship with cities and lands Poland ruled in the interwar period – Lviv in today's Ukraine, Grodno that is part of Belarus, Vilnius now in Lithuania. This historical memory also shapes a dual hostility towards Bolshevism and Russia which had almost ended the life of the reborn Polish state that had disappeared for 125 years.

Few historians would contest that Polish attitudes to Russia were generally negative in both the interwar period, when Bolshevik Russia was viewed as a threat, and the Communist era, when Russia was seen as the country's occupier and oppressor. In terms of foreign policy, however, if, under the Polish Second Republic between 1918 and 1939, Piłsudski and the subsequent Colonels' regime regarded Russia as a threat, after 1945 the People's Republic of Poland as a member of the Soviet bloc had no independent foreign policy and could not be associated with anti-Russian politics.

Of the historical grievances that Poles hold about Russia, one trauma in particular, suffered during World War II, may be the deepest. There are many others. In September 1939 the Soviet Union invaded Poland two weeks after Nazi Germany had, fulfilling the secret protocol of the 1939 Ribbentrop–Molotov Pact which divided occupied lands between Germany and Russia.

An estimated half a million Poles, including prisoners of war treated as rebels against Soviet rule or as untrustworthy kulaks (rich peasants), were arrested by Soviet occupying forces early in the war, before Germany attacked the USSR in June 1941.

Four waves of mass deportations of Poles to Central Asia and Siberia were carried out in 1940–41 encompassing over a million Poles. Half a million may have died. The 1944 Warsaw Uprising, costing over 200,000 lives, was a human and political tragedy, in part because Soviet troops positioned on the other bank of the Vistula lent no support to it. The 1945 Yalta agreement, which allowed Stalin a free hand in postwar Poland and elsewhere in Eastern Europe, condemned the region to Soviet rule for the next forty-four years.

But the wartime trauma most powerfully instrumentalized and engraved in historical memory is the Katyn massacre of 1941 in which between 12,000 and 22,000 Polish officers were executed by the Soviet military in several locations in the USSR. These officers had been rounded up, promised that they would lead a reconstituted Polish army against Nazi rule in Poland, then summarily shot on Stalin's orders when they refused to believe in the promise. The most important of their grave sites is Katyn, near Smolensk, but others are found in Starobielsk, Kharkov, and Ostashkov.

Former Polish Foreign Minister and Russia specialist Adam Rotfeld has contextualized this tragedy. He has argued that the Katyn massacre "was not a crime of the Russians but that of a criminal regime whose victims along-side Poles included Russians, Ukrainians, Belarusians, Jews, and many other nations of the USSR."[37] Yet it is fair to say that conjuring up the memory of the Katyn massacre, underscoring its symbolism for Russia's historical attitude to Poland, and instrumentalizing this event across Poland's ideological lines, is arguably the single most important cause of russo-hypopsia in Poland today.

There can be no fear, suspicion, or hatred of Russia without history, then. The difficult task is to flag examples of elite-manipulated, anti-Russian sentiments – the politics of fear from above – rather than historically legitimate fears of Russia.

THREAT PERCEPTIONS

In the case of much of Central and Eastern Europe, fear of Russia has historically represented the greatest and most influential national fear. It represents the "xenophobia of choice" resulting from multifold reasons for distrusting Russia.

Writing before the Ukraine conflict, two journalists noted: "Russia appears menacing but not infrequently the real reasons for these threats lie in Warsaw and not Moscow."[38] That is to say, Polish leaders have only themselves to blame for indulging Russia's threatening behavior.

Russia's irredentism appeared starkly in March 2014 when Crimea, which had been part of Ukraine for sixty years, was annexed. The move was not consistent with a foreign policy agreement signed just four years earlier with Ukraine which extended Russia's lease of naval facilities in Sevastopol until 2042. The annexation may then have an unintended consequence. The NATO charter prevents members from having foreign military bases on their territory so the abrogation of the 2011 treaty on Sevastopol legally clears the way for NATO membership for Ukraine well before 2042.

An overlooked process by which Russia has appeared threatening to other states is its malleable understanding of who Russian compatriots abroad comprise.[39] A changing understanding of what the Russian nation entails and who its compatriots are began to expand after 1999. Broadening of the Russian мы ("we") seemed of scholastic interest until the 2013 crisis in Ukraine when its significance became known. Russian-speaking communities in southern and eastern Ukraine, living in a region Putin called *Novaya Rossiya* were identified as мы.

Outworn stereotypes of nations abound in popular consciousness. As a centuries-old empire, Russia has attracted more than its fair share of these. The image of Russia's ruthless pursuit of expansionist and imperialist agendas is commonplace. Russian expansionism has been linked to the imperial ideology undergirding the Third Rome idea.[40] Polish science fiction writer Stanisław Lem observed that the "Russian character . . . holds within it the foreboding of trouble, disorder and state collapse."[41] It was an apt summary of Russia's internal history.

Over a decade ago, policy analyst Anatol Lieven wrote that

> Russophobia today is rooted not in ideological differences but in national hatred . . . In these architectures of hatred, selected or invented historical "facts" about the "enemy" nation, its culture, and its racial nature are taken out of context and slotted into prearranged intellectual structures to arraign the unchanging wickedness of the other side.[42]

Among the disparaging myths about Russia are that its unique culture dooms it to perpetual backwardness, it lacks the cultural requisites for democracy and a market economy, and it is inherently anti-Western.[43]

Associating an entire nation with the policy of particular leaders serves a xenophobic purpose. Using the term "Russians" instead of "Soviets" to identify the oppressor of Eastern Europe after World War II nurtured russophobia. Onetime Foreign Minister Rotfeld recalled his surprise in the 1960s when, while translating minutes of the Yalta, Teheran, and Potsdam conferences, he found that almost no one – not Churchill or Roosevelt or Stalin – employed the term Soviet Union. They said "Russia." The Soviet Army was called Russian and the Soviet nation Russian. Stalin's statements in these minutes constantly invoked the idea of Russia. He considered himself unequivocally the continuator of the Russian idea.[44]

Today much of the West remains skeptical about whether Russia has really become desovietized, and associating Russia with authoritarian practices continues. Russophobia may be primarily a political construct, therefore, but it is regularly confounded with an ethnic understanding. It does not help that both tsarist Russian and Soviet Russian foreign policy "continually pushed Russia's frontiers outward, impervious to considerations of ethnicity."[45]

FOREIGN POLICY 1997–2005

Elections in 1990s Poland were contested by a multitude of parties and electoral alliances jockeying for power. Leaders followed foreign policy objectives that met with the approval of voters, fulfilled partisan objectives, and contributed to intragovernmental cohesion.[46] A good example may be the post-1989 foreign policy achievements recorded under Foreign Minister Bronisław Geremek between 1997 and 2000, one of which was closer relations with Russia. A 2000 Polish government document titled *Assumptions for Polish Foreign Policy towards Russia* offered a road map for improved relations with Poland's eastern neighbor.[47]

One foreign policy specialist identified four conditions which, at the turn of the twenty-first century, Polish foreign policy on Russia needed to fulfill: 1. avoid anti-Russian rhetoric and russophobic assumptions; 2. avoid fractiousness with Russia hindering Poland's relations with the European Union; 3. prevent Russia from controlling Belarus and Ukraine; and 4. promote cooperation with Russia and support its rapprochement with Europe.[48]

Another Poland expert, Joanna Gorska, reached counterintuitive findings in her analysis of Polish relations with Russia between 1989 and 2004.[49] On the issue of withdrawal of Soviet forces from Poland after 1989, relations had been largely cooperative though, within Poland, the topic had proved divisive. A conciliatory president squared off against a russo-hypopsic prime minister and Lech Wałęsa succeeded in removing his opponent, Jan Olszewski, from power. The cooperative negotiating model for removal of Soviet troops from the country was pursued. But twenty-five years after the cooperative model had won out over the non-cooperative one, the cleavage over how to deal with Russia continues to mark Polish politics. Russian military intervention in Ukraine served to draw all parties to the non-cooperation option after 2013.

On NATO membership Polish authorities adopted non-cooperative policies towards Russia based on power politics considerations. Most leaders gave high priority to NATO accession as a means to increase Poland's say in security matters ("influence gains") on the one hand, while preventing dependence on Russia ("autonomy gains") on the other. But they also advocated engaging Russia in European security processes in order to restrict Russia's own influence-seeking. Thus, in the run-up to the NATO summit in Madrid in 1997, when Poland was invited to join the Atlantic Alliance, Polish leaders opposed Russia's wish to create a NATO–Russia Council. In sum, no tangible cooperation with Russia on Poland's NATO membership bid took place. The 2013 Ukraine standoff which Ukraine's pro-Western rulers framed as a desire to join Europe, but Russia framed as a further stage of NATO expansion, revealed the longer-term effects of non-cooperation over the NATO issue that began in Madrid.

Gorska also reported that, on energy policy, the Polish government took a cooperative approach towards Russia because of material power considerations. Most Polish politicians endorsed the dual objectives of ensuring regular, adequate energy supplies (influence gains) as well as supply source diversification (autonomy gains). On this issue, initial cooperation with Russia was reversed in 2013–14 when the Kremlin threatened Ukraine with an energy embargo which would have a ripple effect on the European Union.

Up to 2004, then, Poland's Russia policy was based primarily on power politics calculations which sometimes dictated cooperation with Russia, at other times non-cooperation. The realist model shaped not only the "easy" cases of "high" politics, such as removing the Red Army from Polish soil, but also "hard" cases such as cooperating on writing a Katyn narrative explaining what had happened there in 1940.

A combination of realist, but also ideational, considerations explained Poland's vigorous support for the pro-Western leaders of the Orange Revolution in Ukraine in 2004. On the eve of the Kaczyńskis' election victories, Poland had already become Ukraine's leading advocate in European forums urging its admission into European structures. Relations between Russia and Poland had deteriorated, therefore, before the Law and Order party (PiS) took power later in 2005. Overall ideational factors had only limited influence on foreign policy in this period.

FEARS IN THE KACZYŃSKI INTERREGNUM: 2005–07

Ideational factors played a more influential role in the formulation of foreign policy towards Russia from 2005 through 2007 when PiS formed the government. Social construction of Russia as adversary proved critical to the 2005 election, then to the political survival of this nationalist government. To be sure, Lech Kaczyński, one of the PiS founders, had repudiated charges of inherent anti-Russian orientations: "We are not a party of russophobes. Good relations with Russia would be highly beneficial for us. However, we know history all too well."[50] Without history there is no xenophobia.

Once elected president in 2005, however, Lech Kaczyński spearheaded hostility towards both Russia and the countries deemed soft on Russia. This raised problems in Polish–EU relations. During the 2008 Russian–Georgian war, Kaczyński attacked Germany and France for their pliability and for pursuing a "very typical" relationship with Russia because of their governments' willingness to facilitate "the historical experiences and interests of corporations" looking to make "big money" in Russia.[51] Perhaps the most theatrical of his anti-Russian acts was joining with Georgia's President Mikhail Saakashvili in accusing Russian forces of shooting at them in 2008 while they were inspecting the border between Georgia and South Ossetia.[52]

Twin brother Jarosław was at the head of the PiS party which won legislative elections in 2005; it was defeated in early elections in 2007. He served as prime minister in 2006–07, a short interlude when the twins governed Poland together. Pursuing erratic foreign policies towards the European Union, Germany and Russia, Poland was dubbed the "Trojan ass" of the EU.[53]

It was not just the Kaczyński brothers who created a culture of fear, especially of Russia. International relations expert Roman Kuźniar pointed to the key role played by pro-PiS political pundits:

> For all that the official policy towards Russia nearly always made use of measured and restrained language, the tone adopted by Polish commentators in accompanying Polish–Russian relations was mostly aggressive, harsh and inclined to make clear which of various complexes the writer was suffering from.[54]

Personal animosity between the Kaczyńskis, on the one hand, and President Putin and Chancellor Merkel, on the other, exacerbated deteriorating relations. To be sure, Polish leaders confronted an intractable dilemma in managing these bilateral relations: the more it appeared that Germany was Russia's last strong link with the West, the more the German leadership strove to maintain good relations with it.[55] Poland's interests were invariably ignored, it seemed.

PiS took power a year after Poland joined the European Union under a postcommunist government led by the Democratic Left Alliance (SLD). In its desire to demonstrate how "un-communist" the party now was, the SLD-led government had agreed in 2003 to have Poland manage one of three "administrative zones" of occupied Iraq (the other two were American and British). More than that, it had cooperated with the CIA in facilitating extrajudicial rendition flights of suspected Islamic terrorists. An airport and building in Szymany in the Mazurian Lakes region of northern Poland became one of the "black sites" where alleged torture of suspected terror-ists took place. First news of its existence was reported in 2005 and years of stonewalling and denial about the site by Polish authorities ultimately proved ineffective. In 2014 the European Court of Human Rights (ECHR) ruled that Poland had violated the European Convention on Human Rights by allowing the CIA in 2002–03 to transfer, hold, and torture two Saudi suspects in Szymany. Both had ended up in the detention camp at Guantanamo. In the 2014 ECHR judgment each was awarded €100,000 in damages from Poland.

These circumstances – a government composed of many former Communist Party members which became involved in "Bush's war" in Iraq and CIA torture activities in Poland – helped the nationalistic PiS sweep the fall 2005 parliamentary and presidential elections. The Kaczyńskis turned their atten-tion to the Kremlin as threat: "The leadership of PiS – particularly Jarosław Kaczyński – criticized their predecessors for not having done enough to defend Poland's interests in the face of Russian pressure."[56] While in power, neither of the Kaczyńskis held a summit with Putin. The meetings that took place with Chancellor Merkel were awkward and unproductive.

Outer Europe

In 2005 Germany and Russia decided on routing North Stream, a gas pipe-line, under the Baltic Sea and outside of Polish control. PiS Defense Minister Radosław Sikorski compared the decision to the secret agreement between Hitler and Stalin to carve up Poland in 1939.[57] This analogy did nothing to improve Polish relations with Germany and Russia though, as described below, Sikorski's diplomatic career was just beginning.

Another consequential Polish foreign policy move came at the European Union's 2006 Helsinki summit: it torpedoed the start of negotiations about an EU–Russia partnership. The reason was ostensibly Russia's embargo on the import of Polish meat and vegetables because of health concerns.[58] The summit put on a show of unity backing Poland but EU relations with Russia were to be affected for years: to date there is no institutional EU–Russia partnership agreement as there is a NATO–Russia council. Its absence contributed to difficulties in relations between the two actors as the crisis in Ukraine grew.

Under the Kaczyńskis' rule, Poland became the lightning rod in the EU's relations with Russia. How to deal with Russia became an issue polarizing Eastern and Western European states. Polish leaders were convinced that they were voicing the concerns of its neighbors: as one observer put it, "CEE [Central and Eastern European] representatives and their publics often per-ceive Western European members of the EU as appeasers of Russia, while

Western Europeans view CEE members as too hostile toward Moscow."[59] In some measure, this divide disappeared when Russia annexed Crimea in 2014.

The PiS government endorsed exclusionary, xenophobic nationalism. Balibar's concept of an outer Europe seemed particularly applicable to Poland in this period. Deep elite suspicions of the Kremlin (which retrospectively may seem prescient) were mistaken for those of average Poles. But survey data (reported below) did not bear out the association: respondents seemed largely indifferent to ratcheted-up anti-Russian rhetoric.

At the first opportunity they had, in 2007, Poles voted out one of the Kaczyńskis. Overcharged nationalist discourse and exploitative fears directed at Russia and Germany ultimately produced a positive outcome. The cathartic experience of nationalist politicians expressing deep animosities towards neighbors was the basis upon which their liberal opponents could come to power and turn Poland into a mainstream EU member.

The Kaczyńskis' legacy

The distinctive character of the Kaczyńskis' interlude between 2005 and 2007 is more profound than the detail that identical twins rarely in human history have ruled a country in tandem. For purposes of this study it was exceptional how their interregnum marked a high point of the politics of fear from above. It stands in contrast to a pragmatic foreign policy open to constructive relations with other countries after 2007.

Lech Kaczyński, elected president in 2005, did not complete his term. He was killed in 2010 while flying to Smolensk to commemorate the seventieth anniversary of the deaths of Polish officers executed and buried by the Soviet military in 1940 in the Katyn forest. His presidential airplane, a twenty-year-old Russian-built Tu-154 with out-of-date American navigation equipment and piloted by a Polish crew, crashed in thick fog killing all ninety-six on board.

The nationalist policies of the PiS leadership were reflected in its foreign policy. Two foreign policy specialists explained that if Poland's image in the European Union had been tarnished, "the most significant factor is what could be classed as serious damage done to the Polish–German relationship under the Law and Justice-led coalition of 2005 to 2007." Thus, "Poland under the Kaczyńskis, perhaps unfairly, lost much of its credibility as a reliable European partner," in part because of a Western media offensive against them.[60]

To be fair, one study concluded that "the foreign policy of the PiS government broadly continued the policies that previous administrations since 1989 had pursued; there was, however, a marked change in the *style* of the diplomacy that the government adopted."[61] Of the Kaczyńskis' interregnum in 2006–07, celebrated oppositionist thinker Adam Michnik observed at the time: "Rather than seize on its European Union membership to catapult the country forward, Poland's coalition government finds itself looking, and moving, backward." He cited an example. "During a dry summer, a group of [PiS] coalition legislators called upon the Parliament to pray for rain. A similar group proposed that the Parliament vote to declare Jesus Christ the King of Poland."[62]

FOREIGN POLICY AFTER 2007

The main cause of Poles' russo-hypopsia has been sensitivity to the Russian state's international behavior. Shortly before the 2008 Russian attack on Georgia, a survey found that 54 percent of Polish respondents believed that Russia was seeking to regain influence in Eastern Europe; just 20 percent said it was not.[63] These views were not out of line with global attitudinal trends. After the war with Georgia, a 2009 report found that "substantially more people now have a negative view of Russia's influence – 44 percent negative versus 31 percent positive – and that was before the recent disruption in Russian gas supplies to Europe." The inference from these data was straightforward: "the more it acts like the old Soviet Union, the less people outside its borders seem to like it."[64]

In May 2010, a month after the plane crash in Smolensk, Poles were asked about bilateral relations with Russia. In reply to a rare question specifically asking about fear – "Which state should Poland fear the most?" – a half of respondents duly identified Russia. This was double the percentage recorded in 1990 for the USSR when it was in its death throes but down from the peak of two-thirds in late 2005.[65] The next most feared country was Germany (17 percent, dramatically down from 88 percent in 1990 when German reunification negotiations were taking place). Equal third was a residual category of Islamic states, such as Afghanistan and Iraq, and the United States (7 percent each, a high for the US). One-fifth of Poles in 2010 claimed they had no enemy. A counterintuitive finding was that older people expressed least fear of Russia. Respondents who completed higher education were more inclined to express fears about both Russia and Germany.

Poles' threat perceptions of Russia may be influenced by cultural factors. Survey researchers have argued that Poles' attitudes towards other nations are shaped mainly by positive stereotypes of the wealthy civilized "West" and negative ones of the poor culturally lagging "East." But such alleged economic-cultural determinism is only part of the story. The cleavage may also be influenced by racial and religious factors. In 2014 the top eleven nations Poles identified as liking were European ones which are predominantly Roman Catholic or Protestant (Table 5.1).

Table 5.1 Attitudes of Poles towards Other Nations in 2014

Nations	How would you describe your attitude towards other nations? (in percentage)				
	A liking	Indifference	A dislike	Difficult to say	Mean on a scale from +3 to −3
1. Czechs	50	27	17	6	0.72
2. Italians	48	30	15	7	0.73
3. Slovaks	47	31	15	7	0.69
4. Spaniards	46	30	14	10	0.73
5. Irish	46	29	15	10	0.70
6. French	44	31	18	7	0.54
7. Norwegians	43	32	14	11	0.67
8. Hungarians	43	31	17	9	0.61
9. English	43	30	20	7	0.49
10. Swiss	42	30	17	11	0.57
11. Swedes	41	31	17	11	0.55
12. Americans	41	31	21	7	0.45
13. Dutch	40	33	17	10	0.55
14. Austrians	39	32	19	10	0.46
15. Germans	39	27	30	4	0.21
16. Croatians	38	30	20	12	0.45
17. Brazilians	37	30	17	16	0.53
18. Belgians	37	33	18	12	0.49
19. Greeks	37	30	23	10	0.35
20. Japanese	37	28	23	12	0.32
21. Lithuanians	34	31	27	8	0.18
22. Ukrainians	34	27	33	6	0.03
23. Georgians	31	31	25	13	0.17
24. Bulgarians	31	30	28	11	0.11
25. Estonians	30	31	22	17	0.24
26. Belarusians	29	30	31	10	−0.03
27. Jews	29	28	33	10	−0.11
28. Egyptians	25	31	27	17	0.05
29. Chinese	25	29	36	10	−0.18
30. Russians	25	28	42	5	−0.35
31. Vietnamese	24	29	35	12	−0.20
32. Turks	24	26	38	12	−0.29
33. Romanians	21	26	45	8	−0.52
34. Roma (Gypsies)	20	20	55	5	−0.85

Source: Centrum Badania Opinii Społecznej, "Stosunek polaków do innych narodów" (Warsaw: CBOS, February 2014), BS/20/2014, p. 2, www.cbos.pl

The nine most disliked nations (and fourteen of the bottom sixteen) happened to be either non-European or, in religious terms, not Catholic or Protestant. In fact seven are predominantly Orthodox. The survey analysts' claim that "nations culturally far removed" from Poland make up part of the group of least liked peoples raises questions of their own. Russia ranked thirty of thirty-four. In explaining patterns of sympathy and antipathy of Poles towards other nations, researchers agreed that history, current political events, and personal experiences had significant influence.[66]

The breakup of the Soviet bloc did change Polish citizens' attitudes to Russia. Evidence from public opinion surveys and discourse of political elites points to a steady decline in expressed antipathy towards Russia after 1989. Thus, Russia's overall ranking among favorite nations was low but, in 2014, only slightly more respondents expressed a dislike of it (28 percent) than a liking for it (25 percent).[67] This trend may have undergirded conciliatory foreign policy towards Putin's Russia that a center-right liberal government headed by prime minister Donald Tusk (head of the Civic Platform party, or PO) pursued after 2007. That changed when the crisis in Ukraine broke out in late 2013. It cannot be ruled out that Poles' more favorable images of Russia were products of the Kremlin's own efforts to propagate a more positive image in Poland up to 2013.[68]

Tusk's turn

In 2007 the Kremlin's shortlist of what it regarded as provocative Polish foreign policy towards Russia included the following: 1. its support for NATO membership for Georgia and Ukraine; 2. veto of EU–Russia partnership negotiations at the 2006 Helsinki summit; 3. agreement for a United States anti-missile base in Poland signed in 2007; and 4. calls for the establishment of an "Energy NATO." A year later the Eastern Neighborhood Initiative promoted jointly by Poland and Sweden was added to the list. Prime Minister Kaczyński may have been turned out of office but President Kaczyński had years to go in his term.

Under PiS leadership, political rhetoric had exacerbated issue-based Polish–Russian disagreements. Political scientist Jerzy Wiatr suggested that "It is not important whether Jarosław Kaczyński, Anna Fotyga [foreign minister] or Antoni Macierewicz [deputy defense minister] seemed to be russophobes or were seeking to accrue political benefits. What is important is that they introduced a negative and dangerous tone into Polish–Russian relations."[69] Fotyga's appointment as foreign minister was particularly controversial since she had no experience in foreign affairs. As a close friend of President Kaczyński, her role became carrying out his foreign policy agenda.

Civic Platform's 2007 parliamentary victory ended the Kaczyńskis' stranglehold on power. Many issues shaped the election outcome but hostile rhetoric towards Russia made Polish voters aware of how "like any other inherited hatred, blind, dogmatic hostility toward Russia leads to bad policies."[70]

Months after taking office Tusk visited Moscow to meet Putin. The Polish prime minister spoke of reconciliation between the two countries: "both sides are fed up with the 'cold' atmosphere." The United States Embassy in Warsaw described the meeting as a thaw in Polish–Russian relations though it harbored no illusions that a real "new opening" between Warsaw and Moscow would be hamstrung by disagreement over the North Stream pipeline, the anti-missile shield, and other issues.[71]

Tusk and Putin met again several times. At the World Economic Forum in Davos in 2009, they agreed to a series of regular consultative meetings. To be sure, a scheduled 2009 Putin visit to Warsaw to discuss a "broad formula" for issues of the kind nations conduct with their "most important partners" was put off. Instead, Putin came to Gdańsk a few months later to commemorate the seventieth anniversary of the outbreak of World War II. It carried great symbolism, like Putin's 2005 visit to Auschwitz to mark the liberation of the death camp.

The Gdańsk visit highlighted Putin's skills in symbolic politics: "Putin's performance in Poland drew praise from many erstwhile critics of Russia, if not completely fulfilling Polish demands for Russian accountability."[72] He pleased many Poles by emphasizing how "Russia has always respected the bravery and heroism of the Polish people, soldiers and officers, who stood up first against Nazism in 1939." In contrast, President Kaczyński used the occasion to raise historical grievances. He described the Soviet invasion of the country in September 1939 as "a knife in the back of Poland." Equating Soviet actions during the war, however brutal or cynical they were, with Nazi crimes will inevitably trigger a strident Russian backlash.

Tusk's government inherited the thorny issue of siting United States missile interceptors and radar bases in Poland which Prime Minister Kaczyński had negotiated. At the time, it was the most divisive issue in Polish–Russian relations. The Kremlin retaliated by withdrawing from the 1990 Conventional Forces Europe (CFE) Treaty which had set limits on troop levels in Europe. It also threatened to station its own missiles in the Kaliningrad region north of Poland.

Tusk and Sikorski, who had switched parties and portfolios after the 2007 election, signed a scaled-down agreement in 2008: the United States would locate a base with ten interceptor missiles and related Patriot air defense systems in Poland. Foreign Minister Sikorski took part in the signing ceremony in London alongside US Secretary of State Condoleezza Rice and used the occasion to scold the British (he had British citizenship) about

World War II, too. Explaining the rationale for the anti-missile agreement he referred to history: "The British didn't come through in 1939. You declared war but you didn't go to war. That's why we're demanding capabilities, 'boots on the ground,' not just parchment." He added: "we hope that this time our allies help us to even out the risks."[73] As if to prove Sikorski's point, Putin added a new national Russian holiday which celebrated the expulsion of Polish armies from Moscow in 1612.

Public opinion did not back the missile shield. Even after the Georgia–Russia war in late summer 2008, Polish opponents outnumbered supporters by 46 to 41 percent. By spring 2009, the gap had returned to pre-war figures: 53 percent were against and only 29 percent for the shield.[74] Such "pacifist" sentiment does not point to a russophobic Polish public. It also does not indicate endorsement of a national role conception for Poland as the last line of defense of Western civilization which the missile shield could be construed as symbolizing.

Under Tusk a contentious new issue in Polish–Russian relations emerged. The Eastern Neighborhood Initiative, launched in 2008 by the unlikely alliance of Poland and Sweden (though both countries were governed by center-right parties having outspoken foreign ministers), sought to promote closer European Union relations with former Soviet republics on Russia's borders. By summer 2009, Armenia, Azerbaijan, Belarus, Georgia, Moldova, and Ukraine had signed up to the EU initiative. At an EU–Russia summit in Khabarovsk in 2009, then Russian President Dmitri Medvedev presciently cautioned that Russia did "not want the Eastern Partnership to turn into partnership against Russia . . . I would simply not want this partnership to consolidate certain individual states, which are of an anti-Russian bent, with other European states."[75]

Foreign Minister Sikorski found a like soul in Sweden's Foreign Minister Carl Bildt (discussed in the next chapter). Both were accused of holding russophobic attitudes but these were more subtle than that. Sikorski articulated a dualistic approach to Russia: "Open and pragmatic dialogue with Russia cannot be replaced but it has its limits. NATO should not surrender its turf to Russia."[76] After Russia's intervention in Georgia he traveled to Washington to announce a "Sikorski Doctrine." It called for NATO military action if Ukraine was invaded as Georgia had been: violation of existing borders by Russia would constitute a *casus belli*. He renounced that doctrine in 2009 when he realized that his russophobic image damaged his chances of being appointed NATO Secretary General. Indeed, he went to the other extreme and called for Russia's admission into NATO.[77] A long-serving Danish prime minister who had involved his country in the Afghanistan war got the job.

Sikorski was prone to making alarmist statements. *WikiLeaks* reports a 2008 telegram from the United States embassy in Warsaw which cited Sikorski's warning that a Russian attack on Poland was possible within the next ten to fifteen months.[78] In 2011 in Berlin, he made a major foreign policy speech in which he asserted: "I fear Germany's power less than her inactivity." He believed he was the first Polish diplomat in history to call for Germany taking a stronger leadership role in then euro-troubled Europe.[79]

Poland's foreign minister was engaged in numerous diplomatic initiatives in 2013–14 related to the Ukraine crisis, and was a regular visitor to Kiev where he met with Ukraine's pro-Western leaders. For the Kremlin he was not an impartial mediator. At important "road map" meetings in 2014 of the foreign ministers from Russia, Ukraine, Germany, and France held in Berlin, Sikorski was conspicuously left out.

In Warsaw in 2014 he was secretly taped saying that Poland's security relationship with the United States was "worthless" and "even harmful as it gives Poland a false sense of security."[80] He also criticized British Prime Minister David Cameron for his erratic remarks about the European Union. This was at a time when Oxford-educated Sikorski was after another job – European High Representative for Foreign Affairs and Security Policy. His candidature was thus crafted around a firm stance opposing Russia's intervention in Ukraine, his endorsement of German power, and his apparent distancing from both the United States and Britain. Not only was he passed over in fall 2014 for the European Union position in favor of a young Italian diplomat who held out the promise that she could establish a modus operandi with Putin, Sikorski was removed as Poland's foreign minister in a government reshuffle and "booted upstairs" to serve as Marshal of the Sejm (Speaker of Parliament).

Public opinion

Surveys of Poles' attitudes towards their neighbors during Tusk's tenure as prime minister raise questions about whether style and tone had been the only flaws in PiS foreign policy. Results of opinion polls carried out in April 2007, when both the Kaczyńskis held high office, and in April 2010, two weeks after Lech Kaczyński had been killed in Smolensk, showed marked changes in popular attitudes.[81] Thus, in 2007, 62 percent of respondents regarded Poland's relations with Russia as very bad or bad; three years later the proportion had fallen to 32 percent. Similarly, in 2007, 27 percent had said that Poland's relations with Germany were very bad or bad; in 2010 the figure was down to 10 percent. Clearly perceptions of the two neighbors improved significantly in the first three years of the Tusk government.

When asked if they agreed that the policy of Russia and Germany was anti-Polish, in 2007 in the case of Russia, 53 percent of respondents said decidedly or somewhat yes; by 2010, only 33 percent believed Russia's policy was anti-Polish. That Germany conducted an anti-Polish policy was accepted by about 20 percent in both 2007 and 2010.

Closely related survey questions probe russo-hypopsia more closely. In 2007, as the PiS government was falling, one-third of respondents decidedly or rather accepted that "Poland's policy is anti-Russian." The proportion was down to one in five after three years of Tusk's government. The respective results inquiring into perceptions of anti-German policy were 23 percent and 16 percent. Comparing the two sets, we see slightly more widespread perceptions of Poland being ill-disposed towards its eastern rather than its western neighbor. On the related statement that "there is a lot of sympathy for Russians in Polish society," those somewhat or decidedly agreeing went up from 36 percent to 47 percent over the three years of PO government. These figures were nearly the same about Germany.[82]

The author of this study cautioned that perceptions of improvements in bilateral relations with Poland's two neighbors were not the result of real changes in foreign policy; not enough time had elapsed for the Tusk-led government to have carried out major policy changes. Instead, they reflected respondents' impressions of these relations as well as of their symbolism in framing domestic party competition.[83]

Former dissident Karol Modzelewski was also unprepared to credit a change of government for perceived better relations with neighbors. Poland's relations with neighboring nations were weighed down by memories of inflicted pain and suffering at their hands, he claimed. That is why

> For every Polish government – regardless whether Kaczyński or Tusk is the prime minister – overwhelming hostility towards Russians, Germans, or Ukrainians will be like a shackle around the leg not allowing Poland to organize mutual economic and political relations in the best understood sense of national interest.[84]

Modzelewski, for one, was convinced of the harm done by Polish xeno-hypopsia to Poland's international politics.

Twenty years after Communism's fall, views of Russia differed widely in the region. Many of Russia's neighbors in Eastern Europe saw its influence as a bad thing, reflecting concern over resurgent nationalism in Russia. In 2009, nearly six in ten Poles (59 percent) saw Russia's influence as negative, the highest percentage of any country in the region. In the Czech Republic, Hungary and Lithuania, pluralities regarded Russian influence on their countries as a bad thing. Back in 2009, conversely, more Bulgarians and, surprisingly, Ukrainians viewed Russia's impact as positive rather than negative; in Western Europe the balance of opinion was that Russian influence was negative.[85]

What the West found alarming about Russia's international politics Russians found reassuring. In 2009 a majority of Russians (54 percent) agreed with the statement "Russia should be for Russians;" in 1991 just 26 percent had agreed with that statement. Fifty-eight percent agreed "it is a great misfortune that the Soviet Union no longer exists." Nearly half (47 percent) believed "it is natural for Russia to have an empire."[86] Little wonder, then, that in August 2014, Putin's imperial thrust into Ukraine elicited the support of 87 percent of Russians approving of his policies and 82 percent declared their intention to vote for him in the next presidential elections.[87]

Halting the thaw with Russia

Prime Minister Tusk's efforts to return to a productive relationship with the Kremlin was not without its critics in Poland, or in the region generally. In 2009, former presidents Lech Wałęsa and Aleksander Kwaśniewski, together with former defense and foreign ministers, signed "An Open Letter to the Obama Administration from Central and Eastern Europe." Endorsed by many other former leaders of countries in the region, it was published a week after the United States president's summit in Moscow with Russia's leaders.[88]

The letter claimed that American foreign policy no longer valued the region. To make things worse,

> . . . there are fewer and fewer leaders who emerged from the revolutions of 1989 who experienced Washington's key role in securing our democratic transition and anchoring our countries in NATO and EU. A new generation of leaders is emerging who do not have these memories and follow a more "realistic" policy.

The suggestion was that the anti-Soviet and arguably anti-Russian generation was losing influence. This was occurring just as Russian revanchism was increasing (Box 5.1).

Box 5.1 An Open Letter to the Obama Administration in 2009

Russia is back as a revisionist power pursuing a nineteenth-century agenda with twenty-first-century tactics and methods. At a global level, Russia has become, on most issues, a status-quo power. But at a regional level and vis-à-vis our nations, it increasingly acts as a revisionist one. It challenges our claims to our own historical experiences. It asserts a privileged position in determining our security choices. It uses overt and covert means of economic warfare, ranging from energy blockades and politically motivated investments to bribery and media manipulation in order to advance its interests and to challenge the transatlantic orientation of Central and Eastern Europe.

Source: "An Open Letter to the Obama Administration from Central and Eastern Europe," *Gazeta Wyborcza*, English edn, 15 July 2009.

For the signatories this was not a time for the United States to succumb to the "realism" of another Yalta agreement:

> ... we want to ensure that too narrow an understanding of Western interests does not lead to the wrong concessions to Russia. Today the concern is, for example, that the United States and the major European powers might embrace the [Russian President Dmitri] Medvedev plan for a 'Concert of Powers' to replace the continent's existing, value-based security structure. The danger is that Russia's creeping intimidation and influence-peddling in the region could over time lead to a de facto neutralization of the region.

A British diplomat added his critical voice to the alleged incorrigibility of Russia:

> The fall of the Soviet Union did not wipe the slate clean. The Russia that we are dealing with today, with its fear of encirclement, its suspicion of foreigners and natural appetite for autocracy, is as old as the hills, long pre-dating communism. It is a Russia that will never be reassured by the West's protestations of pacifist intent as it pushes NATO and the EU ever eastwards.[89]

The letter concluded: "When it comes to Russia, our experience has been that a more determined and principled policy toward Moscow will not only strengthen the West's security but will ultimately lead Moscow to follow a more cooperative policy as well."[90]

Roman Kuźniar, advisor to President Bronisław Komorowski, supported this approach by underlining Russia's exceptionalism: "The incompatibility of political interests and the differences of psychological outlook and of history are so great that if Russia rejects maintaining normal bilateral relations the inevitable result will be total breakdown" of these relations. He added: "Unlike Germany, Russia feels unable to accept that it has in any way been at fault."[91]

As far as the American Embassy in Warsaw was concerned, Prime Minister Tusk was a "natural ally" of the United States because of their shared interests in Eastern Europe. Both Warsaw and Washington supported the "Europeanization" of Ukraine, Belarus, and states in the south Caucasus. A summary of a 2009 telegram revealed by *WikiLeaks* reported that "though anti-Russian sentiments sometimes hurt Polish foreign policy and deform it, Donald Tusk's government has for now shown itself to be a responsible and rational actor." That was because "Warsaw had given up anti-Russian rhetoric, improved relations with Germany, supported the French project of a Southern Partnership in return for support for an Eastern Partnership."[92]

The 2010 Smolensk air crash became politicized over Russia's role in it. Did Russians shoot down the plane or otherwise sabotage it? One very strange theory claimed that Russian scientists had manufactured the fog that caused it to crash. Was Polish Defense Minister Bogdan Klich negligent (he was sub-sequently made the scapegoat) in allowing an old Russian-built Tu-154, filled with so many top government officials, to fly uninvited to Smolensk? Were Tusk and Putin in cahoots in eliminating the president as a Photoshopped picture of the two exchanging coy smiles near the plane wreckage seemed to show? Since 2010 the surviving Kaczyński twin has created a "Smolensk religion" around a conspiracy theory of Russia having brought down the plane. The 2014 shooting down of a Malaysian passenger airline over Russian-controlled eastern Ukraine was cited by some PiS activists as further evidence in support of this conspiracy theory.

Tusk's more pragmatic modus vivendi with the Russian Federation after 2007 registered with the majority of Poles. In the election campaign to replace his brother as president in 2010, Jarosław Kaczyński was highly criti-cal of Tusk's improved relations with Russia. In a debate between the two run-off candidates, he attacked the proposed gas contract with Russia, that Tusk had negotiated, which would bring ten billion cubic meters of gas a year to Poland through 2037. His opponent, PO-supported Komorowski, backed closer relations with the European Union but also with Russia. Some right-wing foes even dubbed him "Komoruski." In the election, Komorowski defeated Kaczyński by a comfortable, if not overwhelming, margin of 53 to 47 percent. With the defeat, PiS could only protest its fears of foreign countries from the sidelines until elections in 2015.

American diplomats may have praised Tusk in 2009 for his "responsible and rational" approach to Russia but PiS did not give up vilifying his and President Komorowski's supposed russophilism. A consensus emerged across the major parties to stop Russian aggression in Ukraine in 2014 but, even then, Tusk's dovish approach was singled out. A disparaging story, titled "Moscow prefers Tusk", explained how, in 2009, the Polish prime minister had signed a deal with Gazprom favorable to the Russian energy company; in 2010, his efforts to obtain access to the Smolensk crash site, which Russia had blocked off, proved futile; in 2011, he laid the cornerstone for a new gas port in Świnoujście that would make Poland more energy independent but completion of the project was delayed until 2017. In 2013 the Ukraine crisis caught Tusk off guard.[93] If the conservative Polish opposition found failings in Tusk, the European Council did not; he became its president in late 2014.

The Polish Strategic Yearbook affirmed that "The Ukraine crisis provided proof of the weakness of Polish–Russian relations." Polish authorities were able to communicate with all sides to the crisis "but they were not able to conduct any kind of discussions with Russian authorities."[94] For Moscow, then, Tusk's continuation in power provides "warm water in the taps."[95] The charge against him is that in his foreign policy he has not conveyed the fears and distrust of Russia that purportedly pervade Polish society.

Poland's post-2007 upswing in the European Union

A way to check whether Tusk's diplomacy had raised Poland's image and influence after the Kaczyńskis' interlude is to assess the credibility and clout Poland brought to the EU foreign policy discussion table.

In a study measuring Poland's power and influence in the European Union on policy towards Eastern Europe, Nathaniel Copsey and Karolina Pomorska measured its performance on six variables. They recognized that it was this subject that could be "the Polish speciality in the EU" and on which Poland had "no competition in Europe." Supporting this idea, after joining the European Union in 2004 "Polish diplomats were assigned the goal of raising the problems of the region on the EU agenda."[96] Combined with foreign policy consensus across political parties, Poland scored highly for the "intensity" of its Eastern European policy influence on the European Union. But that was where the positive dimension ends. For the authors, the country scored low in skills at alliance building, administrative capacity, persuasive advocacy, and receptiveness of other member states, and it had only a medium score in domestic political strength.

In sum,

> It was not able to convince its partners that its policy on Russia or Ukraine truly represented the Community interest and not a narrow Polish national agenda ... In other words, it appeared that Poland was simply trying to upload its national policy preference onto the EU agenda without sufficient modification.[97]

The Polish–Swedish Eastern Partnership initiative accepted by the European Union represented an exception.

The authors contrasted Poland's lack of foreign policy influence within the European Union on a subject of great importance to it with that of France's strength demonstrated in the high scores it obtained across nearly all the six variables. As suggested in the previous chapter,

> President Sarkozy's *Union pour la Mediterranée* went from what looked like Sarkozy's presidential whim, or an unplanned remark, in 2007, to a bold initiative uniting all the European Union's 27 Member States with all the countries of the South under the umbrella of a Secretariat run by France (and Egypt, the largest southern neighbor) by mid-2008.[98]

A follow-up article by these authors focused on Poland's role in the creation of the Eastern Partnership, an offshoot of the European Neighborhood Policy. Copsey and Pomorska stressed that, after 2007, Polish representatives to Brussels brought improved skills at alliance-building and persuasive advocacy, allowing it to expand its influence. Combined with slightly improved receptiveness of other member states towards Tusk government initiatives, when compared to Kaczyński-led governments, EU officials in the Commission and Council Secretariat judged that "from 2007 the Poles learned to compromise and be more modest in their proposals."[99]

The choice of Sweden, widely viewed as an honest broker (a claim put under scrutiny in the next chapter), and closer relations with Germany were critical to improved alliance building. Poland's persuasive advocacy was paradoxically enhanced by Russia's actions in Georgia in 2008; such "un exogenous event provided a much-needed boost to the credibility of a long-held Polish position."[100]

Increased EU receptiveness to Poland's initiative involved other exogenous factors. Sarkozy's 2007 election win was meaningful because he was more supportive of the Eastern Partnership than Chirac had been. Sarkozy became a cautious backer of European integration and of the Eastern Partnership so long as two red lines were maintained: 1. in discussions with Ukraine, any debate on enlargement was to be banned; and 2. with the establishment of the Mediterranean Union a per capita spending balance was to be struck between eastern and southern neighborhood expenditures; this "balance" would favor the more populated Mediterranean region over the eastern one. Allegedly for this balance to work, for every cent spent on the east two cents more had to be spent on the south.[101]

While not specifically assessing the impact of Tusk's more diplomatic approach to Russia, these studies indicate that Poland's post-2007 foreign policy was more calibrated and, accordingly, more influential in European forums. It also reflected the attitude towards Russia of the majority of Poles. While some continued to express fears about Russia's influence, they did not make Poles exceptional. Russo-hypopsia in Poland before 2013 was measured rather than disproportionate, reasoned rather than irrational.

Poland's improving relations with Russia were set back at the 2013 European Union Vilnius summit. There, Ukrainian President Viktor Yanukovych rejected an association agreement with the European Union because of Kremlin pressure, a decision triggering a protracted conflict in Eastern Europe.

The fact that, in 2014, Poles expressed less confidence in Putin, and had a more negative general image of Russia, showed again how exogenous factors – stimuli from the international system – conditioned russo-hypopsia, not "just" a thousand years of history or incorrigible russophobic attitudes.

Conflict over Ukraine: 2013–14

Distrust of Russia expressed by the Kaczyńskis did not disappear after 2007. It could not be otherwise in Poland. In some ways, this distrust foreshadowed what emerged across most of the European Union after 2013 following the crisis in Ukraine.

A cross-national survey conducted in April 2014 revealed that Poles, more than their counterparts in other Central European states, were most apprehensive about Russia. In answer to the question "Will Russia in the near future strive to regain its influence in our part of Europe or not?" 62 percent of Polish respondents said yes and 21 percent said no. The responses were dramatically different in Slovakia: only 27 percent recognized a Russian bid for greater influence but 51 percent repudiated the idea. Hungarians were split nearly down the middle: 41 percent said yes, 40 percent said no.[102]

Poles' strong (though not exceptional) hypopsia towards Russia is found in other polling data. A Polish survey found close to half of respondents agreeing with the statement that Putin's territorial claims on countries where there are Russian minorities are not limited to Ukraine.[103] In May 2014 Poles rated relations with Russia as the worst they had ever been since polling had begun in 1987: 65 percent said they were bad and only 3 percent claimed they were good.[104]

Compare these results to those in neighboring Germany. In June 2014 *DeutschlandTREND* reported an *increase* in the proportion of German respondents believing Russia was a partner worthy of trust: despite greater bloodshed in eastern Ukraine in the interim it had risen to 21 percent from 14 percent in April 2014. On German foreign policy 89 percent preferred continuation of dialogue between the West and Russia despite the Ukraine crisis; only 9 percent favored far-reaching isolation of Russia. In addition, three-quarters of Germans surveyed opposed increasing NATO's military presence in its eastern member states compared to 21 percent who supported the proposal.[105] We can suggest that Germans set the bar in Europe for *not* exhibiting russo-hypopsic attitudes. Many Poles would claim Poles, not Germans, were realists.

Overall, Polish attitudes were representative of the steadily worsening image Russia had in the world. In June 2014 Poles' negative attitudes towards Russia reached a high of 81 percent from 54 percent in 2013. The increase was more dramatic in the United States, from 43 percent to 72 percent. Britain, Spain, Germany, and Italy also recorded high increases (about 20 percent) in unfavorable images of Russia. Conversely, the greatest improvement in Russia's image between 2013 and 2014 took place in China: in the space of a year, favorable ratings climbed from 49 percent to 66 percent (Box 5.2).

On non-confidence levels in Putin, Spain, Poland, and France led the way (87 percent, 86 percent, and 85 percent respectively) with little or no confidence. For Poles this marked an increase of 12 percent over two years. The

> ### Box 5.2 Fears in a mélange-à-trois
>
> In the highly asymmetrical triangular relationship between Russia, China and the United States, the worst Russian fear is of Sino-American collusion at Russia's expense. Russians have been suspicious of the idea of a Sino-American "G2" emerging. They also fear that the U.S. may attempt to provoke discord between Russia and China. But perhaps they should worry more about a confrontation between the United States and China, which would put Russia between a rock and a hard place. The rise of nationalism in China is the chief reason to worry about a Sino-U.S. confrontation. China-watchers in Russia note that Chinese nationalists clearly view the world in zero-sum terms familiar to early twentieth-century Europe. To some in China, their country is inherently "good," and its actions always "legitimate."
>
> Source: Dmitri Trenin, *True Partners? How Russia and China See Each Other* (London: Centre for European Reform, 2012), p. 11.

figure was 80 percent in the United States.[106] Needless to say, in the armed conflict in eastern Ukraine, Poles sympathized with the side supporting Ukraine's territorial integrity over the separatists by a margin of 48 percent to 4 percent in July 2014. Significantly, however, 42 percent of respondents expressed indifference about the conflict which they attributed to lack of interest, knowledge, or stakes in the fighting.[107]

Analysts seeking to explain Russia's bellicosity towards the post-Yanukovych Ukrainian government have underscored Putin's fear that he, too, may fall victim to opposition at home. His foreign policy gambit to annex Crimea, which boosted his approval ratings in Russia to over 80 percent, furnished a convincing example of how in Russia, too, domestic structures can be shaped by foreign policy.

CONCLUSIONS

In 1993, 17 percent of Polish respondents expressed a liking for Russians and this figure doubled by 2010. In 1994, 59 percent of Poles expressed antipathy to Russians, a total nearly halved (to 31 percent) by 2010.[108] Even at the height of the conflict in Ukraine in 2014 slightly more Poles believed it was more important to maintain good relations with Russia (38 percent) than to engage in close cooperation with countries of the former USSR such as Ukraine and Georgia (34 percent).[109] These data indicate steadily decreasing levels of russo-hypopsia among Polish respondents.

But the existence of russo-hypopsia in Poland is not a myth. It is consistently found in elite discursive practices. At times, as during the Kaczyńskis' power-holding years, it runs counter to Polish public opinion. In my research I could find no evidence of a reverse causal direction – elites' expressed fears sparking public fears. When anti-Russian sentiments did spike, as after 2013, the public was reacting to events occurring in the international system, not to domestic demagoguery.

Since 2000 Russia has conducted a number of military interventions along its borders which have raised threat perceptions and security fears. Russian expansionism inciting fears involves more than military forms. Changing Russian understandings of what the Russian nation entails and who its compatriots are have broadened since 1999. The new round of "in-gathering" of Russian peoples also poses a threat, then: the rationale employed in 2014 for annexing Crimea and for being prepared to protect the rights of Russians and compatriots in post-Soviet space is anchored in a 1999 law titled "On State Policy of the Russian Federation towards Compatriots Abroad."

It may appear that political elites are inclined to follow traditional action scripts and follow old battle lines more than the demos does. This was the case for the Kaczyńskis. But, after 2007, Tusk-led governments were less prepared to be influenced by traditional action scripts singling Russia out as the greatest threat and fear. Average Polish citizens, too, have become Eurocentric in what matters to them.

To a large degree, then, since 2007, policies and attitudes towards Russia have become Europeanized. Poland is prepared to go along with European Union policy on Russia rather than risk being charged with undermining the European Union's relations with Russia because of a supposed russophobia. Its ambition to *lead* opinion-making about Russia has been scaled down. As Kuźniar concisely phrased it, "the attempt at basing Polish policy towards Russia around 'values' had no chance of success."[110]

Disillusion about the future of Russia has deepened: "Today the belief that we can have 'the west on our east' appears to be losing proponents."[111] A product of this is that fear of Russia in Poland has become more contingent. Whatever Moscow decides on has, in the end, less impact on Poles than what Brussels does. On this, Polish public opinion and foreign policy are in agreement.

For a time, between 2005 and 2007, russo-hypopsic Polish foreign policy was divorced from average citizens' views of Russia. After 2007 the Polish government followed public opinion in working towards relations with Russia based on pragmatism, not fear. But this positive development has been set back by Russia's actions in Ukraine, a boon to Poland's limited, but committed, russophobic community.

NOTES

1. Fyodor Dostoyevski, *Dziennik pisarza 1847–1874* (Warsaw: PIW, 1982), vol. 3, p. 293. Quoted in Edmund Lewandowski, *Charakter narodowy polaków i innych*, 3rd edn (Warsaw: MUZA, 2011), p. 54. It is understandable that many Poles regard Dostoyevsky's writings as anti-Polish.

2. Andrzej Nowak, "Rosjanie i Polacy są podobni: rozmowa z Natalią Gorbaniewską," in Nowak (ed.), *Intelektualna historia III RP: Rozmowy z lat 1990–2012* (Warsaw: Sic! 2013), p. 22. For a study of Polish literary figures searching for a non-Soviet Russia see Tadeusz Sucharski, *Polskie poszukiwania "innej" Rosji* (Gdańsk: wydawnictwo słowo/obraz terytoria, 2008).

3. Samuel P. Huntington, *The Clash of Civilizations and the Remaking of World Order* (New York: Simon & Schuster, 1996).

4. Fyodor M. Dostoevskii, *Polnoe sobranie sochinenii v tridsati tomakh* (Leningrad: Nauka, 1972–90), vol. 20, p. 170.

5. Huntington, *The Clash of Civilizations*, p. 138.

6. Artur Dmochowski, "Rosja: mocarstwo schodzące – rozmowa z prof. Andrzejem Nowakiem," in Dmochowski, *Między Unią a Rosją* (Lublin: Wydawnictwo Słowa i Myśli, 2013), pp. 69–70.

7. Andrei P. Tsyankov, "Putin's Crusade," in *New Eastern Europe*, 2, XI, (April–June 2014), pp. 56, 60. See his book which outlines the key structural factors making for American russophobia: Russia's alleged hegemonic political culture, its economic recovery, the relative decline of US power, an uninformed American public plus manipulative US media, and a weak pro-Russia lobby in Washington. *Russophobia: Anti-Russian Lobby and American Foreign Policy* (London: Palgrave Macmillan, 2009).

8. Suna Gülfer Ihlamur Öner, book review of Sevinç Alkan Özcan, *Rusya ve Polonya'da Din, Kimlik, Siyaset* ("Religion, Identity and Politics in Russia and Poland") (Istanbul: Küre Yayınları, 2012), in *Insight Turkey*, 15:3 (spring 2013), p. 206, http://www.insightturkey.com/rusya-ve-polonyada-din-kimlik-siyaset/book-reviews/337

9. See Centrum Badania Opinii Społecznej, "Stosunek polaków do innych narodów" (Warsaw: CBOS, February 2014), BS/20/2014, p. 2, www.cbos.pl.

10. Don Snyder, "Poland Poll Reveals Stubborn Anti-Semitism Amid Jewish Revival Hopes," *Jewish Daily Forward*, 18 January 2014, http://forward.com/articles/191155/poland-poll-reveals-stubborn-anti-semitism-amid-je/?p=all#ixzz3ASzrBMDx

11. See the informative analysis by Irina Tomescu-Dubrow and Kazimierz M. Słomczyński, "Development, Inequality, and Discrimination in Europe: A Comparison of Post-Socialist and West European Democracies." Paper presented at the XVIII World Congress of Sociology, Yokohama, Japan (18 July 2014).

12. Volker Rittberger (ed.), *German Foreign Policy since Unification: Theories and Case Studies* (Manchester: Manchester University Press, 2001), p. 29.

13. Étienne Balibar, *We, the People of Europe? Reflections on Transnational Citizenship* (Princeton, NJ: Princeton University Press, 2004), p. 169.

14. Quoted in Lewandowski, *Charakter narodowy polaków*, p. 125.

15. Rafał Kalukin, "We władzy demonów," *Wprost* (30 January 2011), http://www.wprost.pl/ar/228345/We-wladzy-demonow/

16. I am grateful to Cas Mudde (University of Georgia) for raising this question.

17. Tsygankov, *Russophobia*.
18. Tomasz Zarycki, "Uses of Russia: The Role of Russia in the Modern Polish National Identity," *East European Politics and Societies*, 18 (2004), pp. 599–600. See also his *Ideologies of Eastness in Central and Eastern Europe* (London: Routledge, 2014).
19. Andrzej Nowak, "The Russo-Polish Historical Confrontation," *Sarmatian Review*, 1 (January 1997), http://www.ruf.rice.edu/sarmatia/197/Nowak.html/
20. Paweł Boski, "Rosjanie i stosunki z nimi w ocenie Polaków," in Michał Dobroczyński (ed.), *Polacy i Rosjanie: czynniki zbliżenia* (Warsaw-Toruń: Centrum Badań Wschodnich Uniwersytetu Warszawskiego, Wydawnictwo Adam Marszałek, 1998), pp. 111–26.
21. Based on a 1996 CBOS poll cited in Centrum Badania Opinii Społecznej, *Sytuacja Polski na arenie międzynarodowes* (Warsaw: CBOS, June 2001).
22. Zarycki, "Uses of Russia," p. 614.
23. Ibid., p. 620.
24. See "Putins man varnar för svenskt 'rysshat,'" *SvD Nyheter*, 8 June 2014, http://www.svd.se/nyheter/utrikes/putins-man-varnar-for-svenskt-rysshat_3637670.svd The official was Sergei Markov, co-chair of the National Strategic Council of Russia.
25. Adam Balcer and Kazimierz Wóycicki, *Polska na globalnej szachownicy* (Warsaw: Poltext, 2014), p. 302.
26. Andrzej Walicki, "Rosja Putina a polityka polska," *Przegląd* (23 February 2004).
27. Andrzej de Lazari, Oleg Riabow, and Magdalena Żakowska, *Europa i Niedźwiedź* (Warsaw: Centrum Polsko-Rosyjskiego Dialogu i Porozumienia, 2013), p. 11. For a colorful English-language essay focusing on Poland, see Andrzej de Lazari and Oleg Riabov, "The 'Russian Bear' in Polish Caricature of the Interwar Period (1919–1939)," http://cens.ivanovo.ac.ru/publications/De-Lazari-Riabov-Russian-Bear-Interwar.pdf
28. Ryszard Kiersnowski, *Niedźwiedzie i ludzie w dawnych i nowszych czasach: fakty i mity* (Warsaw: PIW, 1990), p. 13. Cited by de Lazari et al., *Europa i Niedźwiedź*, p. 25.
29. Quoted in Karl Moiseevich Kantor, "Kentavr pered Sfinksom," in Kantor (ed.), *Kentavr pered Sfinksom: Germano-rossijskie dialogi* (Moskva: Centr problem kul'tury, Mezhdunarodnyj fond social'no-jekonomicheskih i politologicheskih issledovanij, (Aprel' 1995), p. 36.
30. Gustave Doré, *Histoire de la Sainte-Russie* (Paris: Hermann, 1996).
31. See Ray Taras, "Snow, ice and vertical drops: what is different about the Sochi Winter Olympics?" in Bo Petersson and Karina Vamling (eds), *The Sochi predicament: Contexts, characteristics and challenges of the Olympic Winter Games in 2014* (Newcastle upon Tyne: Cambridge Scholars Publishing, 2013), pp. 20–40.
32. *Globe and Mail*, 29 October 2011, http://www.theglobeandmail.com/sports/russian-bear-getting-its-figure-skating-growl-back/article559602/
33. Sam Cooper, "Sochi Bear mascot 'blows out' Olympic flame to cap off a great Olympics for bears," *Yahoo.com*, 23 February 2014, http://sports.yahoo.com/blogs/fourth-place-medal/sochi-bear-mascot--blows-out--olympic-flame-to-cap-off-a-great-olympics-for-bears-191619654.html
34. de Lazari et al., *Europa i Niedźwiedź*, p. 269.
35. Ibid., p. 305.
36. Quoted by Lewandowski, *Charakter narodowy polaków*, p. 331.

37. Adam Daniel Rotfeld, *Myśli o Rosji . . . i nie tylko* (Warsaw: Świat Książki, 2012), p. 65.

38. Balcer and Wójcicki, *Polska*, p. 303.

39. On a russo-hypopsic backlash to the expanding idea of compatriots abroad (соотечественники за рубежом), see Oxana Shevel, "Russian nation-building from Yeltsin to Medvedev: Ethnic, civic, or purposefully ambiguous?" Paper presented at the annual meeting of the American Political Science Association (3 August 2010), http://papers.ssrn.com/sol3/papers.cfm?abstract_id=1643541##. Also see my papers, "The simultaneous resurgence of Russia and Russophobia: contemporary stereotypes and enemy images." Paper presented at Clare College, Cambridge University (15 October 2010); "Chronic Russophobia in Poland? Elite and Public Attitudes Compared." Paper presented at the International Council for Central and East European Studies (ICCEES) conference, Stockholm (1 August 2010).

40. Lewandowski, *Charakter narodowy polaków*, p. 48.

41. Ibid., p. 326

42. Anatol Lieven, "Against Russophobia," *World Policy Journal*, 17:4 (winter 2000–01), p. 28. For an early study of the phenomenon, see John Howard Gleason, *The Genesis of Russophobia in Great Britain: A Study of the Interaction of Policy and Opinion* (Cambridge, MA: Harvard University Press, 1950).

43. David Foglesong and Gordon M. Hahn, "Ten Myths about Russia: Understanding and Dealing with Russia's Complexity and Ambiguity," in *Problems of Post-Communism*, 49:6 (November–December 2002), pp. 6–9.

44. Rotfeld, *Myśli o Rosji*, p. 287.

45. Jeffrey Mankoff, *Russian Foreign Policy: The Return of Great Power Politics* (Lanham, MD: Rowman and Littlefield, 2009), p. 300.

46. See Helen V. Milner, *Interests, Institutions, and Information: Domestic Politics and International Relations* (Princeton, NJ: Princeton University Press, 1997), p. 86.

47. Roman Kuźniar, *Poland's Foreign Policy after 1989* (Warsaw: Wydawnictwo SCHOLAR, 2009), p. 258.

48. Antoni Kamiński, "Quality of State Structures, Sovereignty and Eastern Policy of Poland," *Yearbook of Polish Foreign Policy 2000* (Warsaw: Polish Institute of International Affairs, 2000).

49. Joanna A. Gorska, *Dealing with a Juggernaut: Analyzing Poland's Policy Towards Russia, 1989–2004* (Lanham, MD: Rowman and Littlefield, 2011).

50. Andrei Lipski, „S Glubokim Priskorbiem Otmechaem," *Novaya Gazeta*, 2005/10/06 2005. Quoted by Gorska, *Dealing*, p. 158.

51. Lech Kaczyński, in *Rzeczpospolita*, 16 August 2008, http://www.prezydent.pl/x.node?id=18543115

52. "'Shots Fired' near Georgia Leader," *BBC News*, 23 November 2008.

53. Quoted in Jacek Lubecki, "Poland in Iraq: The Politics of the Decision," *Polish Review*, L, no. 1 (2005), pp. 69–92.

54. Kuźniar, *Poland's Foreign Policy*, p. 345.

55. See Christopher S. Chivvis and Thomas Rid, "The Roots of Germany's Russia Policy," *Survival*, 51:2 (April 2009), pp. 105–22.

56. Reeves, "Reopening the Wounds?" pp. 530–1.

57. "Polish Minister Attacks Schröder and Merkel," *Spiegel Online*, 1 May 2006, http://www.spiegel.de/international/0,1518,413969,00.html

58. Quoted in "EU, Russia play down discord after Polish veto," *Agence France Presse*, 24 November 2006.
59. Janusz Bugajski and Ilona Teleki, *Atlantic Bridges: America's New European Allies* (Lanham, MD: Rowman and Littlefield, 2006), p. 39.
60. Nathaniel Copsey and Karolina Pomorska, "Poland's power and influence in the European Union: The case of its eastern policy," *Comparative European Politics*, 8, no. 3, (2010), pp. 313, 318.
61. Reeves, "Reopening the Wounds?" p. 519.
62. Adam Michnik, "Waiting for Freedom, Messing it Up," *New York Times*, 25 March 2007.
63. Centrum Badania Opinii Społecznej, "Opinie o stosunkach polsko-rosyjskich i możliwości pojednania polsko-niemieckiego i polsko-ukraińskiego" (Warsaw: CBOS, July 2008), BS/113/2008, www.cbos.pl
64. "Russia and China Seen Negatively," *BBC News*, 6 February 2009.
65. CBOS, "Opinie o stosunkach polsko-rosyjskich."
66. Centrum Badania Opinii Społecznej, "Stosunek polaków do innych narodów" (Warsaw: CBOS, February 2014), BS/20/2014, p. 7, www.cbos.pl.
67. CBOS, "Stosunek polaków do innych narodów," Tables 2-3, pp. 3-4.
68. Valentina Feklyunina, "Russia's foreign policy towards Poland: Seeking reconciliation? A social constructivist analysis," *International Politics*, 49 (July 2012), pp. 434–48.
69. Jerzy Wiatr, *Polsha i Rossija v cvete istorii i sovremennosti* (St Petersburg: Izbranniye lekcii universiteta: 2013), p. 28.
70. Lieven, "Against Russophobia," p. 25.
71. United States Embassy in Moscow, "Polish PM Tusk's visit to Moscow," telegram no. 08MOSCOW410 (15 February 2008), quoted in Alicja Curanović and Szymon Kardaś, *Rosja w WikiLeaks* (Warsaw: Wydawnictwo Naukowe Scholar, 2011), pp. 121–2.
72. "In a Visit, Putin Tries to Ease Rifts with Poland," *New York Times*, 1 September 2009.
73. "Poland and the Missile Shield – an Interview with Radek Sikorski," *Daily Telegraph*, 20 August 2008.
74. Centrum Badania Opinii Społecznej, "Opinia publiczna o tarczy antyrakietowej" (Warsaw: CBOS, March 2009), BS/45/2009, www.cbos.pl
75. "Russia Alarmed over New EU Pact," *BBC News*, 22 May 2009.
76. Quoted in Radosław Grodzki, *Polska polityka zagraniczna w XX i XXI wieku* (Zakrzewo: Wydawnictwo Replika, 2009), p. 303.
77. "Sikorski v. Komorowski," *The European Courier*, 21 March 2010, http://european courier.org/test/2010/03/21/sikorski-v-komorowski/
78. United States embassy in Warsaw, "Poland: a natural U.S. ally on eastern policy," telegram no, 08WARSAW1409 (12 December 2008), quoted in Curanović and Kardaś, *Rosja*, p. 120.
79. Radosław Sikorski, "I fear Germany's power less than her inactivity," *Financial Times*, 28 November 2011, http://www.ft.com/intl/cms/s/0/b753cb42-19b3-11e1-ba5d-00144feabdc0.html#axzz3AabPV9wU
80. "Tapes Said to Reveal Polish Minister Disparaging U.S. Ties," *New York Times*, 22 June 2014, http://www.nytimes.com/2014/06/23/world/europe/tapes-said-to-reveal-polish-minister-disparaging-us-ties.html?_r=0

81. The analysis did not try to track changes in foreign policy itself. In order to control for the emotional impact of the Smolensk tragedy on respondents' opinions, survey results carried out in January 2010 before the plane crash were also presented. They reveal similar results to the April 2010 ones. Sławomir Wiatr, "Stosunki Polski z sąsiadami w świetle badań opinii publicznej," *Myśl socjaldemokratyczna*, XXII, nos 3/4 (2013), pp. 29–45. The polling agency was Mareco Polska.
82. Ibid.
83. Ibid., p. 32.
84. Karol Modzelewski, *Zajeździmy kobyłę historii. wyznania poobijanego jeźdźca* (Warsaw: ISKRY, 2013), p. 424.
85. "The Pulse of Europe 2009: 20 Years after the Fall of the Berlin Wall," Pew Research, 2 November 2009, http://www.pewglobal.org/2009/11/02/end-of-communism-cheered-but-now-with-more-reservations/
86. Ibid.
87. Levada Center (August 2014), reported in "Putin's electoral rating doubles in 2014," in *Russia Today*, 13 August 2014, http://rt.com/politics/179956-russian-putin-rating-doubles/
88. "An Open Letter to the Obama Administration from Central and Eastern Europe," *Gazeta Wyborcza*, English edn, 15 July 2009.
89. Christopher Meyer, "A Return to 1815 is the Way Forward for Europe," *The Times*, 2 September 2008, http://www.thetimes.co.uk/tto/law/columnists/article2047637.ece,
90. "An Open Letter."
91. Kuźniar, *Poland's Foreign Policy*, p. 338.
92. United States embassy in Warsaw, "Rethinking U.S. force reductions in Europe: view from Poland," telegram no. 09WARSAW876 (28 August 2009), quoted in Curanović and Kardaś, *Rosja w WikiLeaks*, p. 121.
93. Bartosz Marczuk, "Moskwa woli Tuska," *Rzeczpospolita*, 25 June 2014, http://www.rp.pl/artykul/1120898.html
94. Agnieszka Bieńczyk-Missala, "Polska polityka zagraniczna: z Unią Europejską na Majdan," Instytut Stosunków Międzynarodowych Uniwersytetu Warszawskiego, *Rocznik Strategiczny 2013/14* (Warsaw: Wydawnictwo Naukowe SCHOLAR, 2014), p. 304.
95. Marczuk, "Moskwa woli Tuska."
96. Copsey and Pomorska, "Poland's power and influence," p. 312.
97. Ibid., p. 317.
98. Ibid., p. 320.
99. Nathaniel Copsey and Karolina Pomorska, "The Influence of Newer Member States in the European Union: The Case of Poland and the Eastern Partnership," *Europe–Asia Studies*, 66:3, (2014), p. 432.
100. Ibid., p. 435.
101. Ibid., p. 437.
102. Centrum Badania Opinii Społecznej, "Wydarzenie na Ukrainie a poczucie zagrożenia w Europie Środkowo-Wschodniej," no. 59/2014 (Warsaw: CBOS, May 2014), Diagram 4, www.cbos.pl
103. Centrum Badania Opinii Społecznej, "O sytuacji na Ukrainie przed wyborami prezydenckimi," no. 78/2014 (Warsaw: CBOS, May 2014), p. 7, www.cbos.pl
104. Centrum Badania Opinii Społecznej, "Polacy o stosunkach polsko-rosyjskich i poli-

tyce wschodniej polski," no. 77/2014 ((Warsaw: CBOS, May 2014), p. 7, www.cbos. pl

105. ARD-DeutschlandTREND (June 2014), http://www.tagesschau.de/inland/deutsch landtrend-104.pdf

106. "Russia's Global Image Negative amid Crisis in Ukraine," *Pew Research Global Attitudes Project* (9 July 2014), http://www.pewglobal.org/2014/07/09/russias-global-image-negative-amid-crisis-in-ukraine/

107. CBOS, "Stosunek polaków do stron ukraińskiego konfliktu," no. 103/2014 (Warsaw: CBOS, July 2014), p. 3, available at www.cbos.pl

108. CBOS, "Stosunek polaków do innych narodów," pp. 3–4, Tables 2–3.

109. CBOS, "Polacy o stosunkach polsko-rosyjskich," p. 11, Table 5.

110. Kuźniar, *Poland's Foreign Policy*, p. 339.

111. Grzegorz Gromadzki, "Rewolucja niewskazana," *Nowa Europa Wschodnia*, 5 (XIII), (September–October 2010), pp. 42, 31.

CHAPTER SIX

Sweden:
the limits of humanitarianism at home and abroad

Acknowledging fearful attitudes towards others is a courageous act. It may be cathartic, too. It is the first step in preempting the development of prejudice against others. A nation that denies it harbors any fears or suspicions of foreigners – even denies there is such a thing as foreigners – is not coming to terms with a weakness innate to human nature.

In 1588 Michel de Montaigne made the much-quoted statement: "That which we should fear the most is fear itself."[1] The bravado lacing his exhortation represents the antithesis of introspective and humble examination of oneself. But a fear of fear, which may exist in Swedish society, is not a sign of bravado. It is more like a metaphor for choosing to take a road paved with unbridled good intentions. At worst, it represents a fear that Swedes will slip up, in the eyes of others, in their pursuit of noble causes.

This chapter examines whether fears of foreigners exist in Sweden despite a social convention that they should not. Sweden has an enviable record of extending hospitality towards strangers including, in particular, asylum seekers who, in other parts of Europe, are a special target of xenophobes.[2] A focus on war refugees coming from Iraq and Syria, where protracted conflicts have driven millions from their homes, can reveal how well Swedish asylum policy has worked. It may make Sweden's reputed tolerant and inclusionary values even more visible. The causal story can go a step further to describe how these values are reflected in the country's liberal internationalism directed towards the countries of origin of these refugees as well as other distressed societies. Does Swedish foreign policy invariably stress humanitarian concerns over realist considerations which often have the effect of exacerbating conflicts and multiplying refugee flows?

Or will the story be different? Will, in fact, a fear of foreigners living in Sweden, framed and assisted by the media, be as palpable, and at times as dark, as Bo Petersson reported in his book *Stories about Strangers*?[3] Will a "caring multiculturalism" of the kind Sarah Scuzzarello described as attentive and responsive to the specific needs of immigrant communities be bogged down by institutional flaws, as she found in the case of Malmö, Sweden's largest immigrant center?[4] Finally, is a deficient multiculturalism also reflected in an oftentimes flawed foreign policy which does place national interests over humanitarian concerns?

STEREOTYPES AND ATTITUDES

Arguably more than about other countries, stereotypes of Sweden abound in the popular imagination. Many of these are superficial, no more sophisticated than images disseminated by a tourist bureau. But, alongside these are the self-images that Swedes have constructed and propagated. One theme presented is that the country holds the moral high ground through the social policies it adopts at home and the humanitarian policies it pursues abroad.

Swedish authorities like to cite cross-national studies showing the country's ranking at the top, or close to the top, of indices of expenditures on foreign aid, intake of war refugees, opportunities for immigrants (like the MIPEX survey measuring the success of integration of immigrants), empowerment of women, and transparency of government. Labor organizations are credited with creating positive social and economic conditions for workers. If that were not enough achievements, Sweden has been consistently ranked by Transparency International as one of the best countries in the world in which to do business. Even when it appears that Sweden has come up short on a certain index – for instance, few members of minority groups hold positions of power – it turns out that it is not all that bad after all. Sweden is the seventh most socially inclusive country in the world; the United States is the twenty-fifth.[5]

One major failing has been in education. Over the decade examined by the OECD's (Organization for Economic Cooperation and Development) Program for International Student Assessment (PISA), presented in its 2012 report, the average performance of fifteen-year-olds in Sweden declined to below the OECD average in the three core subjects measured – reading, mathematics and science. Moreover, in terms of "classroom environment", allowing each student to concentrate on their work in peace without delay or disruption in their lessons, Sweden was ranked worst in the Western world.[6] It was a finding at odds with the positive image the country projects and led to a national debate on how to improve Sweden's school system.

An ambiguous claim in the list of "firsts," and related to this book's focus on minority groups, is that Sweden was the first European country to discard the policy of multiculturalism as a way of managing diversity.[7] Immigration policy has shifted from a universal model, adopted in 1968, to one prioritizing multicultural policy objectives in 1975. Ten years later it was abandoned in

152

favor of a selective model which, in turn, gave way to a return to universal policy objectives in 2000. Discursive practices changed in tandem with these processes.[8]

An ethos associated with Sweden is political actors' willingness to negotiate with one another and serve the public good. Swedes are attached to the perception that, in this and other ways, the country serves as a model for other countries. "Swedes are a conflict-avoiding species," Göran Rosenberg has written; they are shaped by a "spirit of common understanding, *samförsudhulsanda*."[9]

But a culture of consensus becomes problematic if it develops into an ideology preventing functional decision-making. Susan Sontag warned in 1969 of a "national temperament" producing "a collective historical tradition of emotional disablement" in Sweden.[10] The welfare state, criticized by conservative thinkers, was not to blame, however. For political scientist Sven Steinmo, that was because, in a universal welfare state "everyone benefits and everyone pays." The problem arises when the question is raised "What if the recipient of social welfare payment looks less and less like the payer?"[11] The charge of welfare chauvinism has been made by right-wing populist parties seeking to polarize givers and takers in society. "Parties of discontent" have emerged across Scandinavia to exploit this attitude.[12]

A form of rationality ascribed to Sweden is of moderation, captured by the term *lagom* – reasonableness, measured, being middle of the road.[13] Both in domestic and international contexts, the combination of the virtues of moderation and consensus produce *konflikträdd* – conflict avoidance. As Swedish novelist of Tunisian origin Jonas Hassen Khemiri's character in *Montecore* fumed: "Levels! Levels are the most Swedish instrument in the world. Everything in Swedish must be just right, not too much and not too little!"[14]

Conflict avoidance and moderation were characteristics underscored by Danish journalist Mikael Jalving in his critical analysis of Swedish society. In *Absolut Sverige* he observed how the types of quarrels found in Sweden are not found in Denmark: those pitting atheists against believers, monarchists versus republicans, feminists juxtaposed with gossip media. But, for Jalving, Danes debate immigration and integration, Swedes do not. "In Sweden all think alike and dissenting voices are stifled. In Denmark, they are free and sing out."[15] Jalving concluded that "The Sweden we knew just a few years ago is today only a memory, a fairy tale. The Swedes themselves seem not to care."

A complementary perspective is that, because divisive debates in Sweden over immigration, integration, and identity have now begun, the country stands today where Denmark was a decade ago. As Jalving added: "we all have taboos but in Sweden having taboos is preferable to criticizing them. You see this in areas like immigration and the integration of people from

---

Box 6.1 An exchange on being absolute between two Swedish women in a village on a winter's day

Anna leaned across the table and said, "Katri, there is something about you that's too . . ." she searched for the word ". . . absolute. And it leads nowhere."

"Too absolute?" Katri said. "And it leads nowhere?" She put out her cigarette. "If anyone is absolute, it's you. And it leads straight where you want it to lead."

Source: Tove Jansson, *The True Deceiver* (New York: New York Review Books, 2009; first published in 1982), pp. 178–9.

Muslim countries, feminism, prostitution, authority, nationality, crime and punishment, even the approach to schooling."[16]

A study of how Danish and Swedish policies on immigration integration diverged in the late 1960s found that Danish policy-makers "urged immigrants to either adopt ethnic Danes' cultural beliefs and practices or to contain their culture to the private sphere." By contrast,

> In Sweden, cultural policies celebrated ethnocultural difference. Prior to the 1990s, policy-makers operated in accordance with the belief that immigrants' well-being was contingent on them being able to enjoy their cultures. After this period, they promoted the notion of ethnocultural diversity as a source of cultural enrichment – another dimension of the celebration of difference – and more diversity, not less, was posited as necessary to fight xenophobia and discrimination.[17]

Apart from *lagom,* then, another attitude in Swedish customary practices is *absolut* (the word appearing in the title of Javling's book; see Box 6.1). It would not be inaccurate to identify "absolute moderation" as a defining Swedish value. An "ABSOLUT-ly upright Sweden" (to borrow the upper case from a now privatized Swedish vodka brand), is not fiction. Anders Hellström's *Vi är de Goda* ("We are the Good"), a study of the moral panic and righteousness found in Swedish debates about the right-wing Sweden Democrats Party which first won seats to the Riksdag (parliament) in 2010, captures the phenomenon of absolute moderation well.[18]

Challenging positive stereotypes

Sweden enjoys an overwhelmingly positive image abroad even if for historical and cultural reasons Danes, Norwegians, and Finns remain skeptical. The image is at a point when one writer cautioned: "when foreign observers overpraise Sweden, one should take it with a large pinch of salt." English-speaking societies are especially charmed by Swedish myth-making: "some Anglo-Saxon observers tend to find their own version of paradise in Sweden, and Swedes, just like those from any other nation, love to have their own positive prejudices confirmed."[19] Swedes' proficiency in English contributes to the appeal as does appearing to be Americanized through its popular culture.

For a long time the uncontested master narrative was of a postwar Sweden that had become economically and socially the world's most progressive country thanks to the policies of the Social Democratic Party, the welfare state it built, and the non-threatening feel-good socialism it embraced. As a writer parodied, "Put simply, Sweden is the best place in the world and the country's greatness is only jeopardized when the voters are stupid enough to elect non-Social Democratic governments. And when they do, as they have for the last two elections [2006 and 2010], it 'feels like a coup d'état.'"[20] In these terms the 2014 election would mark a return to "greatness."

Perceptions of Sweden as a utopian welfare state, of an affluent but sharing society, and of a welcoming and receiving society for immigrants have been tested by recent developments. "The myth of Sweden as the 'perfect society' could have disappeared in the 1970s when it turned out to be a country with qualities and flaws just like any other. But it did not, and the myth continues until this day."[21] The 1986 murder of Social Democrat Prime Minister Olof Palme is identified as a turning point when Sweden lost its innocence. Soon after, Sweden moved from a one-party-dominant system, led by the Social Democrats, to a competitive multiparty system. With this transition, much of the idealist, even utopian, thought about the country vanished.[22] Sweden's public intellectuals challenge the stereotype of an absolutely moral Sweden in ways that outside observers frequently fail to do. They point to evidence suggesting the presence of xeno-hypopsia in Sweden.

Is Sweden a false utopia, then? For Nima Sanandaji, a Swedish writer of Kurdish background, "An important part of morality is acknowledging immorality and social issues. Sweden does not do this. Instead, the country suffers from a taboo on taboos." A fear of fear itself, perhaps. "As other countries, it has issues, but unlike other countries, denies them. It has a deep 'phobia of phobias' that leads to very negative attitudes that nobody even thinks of condemning because they pretend that they do not exist." At a basic level "In the social sphere, the Swedish refuse to acknowledge cultural and ethnic differences within the population."[23] Not surprisingly, in 2014, Integration Minister Erik Ullenhag went as far as to claim in a television interview: "We know that different human races actually do not exist." The policy consequence is that, by the end of 2015, all references to race are to be removed from Swedish legislation.[24]

Challenging pristine views of Scandinavian societies is the task that "Nordic Noir," the crime fiction wave originating in Sweden and its neighbors, has undertaken. Grotesque imagery of these countries' under-worlds evokes and exaggerates the unspoken fears pervading them. One novelist disingenuously claimed that Nordic states produce so much crime fiction because there is so little crime in the region. But another writer, Henning Mankell, held the opposite view. He insisted his novels were about reality: "What I try to do is maybe give a more realistic view of Sweden . . . Sometimes it's needed to take a torch and look into the dark corners" of what he maintained was a "very decent country." In this way he wanted to be part of "Sweden's conscience."[25]

Stieg Larsson, journalist and author of the Millennium trilogy, sensational-ized the dark dealings of Swedish authorities more than anyone. His focus was on the corrupt, criminal practices of the country's closed social and political establishment. In the 1980s

> To enter the world of Swedish politics and policy is to enter a small, ingrown realm of group decision-making, in which a professional class of politicians, administra-tors, and interest-group functionaries must constantly expect to keep dealing with one another.[26]

The center-right Bonnier media consortium contributes to a perception of hermetic groupthink found in Stockholm-based elites. One Swede-hypopsic writer observed: "The Sweden of Henning Mankell and Stieg Larsson – all shadowy rightwing conspiracies and prostitution rings – might not be so far from the truth."[27]

A special concern of Stieg Larsson's was the vulnerability of women in the world's purportedly most feminist society. Sweden consistently ranks among the top countries in empowerment-of-women measures. This positively affects its foreign policy, the argument persuasively elaborates, because "states with empowered women *do* make better global citizens in certain critical areas. More sex-equitable countries are more likely to support international commitments against state violence against individuals."[28]

Exposés of Swedish pathologies had been published well before the Millennium trilogy. None was more traumatic and dystopian than novelist Karin Boye's *Kallocain* appearing in 1940. A Swedish *Brave New World*, the story's main character is Leo Kall, a chemist who develops a truth drug in the service of the early surveillance state:

> And please do not think my opinion originates from some civilian superstition that the State exists for our sake, instead of we for the State, as is indeed the fact. I only mean that the kernel of the matter, the individual cell's relationship to the state-organism, lies in the hunger for security.[29]

The panopticon that Boye was describing could have been the Sweden of the 1930s, though more likely it was the German Third Reich or Stalinist

Russia. Fears, suspicions, and the search for security were as palpable in Linda Kall's life with an inscrutable mad scientist working for the state in *Kallocain* as with Larsson's main character, Lisbeth Salander, in *The Girl with the Dragon Tattoo*. Or, more bluntly, as an immigrant father despaired in Jonas Hassen Khemiri's novel, *Montecore*, "For this is the truth about the country we call Sweden, civilized on the surface but barbaric in the structure of thought."[30]

Literary dilettantes have highlighted the fears, suspicions, and threats of average people living in Swedish society. A special group of mavericks comprises hackers who also challenge positive stereotypes of Sweden. These include *WikiLeaks* founder, Julian Assange, and *Pirate Bay* pioneer, Gottfrid Svartholm Warg, who were both pursued by Sweden's justice system. As a result, despite its impressive human rights record "the incestuous nature of Swedish elites – and the country's burgeoning right wing – formed a perfect storm that helped create the peculiar sex-related charges against Assange."[31] Sweden was also identified as a "slacker" in reacting to the Snowden revelations about US National Security Agency (NSA) spying.[32] United States lobbying in Stockholm on surveillance and data-collection rules shaped a Swedish approach which was in denial that hackers have human rights.

Sweden has one of the highest rates of cases brought to the European Court of Human Rights relating to Article 6.1 – the right to a fair trial. Many trials are not held in public, jury selection can be arbitrary, and political interference in reaching verdicts is not unknown. Pre-trial detention in a prison may be lengthy and harsh.[33] The judicial process appears at odds with the fundamental Swedish sense of fairness.

Foundations of stereotypes

The diaries of Gustav Badin, an eighteenth-century Afro-Caribbean slave who, by good and bad fortune, found himself in the Swedish royal court, offer a rare and at times troubling insight into the remembering and forgetting of the stereotyped, in contrast to the richly documented selective memory of those who do the stereotyping. Badin was infrequently mentioned in history books on Sweden of that period.

The country's history is enviable compared to that of France or Poland. "By escaping wars since the Napoleonic Era and moralizing to the world about correct values and courses of action, Sweden has gained an enviable reputation as a nation above many of the problems afflicting other lands."[34] Political scientist Ulf Bjereld emphasized how "Sweden is unique in Europe in that we have not been in a real war in 200 years. This long period of peace has for many come to be associated with Sweden's freedom from military alliances and the neutrality policy that characterized Swedish security policy." As a result, "Neutrality and non-alignment have become part of the Swedish self-image and a valued expression of the country's independence and autonomy. These types of national self-images tend to stick and are difficult to change."[35]

In their look at nineteenth-century Sweden, anthropologists Jonas Frykman and Orvar Löfgren focused on the idea of Swedish morality: "In their development of a new moral system the bourgeoisie tried to distance themselves from the classes above and below them, from the old nobility with its prodigal life-style and from the gray mass of the people with their lack of discipline and culture."[36] But the peasantry was also stereotyped as embodying honesty and honor, and this peaceful countryside image was promoted as the basis for a common national identity. By the turn of the twentieth century identity-making was usurped by the state: "Sweden's government possessed the dual roles of provider and liberal teacher."[37]

After World War I fear of the consequences of nationalism and exclusionary national identity sapped Swedish interest in defining its own self. According to Leigh Oakes, "The breakthrough of social democracy in Sweden in the 1920–1930s, coupled with the racial theories developed by the Nazis, led to the discrediting of the concepts of national identity and nationalism. In short, it became more or less taboo to discuss Swedishness."[38] If an identity was constructed, it was of a political rather than ethnic kind: "Swedish national identity has come to be tightly linked to the welfare state, understood not simply as a set of institutions but as the realization of *folkhemmet*, the 'people's home'". This people's home was quickly to develop into a *folkstat*, or people's state.[39] (Box 6.2)

Per Albin Hansson, Social Democratic prime minister heading a national unity government in the 1930s, first introduced the concept of *folkhemmet*

Box 6.2 Euro-hypopsia in 1930s Sweden

Swedish national identity has become tightly linked to the welfare state. Swedes came to see themselves as the most modern of peoples, inhabiting the very model of the future. The deep-seated suspicion of Europe that is so characteristic of the Swedes can be viewed as the reversal of the German desire to become European. From the vantage point of the most democratic and equal nation in the world, Europe to the south of Denmark could only be imagined as a bastion of neo-feudalism, papism, patriarchy, hierarchy, disorder, and inequality. This attitude is reinforced by the extreme statism of the Swedish social contract, which involves a marked hostility towards continental notions like federalism, subsidiarity, or civil society.

Source: Nina Witoszek and Lars Trägårdh, "Introduction," in Witoszek and Trägårdh (eds), *Culture and Crisis: The Case of Germany and Sweden* (New York: Berghahn Books, 2002), p. 7.

in 1928. He also made Sweden's democratic values a pillar of its neutrality policy which "sought to offset a concrete danger (invasion) with a rhetorical glorification of the 'essence' of the nation."[40]

The evolving Swedish model was "built on a social contract between a strong and good state, on the one hand, and the emancipated and autonomous individual, on the other . . . The state and the people were conceived of as intrinsically linked: the *state* was imagined as the institutional hard shell of the homely domain of *national* community."[41] The state became a quasi-religion, the church became *statskyrka* (a state church), Social Democratic principles became sacralized, and the *folk* (or ethnos) became the demos, the central metaphor of the national socialist welfare state.[42] A Social Democratic poster from the 1930s put it concisely if not humbly: "the way of democracy is the Swedish way."[43]

But Oakes found that

> there was nevertheless a certain irony in the playing down of [ethnic] Swedish nationalism in the 1930s to 1980s. Sweden exhibited a new type of nationalism, portraying itself as the world's conscience and a model for other countries to follow. Economic success and consequent high standards of living served only to reinforce this self-righteous and ethnocentric image.[44]

A non-ethnic conceptualization of self led paradoxically to universalist pretensions.

Sweden has no history of developing an exclusionary national identity. Its self-image is of a non-national (therefore civic), rational, independent, egalitarian society held together by solidarity. Steinmo pointed to the connection between this self-image and its future immigration policy: "the Swedish sense of self required that they open their borders to huge numbers of political refugees and immigrants."[45]

Swedish Social Democracy can be summarized in five ideological precepts: integrative democracy, the people's home, the complementarity of equality and efficiency, a socially controlled market economy, and the public sector as means to freedom.[46] *Jantelagen* – Jante's law – is often cited as the basis of egalitarianism: it criticizes overachieving behavior as inappropriate and undignified. Similar to the 1930s Soviet idea of *uravnilovka* or leveling down, the norm appears across Scandinavia; indeed, it was Aksel Sandemose, a Danish–Norwegian novelist, who conceived of the law in 1933.[47] As for the importance of a regulated market and vibrant public sector, it is argued that "even liberal values require large doses of social policy and public intervention in the economy if citizens are to enjoy freedom in anything more than an empty formal sense."[48]

For popular writer and psychiatrist, David Eberhard, Swedish society exhibits an exaggerated need for security and control. This has produced a "national panic syndrome" causing a Swedish addiction to safety at all times and to living insulated lives.[49] The state's chief responsibility is to provide security and certainty – *säkerhet*. This has led to learned helplessness and other pathologies among average citizens.[50]

Domestic factors that typically create conditions for the growth of xenophobia – cleavages based on religion, region, and ethnicity – have largely been absent in Sweden. International divisions have been breached, too. By the 1960s, Sweden had become a non-aligned state committed to international aid, disarmament, and decolonization. But Alan Pred caught the double-sidedness of this image:

> ... most adult Swedes, whether deeply committed to Social Democratic notions of solidarity and social justice or to liberal humanitarianism, had long viewed themselves as the most egalitarian of egalitarians, as truly True believers in tolerance, while regarding their country as a champion of the elsewhere oppressed, as a moral superpower on the world stage, as the world's most fearless voice against racism, as the world's most active opponent to its practice in South Africa and the United States.[51]

The image of selflessness is pivotal. It shapes policy on accepting, integrating, and empowering immigrants. Its message is to ask not what immigrants can do for Sweden but what Sweden can do for immigrants.[52]

One effect of striving to be a normative superpower is that admitting to prejudice may tarnish this effort and is taboo. In some ways, then, a taboo on taboos has been enforced in Sweden.[53] Fear of showing fear is linked to the taboo. Displaying fear is considered inappropriate when waging a grander moral battle. Some historians and sociologists attribute this rationale to a stoical Calvinist streak in the national character but I identify selective instrumentalization of traditional images and self-images as the main cause. Thus, acknowledging fear of foreigners is not politically correct and it also is socially inappropriate behavior.

The principle of ethical treatment of foreigners has gained in importance as the numbers of war refugees coming to Sweden, most recently from Iraq and Syria, grow. The Swedish state's policies on their reception and integration, as well as on dealing with the governments of their countries of origin – why these refugees were caught up in internal wars and forced to flee – are connected to the humanitarian goals that Sweden has set for itself.

STRANGERS IN SWEDEN

If Sweden was a homogeneous society up to 1945, it became diversified as refugees, at first mainly from other Nordic countries, returned home after World War II. Labor needs in the 1960s and 1970s were filled by Europeans, though a guest worker program of the kind developed in Germany was never adopted. From the 1970s on refugees became the most important component in the country's migration inflow. As Pieter Bevelander and Inge Dahlstadt observed,

> Major contributors to the immigrant population in the 1970s were refugees from Chile, Poland and Turkey. In the 1980s, the major immigrant groups came from Chile, Ethiopia, Iran and other Middle Eastern countries. In the 1990s, immigration from Iraq, former Yugoslavia and other Eastern European countries dominated. A similar pattern has been observed for the past decade, with Iraqis, Iranians and people from the former Yugoslavia and Somalis being the major immigrant groups.[54]

A 1975 parliamentary bill set three principles for immigration policy: 1. immigrants' equality in terms of rights and obligations; 2. their freedom of cultural choice (retaining their homeland culture, adopting Swedish culture, or accepting a blend of the two); 3. cooperation and solidarity between Swedes and ethnic minorities. Perhaps consciously, perhaps not, these three principles corresponded to the ideas of *liberté, égalité, fraternité* of the French Revolution.[55] A 1999 government report identified an additional imperative: recognition of the complex makeup of modern identities.[56]

For Scott McIver, transforming aliens into citizens is the embodiment of a trinity of ideas: integration, equality, and belonging.[57] More than in other receiving countries, conferring citizenship on new arrivals is the cornerstone of Sweden's policy of integrating immigrants. In 1999, the Riksdag passed a bill titled "Sweden, the future and diversity: from a politics for immigrants to a politics for integration." It shifted the policy agenda from managing immigration to promoting integration. Conferring Swedish citizenship and recognizing dual citizenship were means towards this new primary goal.

The post-1999 emphasis on integration could be understood in many ways but a key was diversity (*mångfald*) rather than multiculturality (*mångkultur*) as the basis of the new integration strategy (Box 6.3). Although there was some pushback under the Moderate Party-led governments from 2006 to 2014, the political incorporation of immigrants through citizenship remains a vital component of social integration policy alongside labor market participation and access to housing, education, social security, public services, and cultural life.[58]

Between 1980 and 2010 the immigrant population nearly doubled. In 2010 the foreign-born share of Sweden's total population was nearly 15 percent and another 4.4 percent were descendants of immigrants. About a quarter of the immigrant population was of Nordic origin (the largest was 12 percent from Finland), a third originated from other European countries (Yugoslavia

---

Box 6.3 Integration labyrinth

[What followed the 1999 Swedish parliamentary act was] a move from
what might be termed "exclusive multiculturalism" – a society divided
between "us and them" where we (the majority and native population)
tolerate them – towards "inclusive multiculturalism," where "us and them"
becomes "us" characterized as a diverse group. In this way, emphasis on
"integration" thus becomes integration to a pluralist society, as opposed
to assimilation to a monocultural host society. And multiculturalism is
about supporting integration and diversity rather than a toleration of others
living separately but alongside the majority society.

Source: Scott Iain McIver, "Conceptualizations of citizenship in Sweden and
the United Kingdom: An empirical study and analysis of how 'citizenship' is
understood in policy and by policy-makers." PhD thesis, Politics, School of Social
and Political Studies, University of Edinburgh, 2009, pp. 35–6.

---

and Bosnia together made up 9 percent, Poland 5 percent), and the remain-
der from non-European countries (led by Iraqis with almost 9 percent).[59]

Large numbers of asylum seekers from the former Yugoslavia and Somalia
were admitted in the 1990s. But I concentrate here on asylum for refugees
from the wars in Iraq and Syria during the first and second decades of this
century. Today Iraqis (over 125,000 who were born in Iraq) make up the
second largest minority group (Finns remain first with half a million, only
160,000 of whom were born in Finland). The size of the Iraqi community
doubled between 2002 and 2009. About 15,000 Syrians (out of a total Syrian
refugee total of over two million since the civil war started in 2012) were
taken in by Sweden by mid 2014. The Swedish government granted permanent residency to all refugees from Syria making it the first European Union
member state to do this.

Can we identify fear and distrust among the Swedish public towards these
groups of immigrants and refugees? If so, has it also had an impact on the
country's policies towards war-ravaged Middle Eastern states?

Attitudes towards immigrants

Immigration in Sweden is not seen as important an issue as welfare, health,
and education. In contrast to Denmark and Norway, it is not a valiance
issue pitting those supporting a restrictive policy against others preferring a
generous approach. Swedish attitudes have been characterized by tolerance
towards immigrants and refugees: indeed, much Swedish research highlights

these favorable societal attitudes. Since 1986, the SOM Institute ("Society, Opinion, Media") at Gothenburg University has measured these attitudes. Before then, as early as the 1960s, qualitative data suggesting discrimination towards almost all immigrant groups and minorities could be found. One study, focusing on the 1990s, chronicled systematic Swedish discrimination towards immigrants, that is, "invandrare, originally Swedish for immigrants but by 1990 an almost derisive term that is meant to encompass anyone without ethnic Swedish birth or roots."[60]

SOM results indicate a decrease in unfavorable views of immigrants between 1993 and 2004 from 52 percent to 42 percent.[61] The numbers of respondents who completely agreed with the statement "there are too many foreigners in Sweden" fell from 52 percent in 1993 to 36 percent in 2010. Those who completely agreed with the statement "I would not like having an immigrant from another part of the world married into my family" fell from 25 percent to 12 percent in those years.[62] In 2014, an EU-high 91 percent of Swedes agreed or totally agreed with the statement that "immigrants contribute a lot to my country." The EU average was just 48 percent.[63]

Political scientist Marie Demker found that Swedes lent strong support for an assimilationist policy towards immigrants (80 percent in favor) instead of a multicultural model (only 20 percent in favor). High levels of tolerance towards foreigners are linked then to the idea that they will become Swedish. An attitudinal cleavage exists, however, between those of Swedish and those of foreign backgrounds. Nearly half (47 percent) of ethnic Swedes want fewer refugees and immigrants while only 22 percent of non-European-born residents agree. Similarly, 21 percent of ethnic Swedes support cultural recognition of foreigners; 61 percent of non-European born residents are in favor.[64]

Earlier immigrants to Sweden were mainly Lutheran, Orthodox or Catholic but, since the late 1980s, Muslims have represented the major group of settlers. On the subject of religious freedom, then, Swedish opinion has become slightly more restrictive: whereas 41 percent of respondents in 1993 agreed completely that "immigrants in Sweden should be free to exercise their religion" the proportion fell to 38 percent in 2010. The decrease is insignificant but, given that respondents had been expressing more tolerant views on other aspects of immigration, this bucked the trend and probably reflected a more skeptical attitude towards the growing presence of Islam.

A social taboo prevents directly expressing negative views about Islam. When unfavorable attitudes about "foreign" religions are discernable, they are therefore couched in terms of the status of women, religious clothing, food restrictions, and so on, and are decoupled from ethnicity. The religious debate focuses on gender equality, religious education, freedom of speech, clothing, sexuality, food restrictions, and holidays, all of which bring up differences in Christian and Muslim approaches.[65] Municipal Islamophobia affecting Europe's large immigrant-bearing communities is also relevant. Demker concluded that xenophobia in Sweden is decreasing but "has roots in local traditions, local public opinion and local strongholds."[66] Chief among these is Malmö.

Results of a survey of five thousand schoolchildren aged between sixteen and eighteen, conducted in 2009, largely confirmed patterns found in an earlier 2003 poll. But the fact that more than twice the number of respondents (38 percent to 18 percent) expressed positive attitudes towards immigrants than did negative ones seemed to augur well for social cohesion. There is a caveat: respondents of Swedish background had a 34 to 20 percent positive to negative ratio (46 percent were ambivalent). Those of foreign background had significantly more positive attitudes: 55 to 9 percent (36 percent ambivalent).[67]

Disaggregating the data further, ethnic Swedes were more sympathetic to Jews than those of non-Swedish background were. Just the reverse was true about attitudes towards Muslims: ethnic Swedes were more negative, those of non-Swedish background more positive.[68] These patterns in part help to explain why the 1,500 or so Jews living in Malmö, Sweden's third largest city with a population of over 300,000 (of whom as many as a quarter may be Muslim), have been victims of increasing anti-Semitic incidents.

A question probing the sources of Swedishness asked "What is required for someone to be able to say they're Swedish?" In terms of what is absolutely necessary, the breakdown of responses was: respect for Swedish government and laws (68 per cent); Swedish residency (54 percent); being a Christian (3 percent); following Swedish culture and traditions (18 percent); having a job and home in Sweden (25 percent); being born in Sweden (24 percent).[69] Civic qualities were therefore the most crucial.

Are foreigners in the country subject to differential treatment? Officially they are not but a discernable ethnic hierarchy emerges when using a classic social distance scale ranging from 1 (least distance) to 6 (most distance). Respondents in 2010 rated the three other Nordic nations as being less than 2 points in distance. Northern Europeans including English and Germans also comprised an in-group in comparison to more "foreign" nations: Poles, Croatians, Russians, Bosnians, and Serbs (in that order) were identified as 4 to 5 points distant from Swedes. Above 5 came Turks, Kurds, Iranians, Iraqis, Roma, and Somalis. These results furnish no proof of Swedish xenophobia, only of perceptions of difference.

Across Europe, Arab Muslim males are victims of substantial labor market discrimination, and evidence indicates this occurs in Sweden as well. A study of Swedish employers' implicit associations towards this group found significant negative attitude bias revealed by the Implicit Association Test (IAT). It was substantiated by the large number of employers in the sample who *explicitly* associated this group, relative to native Swedish males, with lower productivity. IAT results showed that 94 percent of those tested exhibited slight implicit attitude bias, but 49 percent explicitly reported having more negative feelings towards Arab Muslims than towards native Swedish males. The implicit–explicit discrepancy was even more pronounced for stereotypes of productivity: 78 percent implicitly associated Arab Muslim males with less productivity but only 12 percent explicitly stated this.[70] The fear of expressing fear and bias in Sweden is exposed in these implicit-explicit discrepancies.

A separate study compared ethnic hiring discrimination based on whether the applicant had an Arabic- or Swedish-sounding male name, and whether he appeared warm and/or competent in the personal job application letter. The field experiment involved submitting fictive applications for 5,636 job openings posted by the Swedish Employment Agency. As predicted by the study, substantial discrimination was evidenced in "Arab" applicants receiving fewer invitations to job interviews.

Consistent with stereotypes of Arabs, an applicant with an Arabic-sounding name had to appear both warm and competent in order to be on an (almost) equal footing with applicants with Swedish-sounding names. As the study observed, "Another way to view the results for the Swede is that he needs to disprove both his warmth and competence to have his chances reduced. Importantly, we can also see that gaining only warmth *or* competence provides no (not even marginally significant) increase for the Arab applicant."[71]

In a choice between hiring a cold and incompetent Swedish applicant and a warm and competent Arab one, the first still has higher probability of getting an interview. Again, we find discrimination coded in stereotypes which furnishes signs of suspicion of strangers – xeno-hypopsia. This pattern makes the observation of former prime minister and foreign minister, Carl Bildt, seem inaccurate: "Muslims in Sweden today are as much Muslim as Swedes are Christian. They are Calvinist in their ethics, work, and entrepreneurship."[72]

The state and discrimination

Apart from job discrimination, "foreigners" have increasingly been victims of hate crimes in Sweden. A 2014 report found that "Africanophobia", in particular, has emerged as a problem. Between 2008 and 2012 hate crimes committed against Afro-Swedes, who total about 180,000, rose by 24 percent. Ninety percent of targets were sub-Saharans. This was taking place at a time when hate crimes in general decreased by 6 percent.[73]

Further marring Sweden's migration and integration record is a 2013 ruling by the Council of Europe's European Committee on Social Rights (ECSR) which charged Sweden with failing to guarantee equal rights for foreign guest workers. The ECSR backed up the original 2007 decision by the European Court of Justice. The Moderate Party-led conservative alliance had made it harder for unions to enforce collective action in defense of foreign workers' rights.[74] The ruling recommended strengthening safeguards against mistreatment of migrant workers.

Refoulement – rendering a victim of persecution back to the persecutor – has also caused controversy in Sweden, notably of Iraqi citizens sent back to Iraq. Sweden is charged with regularly violating the *non-refoulement* principle. It is also one of most restrictive European Union states in granting access to rights for irregular migrants. Denial of health care to non-residents, limitations on their human rights, and immigration control measures have made Sweden riskier for migrants to settle in permanently.

Data collected between 2001 and 2013 by Statistics Sweden found that of all EU member states Sweden was the worst to be in for foreigners entitled to stay but looking for a job. It registered the widest gap between locals and non-nationals in "unemployment discrimination." The reverse was true in Poland which had higher rates of unemployment than Sweden. There, foreigners found work more quickly than locals. The Statistics Sweden report suggested patronizingly that immigrants in Sweden are less willing to do "any type of work" than their counterparts in Poland.[75]

In 2012 the unemployment rate among immigrants was 18 percent compared to 7 percent among the native born. This difference was the more significant given unemployed immigrants searched more intensely for work than unemployed Swedes but their job applications were often ignored. Because of their high unemployment levels, 57 percent of welfare payments were directed to immigrant households.[76] Inevitably, in 2013, riots broke out in several Stockholm suburbs having high numbers of foreign-born residents.[77]

Reforms to the system of immigrant integration adopted in 2010 by the reelected conservative alliance government have not produced results, therefore. At the time, newly appointed Integration Minister Erik Ullenhag (from a conservative party allied to the Moderates) reported candidly how

> Today it takes seven years for the average refugee to find work after they've received a residence permit. After three years in the country, only 30 percent of refugees have work. The foreign-born have a 20 percent lower employment rate than the general population, results in school are worse, and there are entire neighborhoods that are in a downward spiral.[78]

Ullenhag blamed two features of the existing integration system for creating these problems. One was that "the policy has been characterized by too much handholding. Refugees and immigrants have been treated as weak

166

individuals, although it is often the most driven people who leave their homelands." Second, the system "was created on the basis that all immigrants need the same support. We have had Swedish language classes for immigrants with standards that are too low."

The December 2010 reforms had been designed to break the hand-holding mentality. New arrivals would register with the Public Employment Service to help obtain jobs rather than with Social Services to file for benefits. Benefits ("compensation") were to become individualized and would be paid in full only when newcomers took part in "establishment initiatives" such as Swedish language classes. "Societal orientation classes", providing a basic understanding of Swedish society, became mandatory as part of new arrivals' "establishment."

Journalist Lars Åberg described the counterproductive tendency in Sweden to depict immigrants as exotic: "In our ambition to be compassionate and sympathetic – good ambitions! – we've created a special sort of being: the more or less immature newcomer." The approach meant that "people are never afforded an individual identity but are instead treated like demanding members of some clan in need of special treatment."[79] Novelist Khemiri lashed out: "what is more 'Swediotic' than to attach people to their ethnicities? Who does this better than the Swedes?"[80]

Åberg argued that an administrative system has been built based on sympathy for those who move to Sweden. Acknowledging that "The rest of the world considers the Swedes to be tolerant and generous," he cautioned that "Only in Sweden is this generosity perceived and portrayed as humiliating, discriminatory, and xenophobic." It is complemented by "condescending tolerance." Åberg concluded: "One can still hear people speak about 'our immigrants' as if they were pets or birds that one feeds in the park."[81]

Ironically, in the twenty-first century, Swedes themselves have, to a degree, become an emigrant nation again (after the nineteenth-century wave to the United States). Many make what some traditional Swedes regard as a humiliating move to wealthy Norway.

> It is bizarre to think of modern Sweden, so often lauded as a paragon of social and economic stability, as coughing up migrant workers. Stranger still is that Swedes migrate in extraordinary numbers to neighboring Norway, which has always been regarded in both countries as Sweden's little brother.[82]

A reversal of roles has taken place. About fifty thousand Swedes live in Oslo making up 10 percent of its population. Many work in the service industry or have other menial jobs. A degree of Norwegian *Schadenfreude* is inevitable, and a popular mockumentary series on Norwegian television is titled "Swedes are People" – mischievously suggesting that Norwegians should not treat them as pets.

FEARS OF FOREIGNERS AFTER 2006

Legislative elections in 2006 led to the ousting of the Social Democrats and the formation of a conservative government alliance headed by the Moderate Party. Campaigning on the unemployment issue and led by a down-to-business politician, Fredrik Reinfeldt, it captured 26 percent of the vote. If, across Europe, anti-immigrant movements were gaining strength, the 2006 election showed that Sweden was not yet part of the trend. Even at the time of the 2010 election, one British journalist insisted that "Against this troubled background, Sweden has long seemed aloof and immune, an oasis of civility and openness, with the most generous welfare, asylum, and immigration policies in Europe."[83]

But there were warning signs of change as an openly anti-immigrant party, the Sweden Democrats (SD), registered an electoral caesura: "with about 100,000 immigrants entering a country of almost 9 million every year, [Jimmy] Åkesson's breakthrough suggests there has been a shift in the public mood."[84] In 2010 this party won nearly 6 percent of the vote and twenty Riksdag seats. Pia Kjaersgaard, head of the anti-immigrant *Dansk Folkeparti*, was pleased enough to exclaim how "Sweden is becoming a normal country." In Sweden itself, the response to SD success was a coalition-building effort across government–opposition lines to ensure SD deputies would be ostracized. But the greatest trauma caused by anti-immigrant forces was inflicted neither in Denmark nor Sweden but in Norway: the cold-blooded killing of seventy-seven people in 2011 by a Norwegian claiming to act in self-defense against the Islamization of Norway.

In 2008 the Moderate Party-led alliance made labor migration policy more flexible by shifting the onus on to employers to assess their foreign labor needs. After all, the logic went, they were in the best position to know what skills were needed. But this shift made no difference to the 80 percent of immigrants who had received residence permits in the past decade and were reuniting family members or refugees rather than labor migrants.

Resettled refugees not joining relatives or friends are the one immigrant group that do not have the option of settling in a municipality of their choosing. If accepted by Sweden, they are issued a permanent residence permit and assigned to a municipality where accommodation is prearranged before their arrival.

In 2011 the governing alliance concluded an agreement with the opposition Green Party to facilitate passage of a law giving illegal immigrants access to health care and education. Green leader Maria Wetterstrand insisted that the agreement reinforced Sweden's generous asylum and immigration policies. This tactical alliance supports Mikael Spång's argument that the two major parties, Social Democrats and Moderates, are usually on the same side, favoring more restrictive refugee and family reunification policy. Smaller parties, such as Greens, Christian Democrats, Lefts, and Liberals, advocate less restrictive policies. So "although Swedish immigration *policy* has become increasingly Europeanized, immigration *politics* have been less affected."[85]

SD leader Åkesson agreed that the Moderate–Green agreement would further liberalize immigration policy. But he was convinced it would then result in a strong anti-immigrant backlash benefiting his party.[86] His thinking was simple: the more immigrants in Sweden, the greater the distrust Swedes will have of them.

Immigration policy adopted by the conservative alliance revealed the tension between the government's right to regulate immigration and the rights of migrants. Spång noted: "The fact that these tendencies are visible in the same time span further suggests that they are causally related."[87] Arguments advanced in the Swedish parliament legitimating restrictions on immigration often invoke the need to protect social and economic rights and political stability, and, for right-wing deputies, to preserve national culture. Yet "Refugee policy has often been thought to be beyond such considerations; a rights-based and generous refugee policy has long been considered a cornerstone of Swedish policy."[88] Thus, the SD's 2014 program spoke of a humanitarian refugee policy, not its abolition.

Parliament has generally preferred more liberal policies than the ones favored by the government. The Riksdag has placed a stronger emphasis on migrants' rights. But immigration is a policy field dominated by government and bureaucracy, with nongovernmental organizations, interest groups, and religious associations preparing and advising on policy.

In the run-up to the 2014 European Parliament elections, Prime Minister Reinfeldt pointed to how Europe's failure to deliver economic growth and jobs had frayed public trust in democracy. It had fostered a nationalist climate that could reward anti-immigration Euroskeptic parties.[89] He was right. The SD received nearly 10 percent of the vote, an improvement of over 6 percent on the previous European Parliament election, and obtained their first two seats. Even better results were to come. In the Swedish General Election of September 2014, the SD became the third largest party in the Riksdag with forty-nine seats after securing 13 percent of the popular vote.

To be sure, unlike in countries where right-wing parties topped the EP vote, such as the United Kingdom Independence Party (UKIP) in Britain, *Front National* in France, and *Dansk Folkeparti* in Denmark, the SD was the fifth largest vote-getter in Sweden in 2014. If it is accurate to say that Sweden lags a decade behind Denmark in experiencing immigration angst, these results are an ominous sign: Dansk Folkeparti took 27 per cent of the vote, becoming the largest Danish party in Strasbourg. It extended its hand to the fledgling Sweden Democrats.

"White Melancholia" may be an insightful encapsulation of the Moderate Party's interlude in power. In 2011, two Whiteness Studies scholars wrote a critical account of Swedish white melancholy:

> Sweden is currently undergoing a double crisis of Swedish whiteness: "old Sweden," i.e. Sweden as a homogeneous society, and "good Sweden," i.e. Sweden as a progressive society, are both perceived to be threatened by the presence of non-white migrants and their descendants. Both the reactionary and racist camp and the progressive and antiracist camp are mourning the loss of this double-edged Swedish whiteness.[90]

The argument is, then, that

> The conflation of race and ethnicity and the equivalence of Swedishness with whiteness is not only encountered by non-white migrants and their descendants, but also by adopted and mixed Swedes of color with South American, African or Asian backgrounds. In spite of being more or less fully embedded within Swedishness on an ethnic, linguistic, religious and cultural level, these people experience racializing practices as a result of their "non-Swedish" bodies.

The authors added:

> The fact of having held the title of the world's most progressive and left-liberal country, combined with Sweden's perception of itself as the most racially homogenous and pure of all white nations, forms a double bind that makes it almost impossible to transform Swedishness into something that will also accept people of color.[91]

Thus, White Melancholia "is as much about the humiliating decline of Sweden as frontrunner of egalitarianism, humanitarianism and antiracism as about the mourning of the passing of the Swedish population as the whitest of all white peoples." But embracing moralistic, tolerant policies perhaps permits Swedish society to be intolerant of those deviating from these norms. Rather than speaking of repressive tolerance, such a culture may foster tolerant-anchored intolerance.

FOREIGN POLICY OF THE CONSERVATIVE ALLIANCE

Sweden was once, and for a long time, an empire. Charles XII spent his entire adult life (admittedly short) fighting wars outside Sweden. Seventeenth-century Swedish invasions of Poland, called "The Deluge" in the novel by Nobel Prize literature laureate, Henryk Sienkiewicz, may have caused more destruction in the southern regions of Poland than Russia under the tsars had. Danish, Finnish, and Norwegian narratives also are attentive to the power of the *Tre Kronor* Swedish monarchy. Without history there is no xenophobia.

Swedish Social Democracy can again be the point of departure in an examination of the country's international politics. It deftly weaves Swedish national and international values into a seamless whole. As far back as the 1880s "The Social Democratic movement combined liberalism's appreciation of the right of nations to self-determination with its own faith in a world of peace, freedom, and progress."[92] Its 1885 program stated: "Although its sphere of activity is mainly within Sweden, the Swedish Social Democratic Workers' Party, mindful of the international character of the workers' movement, shall therefore strive to fulfill all the duties incumbent upon Swedish workers toward their brethren in other nations."[93]

Sweden's longtime foreign minister, Carl Bildt, offered his own distinctive interpretation of the relevance of his country's history to contemporary international politics. After the Thirty Years War (1618–48) "for Sweden the schism was not with the Muslim world but with Catholicism and Eastern Orthodoxy."[94] Gustavus II Adolphus who reigned from 1611 to 1632 "presented himself as a Protestant lion on the bulwark against the Pope in a European *mission civilisatrice*."[95] Protestantism stood for progress, Europe for conservatism and Roman Catholicism.

Under Social Democratic guidance the Lutheran State Church became a cultural institution: "It is not difficult to conceive Nordic-style Social Democracy as a secularized form of Lutheran Protestantism." Swedish Social Democracy became the "prime mover of earthly progress, in a similar manner to that of French republicanism."[96]

Sweden's historic rivals were then Catholic Europe and Orthodox Russia. Indeed, Swedish identification was more with Germany until World War II; Social Democrat historian Värner Rydén even argued that Swedes belonged to the German part of the Aryan tribe.[97] By contrast, Denmark's wars with Prussia in 1848 and 1864 meant that its chief adversary was Prussia–Germany.

Perceptions of Europe as alien and adversarial resulted in a foreign policy of neutrality, a foundation myth which originated with Karl XIV Johan in 1834: "Neutrality connoted welfare, and vice versa."[98] Nonalignment in peacetime was a corollary.

In the 1930s Social Democracy underlined Sweden's Protestant values to mark it off from an alleged Catholic and conservative Europe. In the 1950s this perception was strengthened when Kurt Schumacher announced his four dangerous Cs (Ks in Swedish): capitalism, conservatism, Catholicism and, depending on which source is used, cartels or colonialism.

Beginnings of neutrality

The neutrality doctrine developed by Östen Undén, Social Democratic politician, law professor, and twice foreign minister, prized both caution and consensus in foreign policy-making. But, in 1959, a breakdown in foreign policy consensus occurred when the leader of the Right Party was excluded from Sweden's United Nations delegation because he opposed a policy of alleged appeasement of the USSR. For political scientist Bjereld this was a turning point. Sweden subsequently shifted roles from "balancing between powers to world conscience and international solidarity, from consensus and national consolidation to open and free debate on foreign policy."[99]

Foreign policy mirroring of domestic values was discernible in the 1960s:

> The growing Swedish interest in areas such as the Third World and the environment can be seen as reflections of the state of the "home of the people": although not yet complete, the construction of it was felt to be so far advanced that the citizens could afford to turn their attention beyond their immediate situation.[100]

The implication is that Sweden could now indulge in the luxury of liberal internationalism.

In 1969 Olof Palme became prime minister, and his sometimes morally framed foreign policies, which inserted Sweden into an international anti-Vietnam War coalition, were not always cautious. Palme was less an idealist than a realpolitiker, evidenced in 1971 by his leaning on the neutrality principle to withdraw Sweden's application for membership in the European Communities.

Nonalignment and neutrality can serve many causes. In his study of Soviet perceptions of the supposed neutrality of Western European states in the 1980s, Bo Petersson discovered that

> In discussion of the legal underpinnings of the neutrality of the four states, Switzerland is grouped with Austria and Sweden with Finland. The neutrality of the former pair is held to rest upon solid legal ground, whereas Swedish and Finnish neutrality is given either a non-existent or a poor legal base.[101]

The Soviet narrative emphasized how all these states were never neutral enough.

In turn, Swedes were convinced that their neutrality was based on their own decision.[102] But Soviet media singled out the Social Democrats as the guarantor of neutrality, citing calls during the Cold War for nuclear-free regions. Invariably these media raised concerns when conservative parties held power. Already in the 1980s, these parties were "alleged to represent sinister military and financial interests, the aims of which are to subvert neutrality and push Sweden closer to NATO."[103] This is the context in which the Kremlin's angry reaction to Bildt's launching of the Eastern Partnership with Sikorski of Poland can be understood.

When, in 1991, Prime Minister Ingvar Carlsson resubmitted Sweden's application for EU membership, the Cold War was over, the threat of a shooting war was far-fetched, and neutrality made little sense. The goal of the Social Democratic government was to "Europeanize Sweden" – a blunt repudiation of the "4 Cs" danger Europe supposedly had posed. The 1994 referendum result in favor of membership was just 52 to 47 percent but, as the European Union does so skillfully in its use of conditionality and subsidiarity instruments, Swedes' self-perception as part of Europe was to grow.

Scholar Anders Hellström explained conditionality this way. For Swedes to become "Good Europeans," too much loyalty to, and identification with, the nation was undesirable. "The constitutive split between 'Good and Bad Europeans' implies that 'we want to be good' and make the right choices."[104] Since "the archetypical 'Good European' acts as a 'Good Host' who welcomes 'Good Immigrants' to the European territory," Sweden had to conform to this norm. Moreover "the label of populism works as a floating signifier that knits together a variety of characteristics (e.g. 'anti-globalization'; 'euro-indifferent'; 'nationalistic') of what it means not to be, act and think as Europeans in Europe." Applying reverse psychology, "The populists are also the 'Bad Europeans' that, potentially, enable 'us' to feel good about ourselves as dedicated Europeans."[105]

Sweden's rejection of the euro at the time of EU accession brought Sweden the best of all worlds. It fed "national myths of Sweden as a prosperous welfare state that has managed to secure welfare and peace for a long time."[106]

POST-NEUTRALITY, NATO, AND SECURITY

In Sweden neutrality is intrinsically linked to identity. It is also linked to sovereignty, internationalism, and solidarity. Neutrality can be a way of opting out of polarizing international politics and constitutes a fear-reduction strategy, perhaps even a muted fear of becoming entangled in the international politics of fear.

Realist accounts underestimate the significance of neutrality which they see as a constructivist practice of observing how international actors conceive of their actions and infuse them with their own meanings.[107] The contingent and strategic aspects of neutrality are played down because realists consider them their own. Christine Agius has insightfully conceptualized widening of security agendas in formerly neutral states and reconfiguring their security policies in line with European and NATO security initiatives as a move from the politics of neutrality to that of post-neutrality.[108]

The Moderates outlined their security policy shortly after taking office in 2006. "Sweden will not take a passive stance if another EU Member State or other Nordic country suffers a disaster or an attack. We expect these countries to act in the same way if Sweden is affected."[109] Nonalignment was missing from this doctrine's language.

Increasing talk of NATO membership for Sweden followed. But holdouts claimed it would do more than affect Sweden's image: it could threaten national security by raising the risk that the country would be dragged into military conflicts. Bjereld emphasized that NATO is an organization associated more with war than with peace and security. A further complication for Sweden is its record of supporting nuclear disarmament, which most Swedes strongly favor. Being a party to NATO's nuclear weapons doctrine would contradict this. Only the small *Folkpartiet*, and one in five Swedish survey respondents, support NATO membership. A procedural issue exists, too: "Swedish politicians and military have dragged Sweden to NATO's gate without public debate."[110]

Public opinion is credited with influencing Swedish policy on NATO. Ulrika Möller and Bjereld maintain that "public opinion is one important channel through which a foreign policy receives feedback with regard to both strategy and appropriateness."[111] For example, "Continuity of policy, such as nonalignment, can be the consequence of the presence of positive feedback; shifts in policy may represent weakened feedback (or reinforcement)."

The authors described how "normative feedback concerns whether the policy contributes to an appropriate international role (on the basis of identity as a sovereign state) and a predominant national narrative."[112] After the Cold War Sweden had to demonstrate that it was "not freeriding, but willing to contribute to make international peace and security." What is more, "Sweden is demonstrating a willingness to work for the common good by actively engaging in strengthening the European security community and in showing continuous readiness to make international military contributions."[113] This reinforces the image of Sweden as carrying out an appropriate international role.

To be sure, Sweden's cooperation with NATO increased under the Moderate Party-led government. In 2013, Sweden joined the Steadfast Jazz exercise allowing its soldiers to train with the NATO Response Force (NRF), a multinational force of 25,000 troops available for rapid deployment. The next year a Swedish fighter squadron, minesweeper, and 120 service personnel joined NRF. For 2015 an additional eight Gripen fighters and an amphibious unit were assigned to it. This makes Sweden ready to participate in NATO missions. Sweden also took part in this period in a NATO cyber defense exercise dubbed Cyber Coalition.

Crypto-NATOism has produced a backlash and an organization called "Stop the Furtive Accession to NATO!" was established. One historian complained how "We have long been deceived about Sweden's policy regarding neutrality. Now, the government is misleading us again, this time into the embrace of NATO."[114] Novelist Henning Mankell's 2009 *The Troubled Man* told what the author described as a fact-based story about the supposed foreign submarine incursions into Swedish waters in 1982. In the novel the villain is not the USSR but United States-led NATO.

What of the foreign policy program of the nationalist Sweden Democrats? For the 2014 election, the SD program expressed opposition to NATO membership and an embrace of traditional national principles of neutrality and nonalignment: "Sweden should remain outside NATO when the alignment is the best from a security perspective. We believe in following the motto 'Non-alignment in peace aiming at neutrality in war.' However, we believe that a stronger Nordic defense cooperation would be to our advantage."[115] This foreign policy accurately reflects the social distance scale summarized above.

The SD cautions against joining the eurozone, allowing more power to be transferred to Brussels, or agreeing to give EU membership to Turkey. It calls for Sweden to renegotiate its terms of membership in the European Union, like the British Conservative Party, but not pulling out, as the United Kingdom Independence Party (UKIP) recommends.

Regarding the developing world, SD is concerned about "releasing resources to non-democratic regimes that can be used to increase the repression of its own people or to make war against their neighbors. An important principle in development assistance should also be help to help themselves instead of putting the countries and people in aid-dependence." The SD comes out for what it terms a humanitarian refugee policy.

Russo-hypopsia

Are increasing russo-hypopsic attitudes in Sweden underpinning newfound collaboration with NATO? Even before the 2013 Ukraine conflict, criticism of Russia's international politics was becoming commonplace.[116] In 2007 Sweden, together with Poland and Estonia, strongly opposed the North Stream pipeline carrying natural gas from Russia to Germany; Sweden did change its position in 2009. The Kremlin mantra of Russia's encirclement by NATO was echoed by some anti-NATO activists in Sweden: "If Sweden and Finland become members, it will close the last two open links in a chain being tightened along the Russian border from the Arctic to the Caucasus, and complete the militarization of Europe under USA/NATO command."[117]

Sweden has not always been suspicious of Soviet or Russian motives nor is it always a supporter of the underdog. In the late 1980s and early 1990s as the Soviet bloc crumbled Foreign Minister Sten Andersson made statements belittling the Baltic states' strivings for independence. They represented a "small minority" compared to Russia. But his view may be the exception to russo-hypopsia rather than the rule.

Documents released by *WikiLeaks* in 2011 indicated that Baltic and Nordic countries had sought to drive a wedge between then Russian President Medvedev and Prime Minister Putin. According to the documents, at a meeting in Washington in 2008, Swedish delegates had proposed measures to "build up" Medvedev and distance him from Putin.[118] All nine countries involved in the scheme had experienced difficult diplomatic relations with Russia. Known as e-PINE ("Enhanced Partnership in Northern Europe"), though unfamiliar to most Swedes, this group cooperated in developing a common policy and sharing information about Russia, Belarus, and Georgia.

In 2013 Sweden's defense minister, Karin Enström, acknowledged that Sweden had cooperated with the National Security Agency (NSA) in spying on Russia. Leaked documents from Edward Snowden suggested that information on Russian politicians was collected by Sweden's main signals intelligence agency, the National Radio Defense Establishment (FRA), and was then handed over to the NSA. Intelligence expert, Wilhelm Agrell, said this confirmed a longstanding suspicion that the FRA and NSA had worked closely together on monitoring leaders in Russia.[119] Sweden was also closely integrated into US global SIGINT operations.

It was predictable, then, that, during the Ukraine crisis, one of Putin's personal envoys decried Sweden's hatred of Russia – *rysshat* – as one of the fiercest in Europe. He claimed that it could even lead to World War III. The analogy used was how anti-Semitism had precipitated World War II.[120]

Referring to its relations with Russia, a 2014 report by the European Council of Foreign Relations (ECFR) asserted that "Sweden stood out as the most principled member state." The country had assisted the European Commission in advising Russia to ease its pressure on East European states. Sweden had a strong voice on such issues as the rule of law, human rights, and the free press in Russia. The report even claimed that Sweden had taken "action to pressure Russia to use its leverage to stop conflict in Syria."[121] This was high praise for Sweden's reasoned and effective russo-hypopsia. As incursions into its airspace and coastal waters grew in 2014 after the Ukraine crisis, new Social Democractic Foreign Minister Margot Wallström observed: "Russia scares Swedish citizens."

Pressure from America

In 2013 President Obama became only the second incumbent United States leader to visit Sweden (George W. Bush was the first in 2001). Two issues divided the two countries. Sweden opposed US military strikes against the Syrian government, even though Bildt had accused the Assad regime of using chemical weapons. Prime Minister Reinfeldt adopted a nonconfrontational approach on a second issue of disagreement: the NSA's electronic surveillance program. He accepted that all democracies, even Sweden's security service Säpo, use intelligence gathering to preempt terrorist attacks.

The United States lobbied for greater Internet restrictions in Sweden. The punitive responses to *WikiLeaks* and *Pirate Bay* founders mentioned earlier are illustrative. Cables released by *WikiLeaks* revealed covert arrangements between the United States and Sweden bypassing democratic processes. Sweden secretly agreed to give the United States access to data on Swedish citizens; doing so officially would have triggered a constitutional requirement of parliamentary oversight. The Ministry of Justice was concerned that the "public spotlight would place other existing informal information-sharing arrangements at jeopardy" and would open the government to domestic criticism.[122] This would reveal "the extent of this cooperation [which] is not widely known within the Swedish government."[123] Another embassy cable revealed a six-step US action plan for Sweden to enact stricter data-retention legislation (IPRED) and copyright infringement laws.[124]

Sweden also passed a controversial surveillance law following American pressure. The law authorized Swedish authorities to transfer unfiltered data about ordinary Swedish citizens to the United States. One Riksdag deputy resigned in protest, charging that the Swedish government was selling out its own people to curry the favor of the United States.

Intelligence collusion with the United States has been extensive, then. One diplomatic cable from the US embassy in Stockholm released by *WikiLeaks* described Bildt, in his capacity as Swedish foreign minister, this way: "Carl Bildt: Medium Size Dog with Big Dog Attitude." Why this description? The US cable stated that "Bildt represents a medium-size country (9.5 million, $350 billion annual GDP) that has some major power ambitions and capabilities."[125]

Islamo-hypopsic foreign policy?

Relations with Muslim majority states have varied. A former defense minister contended that military intervention in Afghanistan, which a "mission creep" transformed from peacekeeping into combat operations, represented the most recent example of a longstanding Swedish commitment to international solidarity.[126] A *WikiLeaks*-released United States embassy cable confirmed that four hundred Swedish troops were involved in special operations in four Afghan provinces.

Agrell accused the Swedish government of not explaining to the Riksdag the change of mission from defensive patrol force to counter-insurgency warfare. The shift had been concealed when the Reinfeldt government requested an extension of the mission as part of NATO's International Security Assistance Force (ISAF). But, in 2009, the United States had redefined ISAF's mission from reconstruction to counterinsurgency warfare.

Surprisingly, the US cable claimed that "On the civilian side, Sweden could – and should – do more." That was what Sweden's comparative advantage had been for many years, yet its civil society-building efforts in Afghanistan had little effect. For Agrell "Sweden failed to manage what it should have been best at."[127]

Foreign Minister Bildt raised doubts about the effectiveness of sanctions against Iran, a significant export market for Swedish companies such as Ericsson and Volvo. On Iraq, Bildt had been co-chair of the European branch of the Committee for the Liberation of Iraq, a lobby group with close ties to the White House. A *WikiLeaks* cable revealed that the head of the committee credited Bildt with having "played a decisive role in building a coalition against Saddam Hussein . . . Someone of Carl's stature, with his background – and from Sweden to boot – was of course very important. Thanks to his personal network and his endorsement, we were able to recruit several other [collaborators]."[128]

In 2011 *WikiLeaks* leaked a cable suggesting Bildt and migration minister, Tobias Billström, had made disparaging remarks about Iraqi refugees four years earlier. Bildt had pressed for an agreement with Iraq that would allow the return (*refoulement*) of asylum seekers denied residence permits in Sweden. He also wanted to reduce the overall number of Iraqi refugees arriving in Sweden. These opinions were expressed at a meeting between the two ministers and the United States ambassador to Iraq, Ryan Crocker.[129] Swedish critics saw this as evidence that the Moderates were adopting policies pushed by growing xenophobic forces in the country. But, when a new armed conflict broke out in 2014 between Islamic State rebel forces and Iraqi authorities helped by Kurdish Peshmerga troops, Sweden made it clear it would stay out of the military battles.

Bildt was also at the center of a controversy in 2012 over a Swedish arms deal and munitions factory in Saudi Arabia.[130] He defended the sale of anti-tank missiles to the sheikhdom and refused to comment on the conduct of Sweden's Defense Research Agency which had been the subject of a criminal probe into secret plans to help the Saudis build a weapons plant.[131] Swedish and Arab prodemocracy activists accused Bildt of betraying the Arab struggle for democracy.[132] It was the Swedish defense minister, not Bildt, who was forced to resign over the opaque arms deal.

Finally, a *WikiLeaks* cable summarized United States embassy analysis of Sweden's policy towards Syria in 2009. "On the possibility of an EU association agreement with Syria, Sweden has been in favor . . . It has promised to consult with us [the United States] before pushing for closer ties with Syria within the EU."[133] This inclusionary approach was in keeping with the liberal internationalism Sweden espoused. It may also have anticipated impending conflict in Syria and a subsequent refugee crisis that Sweden's asylum policy would necessarily implicate the country in.

Did Bildt really have a Big Dog attitude? Was he a speaker of inconvenient truths or a concealer of them? Bildt has prophesized that "In thirty years' time Europe won't be the center of the world, it may only be the peninsula of the Asian mainland." If Europe becomes less pivotal, so will Sweden. As Bildt told the United Nations in 2007, a millennium after that era ended: "The Viking days are over in Sweden." Bildt, like Poland's Sikorski, was sidelined in September 2014 from European foreign policy circles. The first foreign policy change introduced by Social Democrat Prime Minister Stefan Löfven was recognition of a Palestinian state. But claims of Islamic state sleeper cells in Sweden inevitably raised questions about longstanding asylum and foreign policies.

Liberal internationalism

In 1945 Gunnar Myrdal offered a grandiose vision of Sweden's national action script: "We are called upon by history and our external conditions to be the advocate of universal interest."[134] In 2003 Social Democrat Prime Minister Göran Persson officially announced that "Human rights promotion is a Swedish foreign policy priority."[135]

Sweden's foreign policy has many objectives but the distinguishing one is what Alison Brysk has called the pursuit of "Global Good Samaritanship." Sweden was among a small number of democratic middle powers – Canada was one before Stephen Harper's Conservative Party took power in 2006 – which was inspired by visionary, principled leaders and globally conscious civil societies to emphasize a connection between its own long-term interests and the common good at home and abroad.

For Brysk humanitarian internationalism was not just episodic altruism but the cornerstone of international politics. While some foreign policy studies highlight how altruistic norms compete with more structural national interests for influence on foreign policy, specific conditions allow the two to be combined.[136] The process may look like this:

> State identities are constructed in relationship to international society . . . These identities then shape foreign policies as they filter perceptions, establish foreign policy roles, build constraining international and domestic institutions, and provide principled rationales and domestic constituencies for political leaders.[137]

In her study of Sweden, Brysk highlighted how, for many years, it had served as the "undiplomatic critic of international injustice:" it condemned the United States war in Vietnam, apartheid in South Africa, human rights abuses and international aggression of the USSR. Its positive contributions include being a major financial contributor to the United Nations High Commission on Refugees, the United Nations High Commission on Human Rights, and the United Nations Children's Fund (UNICEF). Overall then

179

Sweden has a distinguished record of human rights promotion through foreign aid, multilateral advocacy, peacekeeping and refugee reception. Sweden's projection of principled policy is so persistent, multifaceted and well-publicized that it is considered a "gold standard" for international as well as domestic human rights performance. Sweden represents a gold standard in another way as well, in that human rights promotion is grounded in a high level of affluence and security.[138]

The way that domestic structures and foreign policy are interweaved in Sweden is more easily identifiable than in France or Poland. Sweden's Global Good Samaritan role is the product of many factors: its economic development; its geopolitical place in the international system; a series of influential leaders and a robust civil society which was passionate about such an agenda. For Brysk "In a continuous dialogue between domestic ideology and international society, national interest was reconstructed as humanitarian internationalism" and "allowed for the possibility of foreign policy projection of domestic values."[139]

Confluence of asylum and foreign policies

The defining characteristics of Sweden's foreign policy are similar to those of domestic politics: liberal democratic values; solidarity; egalitarianism, as well as international projection of the Swedish model. For Brysk there is logic in this:

> National interest is reconstructed as global interest through the introduction of norms that provide explanations, prescriptions, and bridges between power and principle. Reconstructed interest follows a constructivist logic of norms, in which actors seek guidance from roles and values rather than simply calculating material gains.[140]

Foreign policy shaped by domestic politics is especially palpable in asylum policy which, in Sweden, functions in a distinctive context.

One indicator of Sweden's humanitarian policies is the assistance it gives to poorer countries. The 2013 Commitment to Development Index (CDI) placed Sweden second best in the world among the twenty-seven richest countries across seven policy areas having an impact on poor nations: aid, trade, finance, migration, environment, security, and technology. Sweden received high marks for its foreign aid, finance, and migration policies. It accepted a large number of immigrants from developing countries (ranked nine by share of population); it admitted a large share of foreign students from developing countries (ranked twelve); and it bore a large share of the burden of refugees during humanitarian crises (ranked first). As a Swedish teacher put it about the ethnically diverse class he was teaching: "as long as there

---

Box 6.4 International conflicts, war refugees, domestic costs

Reception of refugees is a key area of human rights policy simply because it directly affects the life and death of large numbers of people. It is also a test of commitment to principled policy, since receiving refugees always involves some domestic financial and political costs – in contrast to international rhetorical or institutional activities. Domestic costs will be especially salient in a historically homogenous society like Sweden, where high potential resources for absorption will be weighed against the high per capita impact of diverse and needy populations in a society initially lacking pluralistic institutions or immigrant host communities.

Source: Alison Brysk, "Global Good Samaritans? Human Rights Promotion as Foreign Policy – the Case of Sweden," Global Peace and Conflict Studies Working Paper, University of California, Irvine, 18 September 2005, p. 17, http://www.cgpacs.uci.edu/cgpacs_working_papers

---

are wars in the world, we have a job." And there are always wars, he pointed out – "right now, in Syria."

Despite Sweden's relatively small population (barely 2 percent of the total European Union population), Eurostat reported that the country took in 19.5 percent of the 135,700 asylum seekers in 2013. Of asylum seekers in Sweden, 46 percent were from Syria. Of the 35,800 Syrians granted protection status in the EU28, over 60 percent were recorded in Sweden and Germany (12,000 and 9,600 respectively). In 2014 a record 100,000 refugees were expected to arrive, primarily from Syria, Libya, Somalia, and Eritrea. Fighting in northern Iraq was likely to swell the numbers. A poll found that a third of respondents wanted the inflow to decrease, 36 percent thought it should remain the same, and a quarter wanted it to be increased (Box 6.4).[141]

A dark side to Sweden's ranking in the CDI was that it was given the lowest possible ranking for security owing to "high arms exports to poor and undemocratic governments" as well as lack of support for the "creation and transfer of technological advances."[142] These peculiarly Swedish problems were flagged earlier in this chapter.

CONCLUSIONS

Sweden's foreign policy has been ranked as very influential among European Union member states; it punches above its weight. The European Council on Foreign Relations's (ECFR) report identified France and the United Kingdom as having the most influential foreign policies in the European Union; Germany and Sweden ranked third.[143] But "Sweden was once again a 'leader' on a wide range of issues – aid contributions, efforts on human rights issues in Russia and Ukraine, relations with Russia on the Syria conflict, and TTIP [the Transatlantic Trade and Investment Partnership being negotiated between the European Union and the United States]." Further recognition was extended of Sweden's "traditional strengths such as welcoming refugees, support for multilateralism, and development aid."

Foreign Minister Bildt expressed satisfaction with the recognition the report gave to his country's foreign policy: "The government works with purpose and effort to make EU foreign policy reflect Swedish values. The ranking shows that this work has paid off."[144]

Yet Sweden did not distinguish itself on key questions related to policy on the Middle East and North Africa which should entail: pushing for a resolution to the conflict in Syria; pressing for a strong EU response to the military takeover in Egypt in 2013; advocating a comprehensive European strategy towards Iran following its 2013 presidential elections; supporting closer security cooperation with North Africa; backing the Middle East peace process and Palestinian state building; and backing French intervention in Mali.[145] Being neutral on these issues did not capture the ECFR's moral high ground.

The balancing act between promoting the ideal of Good Samaritanism and of economic growth surfaced in a policy speech given by Prime Minister Reinfeldt in 2011. He called on Europe to become a beacon of freedom for Eastern Europe as in previous decades it had been for countries in North Africa. But interconnected to this, he argued, was the practical need to attract labor from other parts of the world to promote economic growth.[146] This two-track approach is encapsulated in the formulation contained in the 2011 Statement of Government Policy: "With visions, but without illusions."

The cornerstone of Swedish foreign policy is upholding international law and respect for human rights. Its security policy is based on mutual dependence and collective responsibility within Europe, in other words, a politics of post-neutrality. Its 2008 doctrine states that Sweden's security is built on solidarity with others. Liberal internationalism is evidenced in humanitarian and peacekeeping missions abroad. The country is acknowledged as setting the gold standard in sheltering war refugees.

But, in the twenty-first century, Sweden has also cooperated with the United States in the torture and rendition of terrorist suspects. It aggressively promotes its arms export industry which includes sales of the "meat grinder" flechette Area Defense Munition condemned by Amnesty International. Idealistic, other-regarding rhetoric still has pride of place in domestic and international politics but national security discourse is pushing it aside. Generally international agendas elicit idealistic discourse, regional security a more realistic one.

If United States foreign policy reflects its capitalist morality at home,

Sweden's values-driven foreign policy reflects its liberalism at home, even if it has in many areas been bruised. In this respect, occasionally unprincipled foreign policy covaries with xeno-hypopsic episodes at home.

There is more to fear than fear itself, then. Imperfections in managing growing diversity and diminishing cohesion at home are refracted in a blemished foreign policy stressing self-help. In theory, return to Social Democratic rule in 2014 would reverse these trends because, traditionally, it was the party that reassured rather than raised fears. An expanded refugee program was built into the budget it presented to the Riksdag. But the conservative opposition together with the anti-immigrant SD voted it down. An early election was only averted after a "December agreement" was reached between government and opposition: the latter would have its 2015 budget adopted in exchange for refraining from opposing subsequent Social Democratic budgets until 2022. In response the marginalized SD observed it was now clearly Sweden's only opposition party.

Notes

1. Michel de Montaigne, *The Complete Essays* (Harmondsworth: Penguin, 1993), Book I, Chapter XVIII. Quoted many times, President Franklin D. Roosevelt used the phrase in his 1933 Inaugural Speech.
2. ALLBUS German General Social Surveys have repeatedly shown that respondents rank asylum seekers as lowest among all groups of strangers; http://www.gesis.org/en/allbus/study-profiles/2012/
3. Bo Petersson, *Stories about Strangers: Swedish Media Constructions of Socio-Cultural Risk* (Lanham, MD: University Press of America, 2006).
4. Sarah Scuzzarello, *Caring Multiculturalism: Local Immigrant Policies and Narratives of Integration in Malmö, Birmingham and Bologna* (Lund: Lundsuniversitet, Lund Political Studies 159, 2010).
5. Society for Human Resource Management (SHRM), *Global Diversity and Inclusion: Perceptions, Practices and Attitudes* (London: Economist Intelligence Unit, July 2008), http://graphics.eiu.com/upload/eb/DiversityandInclusion.pdf
6. OECD Programme for International Student Assessment (PISA), *PISA 2012 Results in Focus* (Paris: OECD, 2014), http://www.oecd.org/pisa/keyfindings/pisa-2012-results-overview.pdf
7. Karin Borevi, "The Political Dynamics of Multiculturalism in Sweden," in Raymond Taras (ed.), *Challenging Multiculturalism: European Models of Diversity* (Edinburgh: Edinburgh University Press, 2013), pp. 138–60.
8. Carl Dahlström, *Nästan välkomna: Invandrarpolitikens retorik och praktik* (Göteborg: Statsvetenskapliga Institutionen, Göteborgs Universitet, 2004).
9. Göran Rosenberg, "The crisis of consensus in postwar Sweden," in Nina Witoszek and Lars Trägårdh (eds), *Culture and Crisis: The Case of Germany and Sweden* (New York: Berghahn Books, 2002), pp. 170, 173.
10. Susan Sontag, *Ramparts* (July 1969), p. 38. On the welfare state see Bo Rothstein,

Just Institutions Matter: The Moral and Political Logic of the Universal Welfare State (Cambridge: Cambridge University Press, 1998).

11. Sven Steinmo, *The Evolution of Modern States: Sweden, Japan, and the United States* (Cambridge: Cambridge University Press, 2010), pp. 34, 229.

12. Jenny Kiiskinen and Sigrid Saveljeff, *Populism and a mistrust of foreigners: Sweden in Europe* (Norrköping: Integrationsverkets, 2007); see Chapter 10 for a review of populist parties in Sweden. See also Björn Fryklund and Tomas Peterson, *Populism och missnöjespartier i Norden: Studier av småborgerlig klassaktivitet* (Malmö: Arkiv avhandlingsserie, 1981) for analysis of earlier movements.

13. Hans L. Zetterberg, *Sociological Endeavor, Selected Writings* (Stockholm: City University Press, 1997), p. 329, quoted in Rosenberg, "The crisis of consensus," p. 174.

14. Jonas Hassen Khemiri, *Montecore* (New York: Knopf, 2011), p 117.

15. Mikael Jalving, *Absolut Sverige: en rejse i tavshedens rige.* A Swedish journalist returned the favor by dissecting pathologies in Danish society; see Lena Sundström, *Världens lyckligaste folk: en bok om Danmark* (Stockholm: Pocketförlaget, 2010).

16. "Danes want Swedes to break 'spiral of silence,'" *The Local (Denmark)*, 29 June 2014, http://www.thelocal.dk/20140629/danes-want-swedes-to-break-spiral-of-silence

17. Mahama Tawat, "Danish and Swedish immigrants' cultural policies between 1960 and 2006: toleration and the celebration of difference," *International Journal of Cultural Policy*, 20:2 (2014), first published 11 December 2012, p. 14. See also his "Two Tales of Viking Diversity: A Comparative Study of the Immigrant Integration Policies of Denmark and Sweden, 1960–2006," PhD Thesis, University of Otago, New Zealand, June 2011.

18. Anders Hellström, *Vi är de Goda: den offentliga debatten om Sverigedemokraterna och deras politik* (Stockholm: Tankekraft förlag, 2010).

19. David Lindén, "Tedious praise of 'perfect Swedish society,'" *The Local*, 30 October 2013.

20. Ibid.

21. Ibid.

22. The transformation of Sweden is described differently by Andrew Brown, *Fishing in Utopia: Sweden and the Future that Disappeared* (London: Granta Books, 2009); by Åke Daun, *Swedish Mentality* (University Park, PA: Pennsylvania State University Press, 1999); and by Ulf Nilson, *What happened to Sweden? – while America became the only superpower* (New York: Nordstjernan Förlag, 2007).

23. Nima Sanandaji, "Is Sweden a False Utopia?" *New Geography*, 10 May 2010, http://www.newgeography.com/content/001543-is-sweden-a-false-utopia

24. "Sweden Just Found the Worst Way Imaginable to Get Rid of Racism," *World.Mic*, 9 August 2014, http://mic.com/articles/95872/sweden-just-found-the-worst-way-imaginable-to-get-rid-of-racism

25. Quoted in Pascale Harter, "Extreme world: Is Sweden as clean as it seems?" *BBC News*, 8 December 2010, http://www.bbc.com/news/world-11949956

26. Hugh Heclo and Henrik Madsen, *Policy and Politics in Sweden* (Philadelphia: Temple University Press, 1987), p. 21, Cited In Rosenberg, "The crisis of consensus," p. 177.

27. Andrew Anthony, "Göran Lindberg and Sweden's dark side," *The Guardian*, 1 August 2010, http://www.theguardian.com/world/2010/aug/01/goran-lindberg-sweden-crime-palme

28. Alison Brysk and Aashish Mehta, "Do rights at home boost rights abroad? Sexual equality and humanitarian foreign policy," *Journal of Peace Research*, 51:1 (January 2014), p. 108.

29. Karin Boye, Kallocain (Madison, WI: University of Wisconsin Press, 1966), p. 101.

30. Khemiri, *Montecore*, p. 243.

31. For a critical introduction by a Chilean refugee and professor of medicine resident in Sweden, see Marcello Ferrada de Noli, *Sweden vs. Assange: Human Rights Issues* (Stockholm: Libertarian Books, 2014), https://libertarianbooks.files.wordpress.com/2014/01/sweden-vs-assange-human-rights-issues-by-m-ferrada-de-noli.pdf

32. European Council on Foreign Relations, *European Foreign Policy Scorecard 2014* (London: ECFR, January 2014), p. 120, http://www.ecfr.eu/page/ /ECFR94_SCORECARD_2014.pdf Scorecard

33. Reported on Justice for Assange website, http://www.swedenversusassange.com/Fair-Trial-for-Julian-Assange.html

34. Dennis Sven Nordin, A *Swedish Dilemma: A Liberal European Nation's Struggle with Racism and Xenophobia, 1990–2000* (Lanham, MD: University Press of America, 2005), p. ix.

35. Ulf Bjereld, "Non-alignment is part of Sweden's self-image," *The Local*, 15 January 2013, http://www.thelocal.se/20130115/45632

36. Jonas Frykman and Orvar Löfgren, *Culture Builders: A Historical Anthropology of Middle-Class Life* (New Brunswick, NJ: Rutgers University Press, 2005), p. 27.

37. Nordin, A *Swedish Dilemma*, p. 79.

38. Leigh Oakes, *Language and National Identity: Comparing France and Sweden* (Amsterdam: John Benjamins Publishing Company, 2001), p. 69. See also Åke Daun, *Swedish Mentality* (University Park: Pennsylvania State University Press, 1996), p. 2.

39. Lars Trägårdh, "Crisis and the Politics of National Community: Germany and Sweden, 1933/1994," in Nina Witoszek and Trägårdh (eds), *Culture and Crisis: The Case of Germany and Sweden* (New York: Berghahn Books, 2002), p. 77.

40. Piero Colla, "Race, Nation, and Folk: On the Repressed Memory of World War II in Sweden and its Hidden Categories," in Witoszek and Trägårdh, *Culture and Crisis*, p. 151.

41. Trägårdh, "Crisis," in Witoszek and Trägårdh, *Culture and Crisis*, p. 77.

42. Ibid., p. 83.

43. Marquis William Childs mythologized "democratic Sweden" in 1936 in his *Sweden: the Middle Way* (New Haven, CT: Yale University Press, 1936), p. 91.

44. Oakes, *Language and National Identity*, p. 70. See also Orvar Löfgren, "Nationellas arenor," in Billy Ehn, Jonas Frykman, and Löfgren (eds), *Försvenskningen av Sverige: Det nationellas förvandlingar* (Stockholm: Natur och Kultur, 1993), p. 28.

45. Sven Steinmo, *The Evolution of Modern States: Sweden, Japan, and the United States* (Cambridge: Cambridge University Press, 2010), p. 75.

46. Tim Tilton, *The Political Theory of Swedish Social Democracy: Through the Welfare State to Socialism* (Oxford: Clarendon Press, 1990), p. 280.

47. Aksel Sandemose (under the pseudonym of Espen Arnakke), *En flygtning krydser sit spor* (Copenhagen: Schønberg 1933). The English edition is A *Fugitive Crosses his Tracks* (New York: A. A. Knopf, 1936).

48. Tilton, *The Political Theory*, p. 275.
49. David Eberhard, *I trygghetsnarkomanernas land: Sverige och det nationella paniksyn-dromet* (Falun: Mänpocket, 2011), pp. 19, 38–42.
50. David Eberhard, *Ingen tar skit i de lättkränktas land* (Falun: Mänpocket, 2011).
51. Allan Pred, *The Past is Not Dead: Facts, Fictions, and Enduring Racial Stereotypes* (Minneapolis, MN: University of Minnesota Press, 2004), p. 187.
52. Borevi, "The Political Dynamics," p. 141.
53. I am grateful to Anders Hellström for developing this idea.
54. Pieter Bevelander and Inge Dahlstedt, "Sweden," in Bevelander, Rasmus H. Bilde, Dahlstedt, Marc Eskelund, Line Møller Hansen, Miroslav Macura, Kasper Geluke Pedersen, and Lars Østby, *Scandinavia's Population Groups Originating from Developing Countries: Change and Integration* (Malmö: Malmö Institute for Studies of Migration, Diversity and Welfare, Malmö University, 2013), p. 194.
55. Oakes, *Language and National Identity*, p. 112.
56. "Svenskt medborgarskap" (Stockholm: Statens offentliga utredningar 1999:34, March 1999), pp. 9–10, http://www.regeringen.se/content/1/c4/24/01/7d21de04.pdf
57. Scott Iain McIver, "Conceptualizations of citizenship in Sweden and the United Kingdom: An empirical study and analysis of how 'citizenship' is understood in policy and by policy-makers." PhD thesis, Politics, School of Social and Political Studies, University of Edinburgh, 2009, p. 133.
58. On citizenship see Bo Bengtsson, Per Strömblad, and Ann-Helén Bay (eds.), *Diversity, Inclusion and Citizenship in Scandinavia* (Newcastle: Cambridge Scholars Press, 2010); see especially the chapter by Karen Borevi, "Dimensions of Citizenship: European Integration Policies from a Scandinavian Perspective," pp. 19-46. Also Pieter Bevelander, Christian Fernández, and Anders Hellström (eds.), *Vägar till Medborgarskap* (Lund: Arkiv förlag, 2011); more recently, Pieter Bevelander and Mikael Spång, "From Aliens to Citizens: The Political Incorporation of Immigrants," IZA DP No. 7920 (Bonn: Forschungsinstitut zur Zukunft der Arbeit, January 2014), http://papers.ssrn.com/sol3/papers.cfm?abstract_id=2389288##
59. Bevelander and Dahlstedt, "Sweden," Table 1.4, p. 198.
60. Nordin, *A Swedish Dilemma*, p. 29. See also Pred.
61. SOM-institutet website, http://www.som.gu.se/
62. Marie Demker, "Scandinavian Right-Wing Parties: Diversity More than Convergence?" in Andrea Mammone, Emmanuel Godin, and Brian Jenkins (eds), *Mapping the Extreme Right in Contemporary Europe* (New York: Berghahn Books, 2011), pp. 367–9, 376.
63. European Commission, "Europeans in 2014," Special Eurobarometer 415 (March 2014), p. T67, QD6.3, http://ec.europa.eu/public_opinion/archives/ebs/ebs_415_data_en.pdf
64. Demker, "Scandinavian Right-Wing Parties," p. 370.
65. Ibid.
66. Marie Demker, "Attitudes toward immigrants and refugees: Swedish trends with some comparisons." Paper presented at the International Studies Association 48th Annual Convention, 28 February–3 March 2007, Chicago, p. 36.
67. *Den Mångtydiga intoleransen: en studie av gymnasieungdomars attityder läsåret 2009/2010* (Stockholm: Forum för levande historia, 2010), Table 2, p. 33 and Table 3.1, p. 81.

For a national quantitative study see Pieter Bevelander and Jonas Otterbeck, "Young people's attitudes towards Muslims in Sweden," *Ethnic and Racial Studies*, 33:3 (2010; first published 22 August 2008), pp. 404–25.

68. *Den Mångtydiga intoleransen*, Table 6.1, p. 90; Table 4.1, p. 84.
69. Ibid., Table 2.10, p. 78.
70. Jens Agerström and Dan-Olof Rooth, "Implicit Prejudice and Ethnic Minorities: Arab-Muslims in Sweden," Discussion Paper No. 3873 (Bonn: Forschungsinstitut zur Zukunft der Arbeit, December 2008), p. 10.
71. Rickard Carlsson, "Warmth and competence in implicit stereotypes and discrimination" (Lund: Faculty of Social Sciences, Department of Psychology, Lund University, 2013), pp. 38–9. Examples of warm or competent language in application letters are provided on pp. 36–7.
72. Carl Bildt, "European Union Foreign Policy." Paper presented at the European University Institute, Fiesole, 28 May 2010.
73. Deeq Awil, "Afrophobic hate crime is on the rise in Sweden, and the Somalis bear the brunt of it," *Somalia Online*, 3 February 2014, http://www.somaliaonline.com/afrophobic-hate-crime-is-on-the-rise-in-sweden-and-the-somalis-bear-the-brunt-of-it/
74. "Sweden 'violates the rights' of guest workers," *The Local*, 20 November 2013, http://www.thelocal.se/20131120/european-council-slams-swedens-guest-worker-policy
75. "Foreigners Worst Off for Unemployment in Sweden," *The Local*, 25 November 2013, http://www.thelocal.se/20131125/swedens-jobless-foreigners-level-worst-in-eu; see also an earlier report: Cecilia Englund, "Migrants, minorities and employment in Sweden: exclusion, discrimination and anti-discrimination" (Stockholm: RAXEN Focal Point for Sweden, 2003), http://fra.europa.eu/sites/default/files/fra_uploads/239-SW.pdf
76. Ivar Ekman, "Stockholm Syndrome: How Immigrants are Changing Sweden's Welfare State," *Foreign Affairs*, 19 May 2014, http://www.foreignaffairs.com/articles/141437/ivar-ekman/stockholm-syndrome
77. Sofie Fredlund-Blomst, "Assessing Immigrant Integration in Sweden after the May 2013 Riots," *Migration Policy Institute*, 16 January 2014, http://www.migrationpolicy.org/article/assessing-immigrant-integration-sweden-after-may-2013-riot
78. Eril Ullenhag, "New arrivals need more than a 'pat on the head,'" *The Local*, 24 November 2010, http://www.thelocal.se/30400/20101124/
79. Lars Åberg, "Godhjärtade svenskar ser på invandrare som husdjur," *Dagens Nyheter*, 1 September 2010, http://www.dn.se/debatt/godhjartade-svenskar-ser-pa-invandrare-som-husdjur/. An English version is: "Well-meaning Swedes treat immigrants as pets," *The Local*, 9 September 2010, http://www.thelocal.se/20100909/28890
80. Khemiri, *Montecore*, p. 275.
81. Åberg, "Godhjärtade svenskar," *Dagens Nyheter*.
82. David J. Michael, "Nordic Sibling Rivalry," *Slate*, 11 December 2012), http://www.slate.com/articles/business/dispatches/2012/12/swedish_migrant_workers_and_norwegian_oil_wealth_have_reversed_the_centuries.html
83. Ibid.
84. Pieter Bevelander, "In the Picture: Resettled Refugees in Sweden," in Bevelander, Mirjam Hagström, and Sofia Rönnqvist (eds), *Resettled and Included: Employment Integration of Resettled Refugees in Sweden* (Malmö: Holmbergs, 2009).

85. Mikael Spång, "Europeisering av svensk invandringspolitik," Current Themes in IMER Research, 4 (Malmö: Malmö University IMER, 2006), p. 53.
86. "Sweden in 'historic' deal on immigration policy," The Local, 3 March 2011, http://www.thelocal.se/32374/20110303/
87. Mikael Spång, "Svensk invandringspolitik i demokratiskt perspektiv,", Current Themes in IMER Research, 8 (Malmö: Malmö University IMER, 2008), p. 184.
88. Ibid., p. 181.
89. Alistair Scrutton and Simon Johnson, "Swedish PM warns of nationalist surge as EU elections loom," Reuters, 8 May 2014, http://news.yahoo.com/swedish-pm-warns-nationalist-surge-eu-elections-loom-221745169.html
90. Tobias Hübinette and Catrin Lundström, "White melancholia: Mourning the loss of 'Good old Sweden,'" Eurozine, 18 October 2011, http://www.eurozine.com/articles/2011-10-18-hubinette-en.html. It originally appeared in Swedish in Glänta 2 (2011).
91. Tobias Hübinette and Carina Tigervall, "To Be Non-White in a Color-Blind Society: Conversations with Adoptees and Adoptive Parents in Sweden on Everyday Racism," Journal of Intercultural Studies 30 (2009); Catrin Lundström, "'Concrete Bodies:' Young Latina Women Transgressing the Boundaries of Race and Class in White Inner-City Stockholm," Gender, Place and Culture, 17 (2010); Lena Sawyer, "Routings: Race, African Diasporas, and Swedish Belonging," Transforming Anthropology, 11 (2002).
92. Herbert Tingsten, The Swedish Social Democrats: Their Ideological Development (Totowa, NJ: Bedminster Press, 1973), p. 465.
93. Ibid., p. 467.
94. Bildt, "European Union Foreign Policy."
95. Bo Stråth, "The Swedish Demarcation from Europe," in Mikael af Malmborg and Stråth (eds), The Meaning of Europe (Oxford: Berg, 2002), p. 135.
96. Mikael af Malmborg and Bo Stråth, "Introduction: The National Meanings of Europe," in Malmborg and Stråth, The Meaning of Europe, p. 16.
97. Quoted by Stråth, "The Swedish Demarcation," p. 130.
98. Ibid., p. 140.
99. Ulf Bjereld, Hjälmarsonaffären, ett politiskt drama i tre akter (Stockholm: Nerenius & Santérus, 1997), p. 149.
100. Helena Forsås-Scott, Swedish Women's Writing 1850–1995 (London: Athlone Press, 1997), p. 102.
101. Bo Petersson, "Essay and Reflection: On the Soviet Union and the Neutrals," in International History Review, XI:2 (May 1989), p. 294.
102. See Sverker Åström, Svensk neutralitetspolitik (Stockholm: Svensk Institut, 1983), p. 6
103. Petersson, "Essay and Reflection," p. 296.
104. Anders Hellström, Bringing Europe Down to Earth (Lund: Lunds Universitet, Political Studies no. 144, 2006), pp. 228–9.
105. Ibid., pp. 186, 209.
106. Ibid., p. 137.
107. Christine Agius, The Social Construction of Swedish Neutrality: Challenges to Swedish Identity and Sovereignty (Manchester: Manchester University Press, 2012), pp. 20–4.
108. Christine Agius, "Transformed Beyond Recognition? The Politics of Post-Neutrality," Cooperation and Conflict, 46:3 (September 2011), pp. 370–95.

109. Ministry for Foreign Affairs, "Sweden's security policy," 3 December 2008, http://www.sweden.gov.se/sb/d/3103/a/116839

110. Charlotte Wagnsson, "A security community in the making? Sweden and NATO post-Libya," *European Security*, 20:4 (December 2011), p. 597.

111. Ulrika Möller and Ulf Bjereld, "From Nordic neutrals to post-neutral Europeans: Differences in Finnish and Swedish policy transformation," *Cooperation and Conflict* 45:4 (2010), p. 379.

112. Ibid., pp. 368–9.

113. Ibid., pp. 377–9.

114. Sven-Eric Liedman, quoted in "Should Sweden Join NATO? 'Definitely not!'" 4 March 2010, http://www.stoppanato.se/english/proposal.htm

115. Sverigedemokraterna, "Vår politik – en översikt," http://sverigedemokraterna.se/var-politik/var-politik-a-till-o/

116. For studies of two Nordic states' russophobia, see Anni Kangas, "Beyond Russophobia: A Practice Based Interpretation of Finnish–Russian/Soviet Relations," *Cooperation & Conflict*, 46:1 (March 2011), pp. 40–59; Anni Kangas, *The Knight, the Beast and the Treasure: A Semiotic Inquiry into the Finnish Political Imaginary on Russia, 1918–1930s* (Tampere: Tampere University Press, 2007).

117. Liedman, "Should Sweden Join NATO?"

118. "E-PINE Political Directors, April 30th Meeting in Washington, DC," para. 20, WikiLeaks Updates website, 20 February 2011, http://wikileaksupdates.blogspot.com/2011/02/e-pine-political-directors-april-30th.html

119. "'No Surprise' Sweden Spies on Russia – Minister," *The Local*, 5 December 2013, http://www.thelocal.se/20131205/no-surprise-that-sweden-is-spying-on-russia

120. "Putins man varnar för svenskt 'rysshat,'" *SvD Nyheter*, 8 June 2014, http://www.svd.se/nyheter/utrikes/putins-man-varnar-for-svenskt-rysshat_3637670.svd

121. *European Foreign Policy Scorecard 2014*, p. 119.

122. "Viewing cable 08STOCKHOLM748, HSPD-6 TEAM VISITS TO DISCUSS TERRORIST SCREENING" (07-11-2008), http://wikileaks.org/cable/2008/11/08STOCKHOLM748

123. "Viewing cable 07STOCKHOLM506, SWEDEN: SCENE-SETTER FOR PRIME MINISTER" (04-05-2007), http://wikileaks.org/cable/2007/05/07STOCKHOLM506.html

124. "Viewing cable 09STOCKHOLM141, SPECIAL 301 FOR SWEDEN: POST RECOMMENDATION" (02-03-2009), http://wikileaks.org/cable/2009/03/09STOCKHOLM141.html

125. Ibid.

126. Sten Tolgfors, "Avhopp riskerar Sveriges anseende," *Dagens Nyheter*, 13 June 2010, http://www.svd.se/opinion/brannpunkt/avhopp-riskerar-sveriges-anseende_4856681.svd

127. Wilhelm Agrell, *Ett krig här och nu: från svensk fredsoperation till upprorsbekämpning i Afghanistan 2001–2014* (Stockholm: Bokförlaget Atlantis, 2013).

128. *Wikileaks* cables reported in "Justice for Assange" website, http://www.swedenversusassange.com/Political-Interference.html#USSE

129. "Bildt och Billström KU-anmäls, in *SvD Nyheter*, 21 January 2011), http://www.svd.se/nyheter/inrikes/bildt-och-billstrom-ku-anmals_5882467.svd

130. For a detailed account of the Saudi affair see Bo Göran Bodin and Daniel Öhman *Saudivapen: Hycklande politiker, ljugande tjänstemän och hemliga spioner* (Stockhom: Albert Bonniers Forlag, 2014).

131. "Saudi Arabia a 'Family Business' – Bildt," *The Local*, 4 April 2013, http://www.thelocal.se/20120404/40080

132. "Sweden has betrayed the Arab Struggle for Democracy," *The Local*, 11 April 2012, http://www.thelocal.se/20120411/40210

133. "Viewing cable 09STOCKHOLM266, SWEDISH FOREIGN MINISTER BILDT'S WASHINGTON AGENDA" (29-04-2009), http://wikileaks.org/cable/2009/04/09STOCKHOLM266.html

134. Myrdal quoted by Mikael af Malmborg, *Neutrality and State-Building in Sweden* (London: Palgrave, 2001), p. 158.

135. "Human Rights in Swedish Foreign Policy," Government Communication 2003/04:20 (Stockholm: 30 October 2003), http://www.manskligarattigheter.se/dm3/file_archive/040301/3e2f0d255a5e3a6938c1bc0678ff7d8e/s200304_20e.pdf

136. Roland Ebel, Ray Taras, and James Cochrane, *Political Culture and Foreign Policy in Latin America: Case Studies from the Circum-Caribbean* (Albany, NY: State University of New York Press, 1991).

137. Alison Brysk, "Global Good Samaritans? Human Rights Promotion as Foreign Policy – the Case of Sweden," Global Peace and Conflict Studies Working Paper, University of California, Irvine, 18 September 2005, p. 17, http://www.cgpacs.uci.edu/cgpacs_working_papersGPACS Working Paper. See also her *Global Good Samaritans: Human Rights as Foreign Policy* (Oxford: Oxford University Press, 2009).

138. Brysk, "Global Good Samaritans?" p. 2.

139. Ibid., p. 23.

140. Brysk follows the logic of Ronald Jepperson, Alexander Wendt and Peter J. Katzenstein, "Norms, Identity, and Culture in National Security," in Katzenstein (ed.), *The Culture of National Security* (New York: Columbia University Press, 1996), pp. 33–75.

141. "En majoritet av väljarna vill att Sverige skall ta emot oförändrat eller ökat antal flyktingar," *Novus*, 19 August 2014, http://www.novus.se/nyheter/2014/en-majoritet-av-vaeljarna-vill-att-sverige-skall-ta-emot-ofoeraendrat-eller-oekat-antal-flyktingar.aspx

142. Center for Global Development, "Commitment to Development Index: Sweden 2013," http://www.cgdev.org/page/sweden-2

143. *European Foreign Policy Scorecard 2014*.

144. Quoted in "News: Minister for Foreign Affairs (Sweden)," http://outsourcedinternetmarketing.com/bookkeeping/news/Minister-for-Foreign-Affairs-%28Sweden%29.html

145. *European Foreign Policy Scorecard 2014*, pp. 122–3.

146. "Reinfeldt: EU must open doors to foreign labour – and new members," *The Local*, 7 March 2011, http://www.thelocal.se/32448/20110307/

CHAPTER SEVEN

Summing up

THE BIG PICTURE

Human fears can be both large and small. They can conjure up the imagery of devils and of dust – of terrifying demons and of mundane details which haunt daily life. They are cosmic and they are existential. Fears can be fixated on foreigners and far-away locals living in our society but they can also mystify and dehumanize Others beyond our borders. Domestic politics and foreign policies are punctuated by the fears of citizens and their leaders. Fear indelibly marks the human condition at the same time that it has inescapably metaphysical features.

This book has sought to demystify the part played by this human emotion in political life. I have linked fear to other closely related human attributes, distrust and suspicion. For Thucydides phobia and hypopsia were two of a kind. Today, the first concept is universally known and employed though in a way inconsistent with its original meaning in Greek. The second term is virtually unknown but has the virtue of not being loaded or emotive. It has specific salience in capturing the social relations between natives and strangers.

Fear is the stuff of keynote speeches made by world leaders at important venues (Box 7.1). Hypopsia is left out of such speeches but is the more precise term to employ for capturing the manner in which individuals and human societies relate to each other. There is, indeed, hypopsia in the east and hypopsia in the west, hypopsia up north and hypopsia down south.

Measuring levels of fear is difficult. In survey questions and official discourse a number of proxy variables can stand in for fears: anxiety, distrust, social distance, lack of confidence, suspicion, antipathy. These reactions are better encapsulated by the term hypopsia than phobia.

After the Cold War some political scientists turned to writing on trust. They showed how it creates human capital, horizontal networks, and growth

191

Box 7.1 "Fear in the East, Fear in the West, Fear up North, Fear down South"

Our world today is replete with fear and hope; fear of war and hostile regional and global relations; fear of deadly confrontation of religious, ethnic and national identities; fear of institutionalization of violence and extremism; fear of poverty and destructive discrimination; fear of decay and destruction of life-sustaining resources; fear of disregard for human dignity and rights; and fear of neglect of morality . . .

The prevalent international political discourse depicts a civilized center surrounded by uncivilized peripheries. In this picture, the relation between the center of world power and the peripheries is hegemonic. The discourse assigning the North the center stage and relegating the South to the periphery has led to the establishment of a monologue at the level of international relations. The creation of illusory identity distinctions and the current prevalent violent forms of xenophobia are the inevitable outcome of such a discourse. Propagandistic and unfounded faith-phobic, Islamo-phobic, Shia-phobic, and Iran-phobic discourses do indeed represent serious threats against world peace and human security.

Source: "Statement by H. E. Dr. Hassan Rouhani, President of the Islamic Republic of Iran at the Sixty-Eighth Session of the United Nations General Assembly," New York, 24 September 2013, http://gadebate.un.org/sites/default/files/gastatements/68/IR_en.pdf. The heading is my adaptation of an excerpt about war from "Ethiopian Emperor H.I.M. Haile Selassie's Address to the United Nations," New York, 6 October 1963.

---

in market economies. But in the twenty-first century studying distrust seems more appropriate. In 2014 Oxfam reported that 1 percent of the world's population controls nearly half the world's wealth. The richest eighty-five individuals on the globe own as much as the poorest 50 per cent of humanity. In such conditions, distrust and suspicion are the more natural reactions to political order, not trust. "How did we get to this point?" is the hypopsic question that needs to be asked.

Employing Bruce Springsteen's binary cited in Chapter 1, this study has been less about the devils than about the dust. It represents the effort to advance knowledge of contemporary fears and their wider impact through an exploration of tangible, concrete, palpable evidence. From government sources to *WikiLeaks* cables, attitudinal surveys to politicians' speeches, party programs to electoral behavior, I have connected evidence of fearfulness and hypopsia in a society to international politics. One of my initial research questions was that surely there must be a good explanation for why unprecedented levels of anarchy characterize the international system today.

It cannot be that all the world's countries decided to adopt stupid foreign policies at the same time.

Throughout the empirical research effort, I discovered that academic researchers and political actors themselves regularly acknowledged the interstices of domestic and international politics. The subject was not scholastic but a real concern. It is therefore surprising that no systematic comparative study has been published in this area.

The frequently cited domestic–foreign policy linkage is typically predicated on the existence of different levels of fear, insecurity, distrust, and threat perception occurring concurrently at home and abroad. Applying these concepts empirically led me to the finding that they have been overwhelmingly ethnicized and considered the products of religious and even civilizational differences. In an era of identity politics, that should have been expected from the outset. But fear of strangers and strangeness can take different forms in addition to the recourse to essentialist categories such as ethnicity and race. Differences in personalities, social values, political attitudes, professions and occupations also can cause wariness and mistrust among groups. It is the phenomenon of global migration that has made ethnic, racial, and religious markers most relevant of all.

The "contact hypothesis" holds that interpersonal relations represent an effective way to overcome suspicion and prejudice between majority and minority group members. But migration flows have taken place on such a large scale that interpersonal contacts may now be hard to establish. The impersonal relations that are the alternative do not provide real contact. Intercultural encounters have always been a double-edged sword, sometimes fostering understanding, at other times fueling animosity. Primarily urban fears and hypopsia in Europe discussed in this book suggest that the contact hypothesis is either no longer valid or no longer applicable in contemporary social conditions.

Causal stories: lessons learned

A reasonable research question to pose is whether public opinion embodying fears and distrust *may* influence foreign policy. If it does, it is necessary to do two things: specify under what conditions this can occur, and describe what the effects may look like. In the case studies of France and Poland, caesuras occurred in 2007 when Sarkozy and Tusk were elected to power six months apart. Sweden's had come a bit earlier in September 2006, with the victory of the Moderate party over the Social Democrats.

Has the evidence presented in the three case studies laid an empirical basis for advancing arguments about covariations between domestic fears and foreign policy outcomes? Are there solid grounds to believe that the first

Table 7.1 Summary of Results: Strength of the Domestic–Foreign Policy Linkage in Three Cases

	France after 2007	Poland after 2007	Sweden after 2006
Expressed level of public hypopsia	Significant	Minor	Low
Primary target of distrust	North African Muslims	Russians	Refugees from Middle East
Location of target	At home and abroad	Abroad	At home
Public policy towards group	Discriminatory: Incorporation	Laissez-faire: None	Liberal: Recognition
Influence of xenophobic party	Strong	None	Moderate
Foreign policy towards source	Military interventions	Diplomatic offensive	Business as usual
Covariation in domestic/foreign policies	Occasional	Weak	Significant
Nature of causal inference	Plausible	Implausible	Probable

may constitute a key independent multidimensional variable – though not necessarily exerting influence on its own – producing the results we have described? In Chapter 3 I noted that "The act of imputing causality is the act of identifying rule-based patterns in the phenomena we study." It is difficult to conclude that the three cases reveal such rule-based patterns. Imputing causality to fears in the making of foreign policy is unsustainable. A universally identifiable, rule-based pattern – in the three cases that elected leaders who are foreign policy formulators are invariably responsive to the policy preferences of the electorate – is not supported by the evidence.

But the goal was to tell a causal story in which causal inference organized the narrative. This has led to a more positive result. Table 7.1 summarizes linkages between domestic policies shaped by distrust and fear of singled-out groups and foreign policies towards the countries of origin of these groups.

Certain factors stand out. The presence in France of an electorally successful xeno-hypopsic party (*Front National*) makes a difference: significant negative images of North African and Sahelian Muslims, a traditional assimilationist public policy, more Islamophobic discourse under the Sarkozy and Hollande presidencies, and increasing military interventions in Muslim-majority states make France stand out.

An even more probabilistic linkage between citizens' fears and foreign policy outcomes appears in Sweden. Liberal immigration policy, particularly towards asylum seekers, integration policy giving immigrants considerable freedom of cultural choice (though it became more constrained after 2006), and foreign policy choices, such as perfunctory diplomatic efforts to end the Syrian war and stay out of the 2014 Iraq conflict, are of a piece. They proceed in tandem and, when some pushback occurs to them, as under the Moderate Party-led governments from 2006 to 2014 plus newfound influence of the xeno-hypopsic Sweden Democrats, each of the policies appears equally affected. Civil wars in the Middle East and elsewhere, creating humanitarian and refugee crises, have an immediate and direct impact on Sweden, given its steadfast principle of providing protection to asylum seekers.

The weakest connection between citizens' fears and foreign policy outcomes was found in Poland. The widespread and longstanding perception that Poles are chronically russophobic did not stand up under scrutiny. To be sure, Polish public opinion recognized Russia as a renewed threat with the outbreak of the conflict in Ukraine but it singled out its international politics as a cause. Russians today are not an internal threat as they were when, under Communism, the Kremlin called the shots through its marionettes in Warsaw. But they may become one again because of pursuing revanchist foreign policy.

There is no sizeable Russian community living in the country that can serve as a target of distrust. The number of Russian speakers has steadily increased with arrivals of students, temporary workers, and cross-border merchants but they generally self-identify as from Ukraine, Belarus, and other post-Soviet states. Political parties across the spectrum advocate russo-hypopsic policies but no right-wing xenophobic party of the *Front National* or Sweden Democrats kind holds much sway. To be sure, part of the political elite practices the politics of fear from above but it has had minimal impact on public opinion; the Kaczyńskis' interlude furnishes evidence of this. The Poland case is as close as we get to a null result: weak covariation occurs between limited public russo-hypopsic attitudes, on the one hand, and aggressive diplomatic activity aimed at taking down the Kremlin leadership, on the other. Without covariation there is no causal connection.

Stronger evidence is found in Sweden of the impact of citizen attitudes on foreign policy than in Poland. National action scripts are clearly defined in both cases (respectively, humanitarianism; "Europe's eastern bastion") but greater political continuity in Sweden, attributable to extended periods of Social Democratic rule, have cemented a consensus around embracing liberal values at home and abroad. In France there is occasional covariation in domestic and foreign policies, more discernable under Hollande than under Sarkozy.

Thucydides' Theorem tells us that political actors do not do as they wish in determining a country's international politics. So military interventions in

Muslim-majority states, as with France, diplomatic maneuvering in Ukraine, as with Poland, and admitting refugees from war-torn countries while otherwise conducting business as usual with them (though not making war on them), as with Sweden, are decisions shaped by factors other than leaders' preferences. These include the influence of citizen fears, particularly when such fears are acute, supported by expert opinion, and spurred by international systemic factors.

Democracy itself posits a causal relationship between citizens and leaders. Though cautious about empirical evidence suggesting that citizen fears do affect foreign policy outcomes under specific conditions, I suggest that, as liberal democracies, France, Poland, and Sweden must maintain the semblance of having active civil societies, democratic values, and representative and responsible government in them. This entails promoting congruence in citizens' and elites' values. At times, the lack of congruence is blatantly exposed: France and leaders' personal ties to Arab dictators; Poland and rendition cooperation with the CIA; Sweden and arms deals with Saudis. But citizens' fears and distrust, which could become influential enough at a certain stress point to trigger a moral panic, can restrain leaders' incongruent actions. Fears are a powerful force and get the attention of leaders in democratic countries.

In this book I have considered two of the great phobias marking contemporary state and international politics: Islamophobia and russophobia. Each exists at the individual level, though the study of individual anti-Muslim attitudes is the more commonplace. The reason for this, I suggest, is that anti-Muslim attitudes are products of a politics of fear from below used primarily by populist right-wing parties and movements to increase their influence. The case of France brought out this tendency clearly.

Anti-Russian attitudes show up, above all, among state leaders and other elites. Their politics of fear from above does not always have purchase with average citizens, as the Poland case indicated. Also contributing to this tendency are that citizens across Europe do not encounter, or easily identify, Russians living abroad. They are not a visible group, their diaspora numbers are limited, and wealthy Russians residing in the West usually keep apart. In addition, it is as an actor in the international system that Russia makes its presence felt most. Not surprisingly, then, discursive and media accounts of Russia have revolved around its leader even though 10,000 other officials work in the Russian presidential administration.

The case of Sweden focused on how possibly socially suppressed fears of foreigners – buttressed by government policies aiming preemptively and prophylactically to neutralize fears – were circumscribed at the individual and, as importantly, state level, too. The liberal internationalism characterizing the country's foreign policy for many decades may even be designed to contribute to social engineering which makes expression of fears "not done." That is why the emergence of an anti-immigrant party in parliament seems more traumatic than it really is: the taboo on xeno-hypopsia has been partially pried open.

It may be that a reverse causal direction from international to domestic politics occurs in Sweden, the contrary of what the book's main focus has been on. Humanitarianism, neutrality, Samaritanism are attributes attractive to a society's image of itself. To be sure, today's international opportunity structure, with its exceptional number of conflicts and culture of fractiousness, has given Swedish society's liberal value system the chance to be projected advantageously abroad.

In the three countries a balance in the influence of the three principal approaches to international relations appears. Realism is reflected in France's defense of its economic interests in Africa, Poland's concern with Russian expansionism, and, to a more limited degree, Sweden's business as usual in conflict zones and even rogue states. On the other hand, liberal internationalism is more discernable in Sweden's policy on providing humanitarian assistance in conflict areas and giving shelter to war refugees. France's invocation of the right to protect and Poland's on taking in exiles from Georgia, Chechnya, Ukraine, and Belarus are examples of selective liberal internationalism. Finally, social constructions of allies and foes are employed in roughly equal measure in the three states.

The politics of fear are not utilized evenly across individual, state, and international levels. The efforts of right-wing xenophobic parties to fuse the three together – evidenced in their foreign policy programs analyzed here – are isolated efforts and have had limited success; the *Front National* has been most effective in not just fusing its xenophobic home and foreign programs but has even seen them become "mainstreamed" by other parties.

The three levels of international relations analysis have remained largely compartmentalized in examining the politics of fear. The interstate level of analysis identifies fear as central to the existence of threat perceptions and insecurity. Less highlighted are domestic fears as a factor affecting foreign policy and international relations. The influence of fear on individual foreign policy decision-makers has been a subject of interest for many political psychologists. It is the shortfall in studies of fear at the domestic level that this book wished to redress.

FEAR IN THE UNITED STATES

A *fin de siècle* observation about the United States by France's top diplomat was that it represented a hyperpower. But with hyperpower come hyperfears. By that definition, since 1999, the United States has developed enormous stakes in the international system that can be affected by a changing security environment as well as by a shifting balance of economic power. Hard US military power remains largely unaffected – in this respect the unipolar moment has lasted for well over a decade – despite unsuccessful military interventions in Middle Eastern countries. On the other hand, its soft diplomatic and economic power has eroded as has its sticky cultural power (Box 7.2).

Fears of a less favorable international environment have influenced the making of American foreign policy. Isolationism appears as a panacea and alluring foreign policy temptation but the Obama administration has not

Box 7.2 Global insecuritization

The Fourth of July, for me, is one of those special American holidays that celebrates not religion, ethnicity or sect but rather freedom and the country's unique national identity, which is based on it. But around the world these days, we're seeing the rise of another kind of nationalism, one that can be darker and more troubling . . . You can see this rise of nationalism not just in Europe but also around the world. Consider Japanese Prime Minister Shinzo Abe's plan to reinterpret his country's pacifist constitution. Leaders, such as Vladimir Putin in Russia, Recep Tayyip Erdogan in Turkey and Xi Jinping in China, have made appeals to nationalism a core part of their agenda and appeal . . .

[T]oday we seem to be witnessing mostly a different kind of nationalism, based on fear, insecurity and anxiety . . . It is a strange mixture of insecurity and assertiveness. People worry that their society is changing beyond recognition and that they are being ruled by vast, distant forces – the European Union in Brussels, the International Monetary Fund or the federal government in Washington – that are beyond their control. And by people who do not share their values.

In the United States, we do see one parallel: the rise of the Tea Party . . . I don't recognize my country anymore, say Mike Huckabee, Glenn Beck and many others on the right. The same line could be repeated by every one of those European nationalists who won in the polls in May [2014] . . . The bottom-up force that seems to be moving the world these days is political identity. The questions that fill people with emotion are "Who are we?" and, more ominously, "Who are we not?" Even in America, even on the Fourth of July.

Source: Fareed Zakaria, "Identity, not ideology, is moving the world," *Washington Post*, 3 July 2014, http://www.washingtonpost.com/opinions/fareed-zakaria-identity-not-ideology-is-moving-the-world/2014/07/03/631ff338-02d7-11e4-8572-4b1b969b6322_story.html

succumbed to it. The sense of American declinism is not as pervasive or persuasive as its counterpart in Europe is.

What of the impact of American fears at the individual and national levels, independent of the state of international relations? Are concerns among Americans about national identity, social cohesion, and liberal values growing? Are they shaping US relations with neighboring countries, its allies, and its adversaries?

United States exceptionalism is used to explain many phenomena and can help address these questions. The United States has little reason to fear the loss of a defining and primordial characteristic cementing its society – the English language. Compared to other factors English is in the ascendance, not in decline, across much of the world. Occasional warnings of the incursion of Spanish into American life appear misplaced when much of the rest of the world is promoting educational policies aiming to make citizens proficient in English. The English language is unchallenged in the United States and no federal law is needed to recognize it as the official language. Such a law is needed only in a fundamentally insecure society, such as Ukraine.

The fate of an "American way of life" may be less secure. In the age of globalization, which is usually applauded by liberal thinkers, there is no "way of life" that can be made immune from serious transformation. Moreover, while it is still possible to make credible claims about the desirability of exporting American values and conducting democracy promotion abroad, the idea of projecting an American way of life to other parts of the world is no longer credible or productive. It is a discredited idea and, tellingly then, is vanishing from public discourse.

In contrast to Poland, there is no neighbor that Americans feel the need to fear. Some residual distrust of the thoroughness of Canada's border patrol measures has been expressed. It is framed primarily as a securitization, not immigration, problem.

Anti-immigrant attitudes, directed at Mexicans and Central Americans crossing illegally into the United States from the south, are substantial and oftentimes racialized. But they have not to now fuelled xenophobia of the kind European anti-immigrant parties construct. There is also an informal taboo in the United States on open debate of some of the pathologies of illegal border crossing: for example, the impact of narco-traffickers and human smugglers on criminality and human rights. This serves the intended purpose of fear reduction: American citizens' fears of foreigners are minimal, with the exception of several US border states. In addition, trust remains a currency of American society in a way that distrust is one in other parts of the world, such as that traditionally seen in Cuban society of the United States (Box 7.3).

The causal mechanisms that could link Americans' fears to foreign policy are not as strong as in Europe. The influence of a fearful American public on

199

Box 7.3 José Martí on Cubans' views of the United States

They admire this nation, the greatest ever built by liberty, but they dislike the evil conditions that, like worms in the heart, have begun in this mighty republic their work of destruction. They have made of the heroes of this country their own heroes, and look to the success of the American commonwealth as the crowning glory of mankind; but they cannot honestly believe that excessive individualism, reverence for wealth, and the protracted exultation of a terrible victory are preparing the United States to be the typical nation of liberty, where no opinion is to be based in greed, and no triumph or acquisition reached against charity and justice. We love the country of Lincoln as much as we fear the country of Cutting [A. K. Cutting – adventurer denounced by Martí as being at the root of "all misorioo und prejudices" due to his effort to instigate a war between the United States and Mexico in 1886]

[. . .]

No matter how great this land is or how anointed the land of Lincoln may be for the free men of America, for us, in our heart of hearts, where nobody dares to challenge or take issue with our secret feelings, the América of Juárez is greater because it has been more unhappy, and because it is ours.

Sources: 1. José Martí, "Letter to the Editor," *New York Evening Post*, 25 March 1889, http://college.cengage.com/history/world/keen/latin_america/8e/assets/students/sources/pdfs/76a_marti_letter_to_ny_evening_post.pdf;
2. José Martí, "Mother America," speech given at the Spanish-American Literary Society of New York, 19 December 1889, http://www.fofweb.com/History/HistRefMain.asp?

the country's international politics is slight compared to stimuli emerging in the international arena – a jihadist insurgency in Iraq and Syria that threatens American interests; an Iran on the way to becoming a nuclear power; a Russia violating international law; a China intent on securing energy resources in many parts of the world.

Citizens' fears may place a crucial role in American domestic politics; the Tea Party has demonstrated this for a decade. But little political space is available for fears to make an imprint on American foreign policy. Competing factors are the existence of such powerful institutions as the United States Defense Department. Its high level of expenditures guarantees that the Pentagon believes it has the right to make key decisions on behalf of the public.

The global network of American diplomats, scholars, and teachers established under the State Department's many international programs confirms its prerogative to define and pursue the national interest regardless of American citizens' fears. The United States Commerce Department has a smaller but parallel and far-flung structure. The National Security Agency collects data on citizens and leaders from across the globe. Under these institutional conditions the influence of public fears on foreign policy will be paltry, more so than in other Western democracies.

To end, it is valuable to return to Montaigne's banal saying that there is nothing to fear but fear itself. It has had more resonance in the United States than in Europe because it is associated more closely with President Franklin D. Roosevelt's 1933 Inauguration Speech (ushering in the first of his unprecedented four terms) than with a phrase by a French essayist of the Renaissance. The mantra is an implicit exhortation to bravura. Its assumption is that the quality of fearlessness can be achieved despite the human inclination to display fear. Fearlessness is regarded as desirable even if it runs counter to a practical survival strategy running through human history.

Fearlessness is not a virtue on a continent that has fought two world wars and witnessed a Holocaust plus several other genocides over the past hundred years. By contrast, fearlessness is a much-esteemed quality in the United States which allowed it to expand west and south; its fearless thrust north into Canada in the War of 1812 ended unsuccessfully two years later. Accordingly, it may be fearlessness, not fears, that has traditionally exerted the greater influence on US foreign policy. But the greater social fragility of most of Europe, and beyond, means that fear carries on being a resilient factor continuing to sculpt domestic and foreign politics.

Select bibliography

Christine Agius, *The Social Construction of Swedish Neutrality: Challenges to Swedish Identity and Sovereignty* (Manchester: Manchester University Press, 2012).

Mikhail A. Alexseev, *Immigration Phobia and the Security Dilemma: Russia, Europe, and the United States* (Cambridge: Cambridge University Press, 2006).

Zygmunt Bauman, *Liquid Modernity* (Cambridge: Polity Press, 2000).

Zygmunt Bauman, *Europe: An Unfinished Adventure* (New York: Polity Press, 2004).

Zygmunt Bauman, *Liquid Fear* (Cambridge: Polity Press, 2006).

Ryan K. Beasley, Juliet Kaarbo, Jeffrey S. Lantis, and Michael T. Snarr (eds), *Foreign Policy in Comparative Perspective: Domestic and International Influences on State Behavior* (Thousand Oaks, CA: CQ Press, 2012), 2nd edition.

Bo Bengtsson, Per Strömblad, and Ann-Helén Bay (eds), *Diversity, Inclusion and Citizenship in Scandinavia* (Newcastle: Cambridge Scholars Press, 2010).

Pascal Boniface, *Le monde selon Sarkozy* (Paris: Jean-Claude Gawsewitch, 2012).

Alison Brysk, *Global Good Samaritans: Human Rights as Foreign Policy* (Oxford: Oxford University Press, 2009).

Philippe Burrin and Christina Schori-Liang (eds), *European Right-Wing Populism and Foreign Policy* (Aldershot: Ashgate, 2007).

Brian E. Calabrese, *Fear in Democracy: A Study of Thucydides' Political Thought* (Ann Arbor, MI: ProQuest, UMI Dissertations Publishing, 2008).

Raffaella A. Del Sarto, *Contested State Identities and Regional Security in the Euro-Mediterranean Area* (Basingstoke: Palgrave, 2006).

Nicolas Demertzis (ed.), *Emotions in Politics: The Affect Dimension in Political Tension* (London: Palgrave, 2013).

Roger Eatwell and Cas Mudde (eds), *Western Democracies and the New Extreme Right Challenge* (London: Routledge, 2009).

Michel Foucault, *Discipline and Punish: The Birth of the Prison* (New York: Vintage Books, 1995).

Frank Furedi, *Culture of Fear Revisited* (London: Bloomsbury Academic, 2006).

Joanna A. Gorska, *Dealing with a Juggernaut: Analyzing Poland's Policy Towards Russia, 1989–2004* (Lanham, MD: Rowman and Littlefield, 2011).

Anders Hellström, *Bringing Europe Down to Earth* (Lund: Lunds Universitet, Political Studies no. 144, 2006).

Samuel S. Huntington, *The Clash of Civilizations and the Remaking of World Order* (New York: Simon & Schuster, 2011; first published 1996).

Andrew Hussey, *The French Intifada: The Long War Between France and Its Arabs* (London: Granta, 2014).

Jef Huysmans, *The Politics of Insecurity: Fear, Migration and Asylum in the EU* (London: Routledge, 2006).

Peter Katzenstein (ed.), *The Culture of National Security: Norms and Identity in World Politics* (New York: Columbia University Press, 1996).

Milja Kurki, *Causation in International Relations: Reclaiming Causal Analysis* (Cambridge: Cambridge University Press, 2008).

Roman Kuźniar, *Poland's Foreign Policy after 1989* (Warsaw: Wydawnictwo SCHOLAR, 2009).

Jonathan Laurence and Justin Vaisse, *Integrating Islam: Political and Religious Challenges in Contemporary France* (Washington, DC: Brookings Institute, 2008).

Samuel Laurent, *Sahelistan* (Paris: Seuil, 2013).

Christina Schori Liang (ed.), *Europe for the Europeans: The Foreign and Security Policy of the Populist Radical Right* (Aldershot: Ashgate, 2007).

Richard Ned Lebow, *A Cultural Theory of International Relations* (Cambridge: Cambridge University Press, 2008).

Richard Ned Lebow, *Forbidden Fruit: Counterfactuals and International Relations* (Princeton, NJ: Princeton University Press, 2010).

Cas Mudde, *Populist Radical Right Parties in Europe* (New York: Cambridge University Press, 2007).

Andrea Mammone, Emmanuel Godin, and Brian Jenkins (eds), *Mapping the Extreme Right in Contemporary Europe* (New York: Berghahn Books, 2011).

Maud S. Mandel, *Muslims and Jews in France* (Princeton, NJ: Princeton University Press, 2014).

Nasar Meer, *Key Concepts in Race and Ethnicity* (Thousand Oaks, CA: Sage, 2014).

Fatima Mernissi, *Islam and Democracy: Fear of the Modern World* (New York: Addison-Wesley, 1992).

Dominique Moïsi, *La géopolitique de l'émotion: comment les cultures de peur, d'humiliation et d'espoir façonnent le monde* (Paris: Flammarion, 2008).

Ulf Nilson, *What happened to Sweden? – while America became the only superpower* (New York: Nordstjernan Förlag, 2007).

Dennis Sven Nordin, *A Swedish Dilemma: A Liberal European Nation's Struggle with Racism and Xenophobia, 1990–2000* (Lanham, MD: University Press of America, 2005).

Leigh Oakes, *Language and National Identity: Comparing France and Sweden* (Amsterdam: John Benjamins Publishing Company, 2001).

Roger D. Petersen, *Understanding Ethnic Violence: Fear, Hatred, and Resentment in Twentieth-Century Eastern Europe* (Cambridge: Cambridge University Press, 2002).

Bo Petersson, *Stories about Strangers: Swedish Media Constructions of Socio-Cultural Risk* (Lanham, MD: University Press of America, 2006).

Allan Pred, *The Past is Not Dead: Facts, Fictions, and Enduring Racial Stereotypes* (Minneapolis, MN: University of Minnesota Press, 2004).

Corey Robin, *Fear: The History of a Political Idea* (New York: Oxford University Press, 2006).

Bo Rothstein, *Just Institutions Matter: the Moral and Political Logic of the Universal Welfare State* (Cambridge: Cambridge University Press, 1998).

Richard Sobel, *The Impact of Public Opinion on US Foreign Policy Since Vietnam: Constraining the Colossus* (Oxford: Oxford University Press, 2001).

Raymond Taras, *Europe Old and New: Transnationalism, Belonging, Xenophobia* (Boulder, CO: Rowman and Littlefield, 2010).

Raymond Taras, *Xenophobia and Islamophobia in Europe* (Edinburgh: Edinburgh University Press, 2012).

Fabrizio Tassinari, *Why Europe Fears its Neighbors* (Santa Barbara, CA: ABC-CLIO, 2009).

Andrei P. Tsygankov, *Russophobia: Anti-Russian Lobby and American Foreign Policy* (London: Palgrave Macmillan, 2009).

Mitja Velikonja, *Eurosis: A Critique of the New Eurocentrism* (Ljubljana: Peace Institute, 2005).

Nina Witoszek and Lars Trägårdh (eds), *Culture and Crisis: The Case of Germany and Sweden* (New York: Berghahn Books, 2002).

Tomasz Zarycki, *Ideologies of Eastness in Central and Eastern Europe* (London: Routledge, 2014).

Slavoj Žižek, *Violence: Six Sideways Reflections* (London: Picador, 2008).

Index